ANCIENT ISRAEL

VOLUME THREE

ANCIENT ISRAEL

VOLUME THREE

ANGELO S. RAPPOPORT

SENATE

Ancient Israel Volume Three

Previously published by
The Gresham Publishing Company, London

This edition published in 1995 by Senate, an imprint of
Studio Editions Ltd, Princess House, 50 Eastcastle Street,
London W1N 7AP, England

ISBN 1 85958 172 2
Printed and bound in Guernsey by
The Guernsey Press Co. Ltd

SOLOMON SIGHTS THE MYSTERIOUS PALACE
Page 100

Contents

VOLUME THREE

CHAPTER I

CHAPTER II

CHAPTER III

CHAPTER IV

CHAPTER V

CHAPTER VI

iii

CONTENTS

CONTENTS

CHAPTER XVIII

CHAPTER XIX

CHAPTER XX

Plates

VOLUME THREE

PREFACE

The present and last volume of the work on Myths and
Legends of Ancient Israel deals with the first three Kings of
Israel, Saul, David, and Solomon, and also with the Prophet
Elijah and Queen Esther. Both David and Solomon occupy
an important place in Jewish legendary lore. David is the
elect, the chosen of the Lord, not only during his mortal life
but also in Paradise where he will pronounce the blessing
over the cup of wine, an honour of which the Patriarchs and
even Moses and Aaron will deem themselves unworthy. As
for Solomon, who occupies an even larger space in Jewish
tradition than his father David, the opinions of the Rabbis
differ. Whereas the earlier school frequently criticizes the
actions of the famous King of Israel and dwells on his weak-
nesses and his downfall, the later school glorifies him as the
counterpart of his father David. He is represented as a pious
and wise ruler, the King of Israel *par excellence*, a Prophet
and Judge inspired by Divine wisdom.

In the present, as in the two preceding volumes, we have
once more related the legends not only of purely Jewish
origin, but also those found in Moslem tradition as well as
in occidental literature. In the tradition of the Mohammedans
King Solomon is represented as being far superior to his
father David. He is a Prophet of God, and long before the
birth of Mohammed he had already recognized and rendered
homage to the future messenger of Allah. In Jewish tradition

reference is made to Solomon's future life, but none to his
death, whilst in Moslem lore many legends are found which
relate the details of his death.   The reader will also find in
this volume a chapter dealing with the mediæval literature
wherein Solomon is the central figure.   In the chapters on
Elijah and Esther the reader's attention has also been drawn
to similar legends and tales related in Oriental and European
literature.

ANGELO S. RAPPOPORT.

MYTH AND LEGEND OF ANCIENT ISRAEL

VOLUME III

CHAPTER I

King Saul

Saul, the first King of the Jews—His handsome appearance—The welfare of the public—The lighted streets—Saul and the admiring maidens —The modest hero—Simple life—The Witch of Endor—The story of the King and the cocks—The familiar spirit—Samuel and the dead—Saul in Paradise—The burial of Saul—The famine in Palestine—David's investigations—The sins of the people—The royal coffin—Saul in Moslem legend —The spring in the desert—David and the five stones—Saul's jealousy of David—The suit of chain mail—Saul at the grave of his victims—The King and his twelve sons—The city of the giants—The crowing cocks.

SAUL, THE FIRST KING OF THE JEWS

In Jewish legendary lore King David and his son Solomon occupy a prominent place, but the aureole of legend and myth has also crowned the head of Israel's first King. There are, however, two distinct views in Jewish legend with regard to Saul. Whilst some of the Haggadists treat the first King of Israel with but little sympathy, others depict him in very glowing colours. He was chosen first King of Israel on account of his handsome appearance, his piety, his bravery, his military powers, his innocence and modesty. One of his ancestors, his grandfather Abiel, had received the promise that one of his descendants would ascend the throne of Israel. The merit of

1

this grandfather of Saul consisted in the care he took of the welfare of the public. He was in the habit of having the streets lighted so that people could go to the houses of study after dark.[1] But it was not only on account of the merits of his ancestors that Saul received the crown and was considered worthy to rule over Israel. His beauty was unusual, and when he asked the maidens about the seer and they told him concerning Samuel, these maidens did not seem to be in a hurry to shorten their conversation, but dragged it out so as to have an opportunity to contemplate his beauty as long as possible.[2] Saul, however, was far from noticing the admiring glances, and no pride swelled his pure and innocent heart, for he was as innocent as a babe and pure as a child, free from sin as a one-year child. He had never committed sin when he ascended the newly created throne of Israel.[3] He was a hero, too, for he had already carried off victories over the Philistines when he was called to the throne. And yet, ambition never entered his heart, and his modesty was as great as that of Moses, for he refused to accept the royal crown, and even after he had been anointed he would not accept it until the bright stones in the breastplate of the High Priest announced the decision of Providence. And even when he sat on the throne of Israel, Saul remained as modest as he had been before his election.

THE WITCH OF ENDOR

After the death of Samuel Saul greatly missed the prophet and his advice. He soon found an opportunity to enter into communication with the departed prophet. When he told his servants to find him a necromancer, they wondered greatly. In legendary lore Saul is compared to a king who had given instructions that all cocks be put to death and then inquired of his servants whether there was any cock to wake him up with dawn.

[1] *Leviticus Rabba*, 9.   [2] *Berachoth*, 48.   [3] *Yoma*, 22b; *Leviticus Rabba*.

" Hast thou not given instructions to kill all the cocks in the land?" asked his servant.[1]

Thus Saul, who had removed the witches and necromancers from the land, once more loved what he had formerly hated. Thereupon he went to En-Dor, where dwelt Abner's mother, the witch of En-Dor, wife of Zephaniah. Saul inquired of her for himself by the familiar spirit, and the woman brought Samuel, whose figure appeared upright before them. Then the woman knew that the man who had come to visit her was the King, as for an ordinary mortal the spirit raised from the dead would have appeared feet in the air and head downwards.

Samuel was not alone, for many dead who thought that the day of resurrection had come accompanied Samuel. When the woman beheld the number of dead by the side of Samuel, she became very much confused.[2] Then Samuel, whose voice the witch could not hear, said unto Saul: " If thou wilt accept the judgment of God, to-morrow thou wilt be with me and thy lot shall be with me in the place where I abide, that is in Paradise." [3]

Thereupon the Lord summoned His angels and said: " When a man is invited to a banquet he usually leaves his children at home for fear of an evil eye, but Saul goes out to battle and yet takes his sons with him. He knows that he will meet his death, but he gladly accepts for himself and for his sons the Divine judgment."

And thus Saul died with his sons so that his portion might be with Samuel in the future life and that he might dwell in the prophet's division in heaven.[4]

---

[1] *Midrash Tanchuma*, ed. Buber, III, p. 42a; *Midrash Samuel*; Grünbaum, *Neue Beiträge*, p. 188.
[2] *Leviticus Rabba*, 26; *Midrash Samuel*, 24; *Pirke de Rabbi Eliezer*, Ch. 33.
[3] *Midrash Tanchuma*, ed. Buber, III, p. 42a; *Midrash Samuel*, 24; *Leviticus Rabba*, 26.
[4] *Berachoth*, 12b; *Leviticus Rabba*, ibid.; *Pirke de Rabbi Eliezer*, ibid.

The Burial of Saul

The remains of Saul and his sons were interred at Jabesh Gilead, outside the land of Israel. Now in the days of David a famine arose in the land, lasting three years, year after year.

In the first year of the famine the King said to his people: " Are there some among ye who worship idols?" And he caused an investigation to be made so as to discover whether any idolatry was being practised in the land.

During the second year that the famine prevailed, David said unto his people: " Are there perchance some among ye who are leading immoral lives?" And he again caused investigations to be made for the purpose of finding out whether the punishment had been inflicted upon the people for the sin of lewdness. Investigations, however, proved that such a sin did not prevail in the land.

During the third year that the famine prevailed, David asked himself whether the people were perhaps punished because they had committed the sin of shedding blood. Once more the investigations yielded no result.

Thereupon David prayed to the Lord, and God answered: " It is for Saul. Saul was anointed with the oil of consecration; he abolished idolatry and he dwells in Paradise together with the Prophet Samuel. Yet, ye are in the land of Israel, while he and his sons are buried outside of the Holy Land."

When David heard these words of the Lord, he gathered together all the elders of Israel, all the nobles and scholars, and they all betook themselves to Jabesh Gilead, where they found the bones of Saul and of his son Jonathan. The procession crossed the Jordan, and the coffin containing the bones of the disinterred King was brought to the borders of each tribe. All Israel showed respect to the remains of the dead King, and they were laid to rest in the land of Benjamin. The

THE SPIRIT OF SAMUEL APPEARS TO SAUL

Facing page 4, Vol. III

Lord, seeing the respect paid by the people of Israel to the memory of Saul, had compassion, sent rain upon the land, and the famine ceased.[1]

SAUL IN MOSLEM LEGEND

In Mohammedan tradition Saul is the subject of many legends, the majority of which have been borrowed from the Jews. When Thalut was made King of Israel, he summoned all his fighting men, who numbered seventy thousand, and he led them against the Philistines. Saul started with his army, and his way led through the desert. One day the men had no water, and the heat was great in the wilderness. The soldiers began to murmur against Saul and Samuel. Thereupon the Prophet prayed to the Lord and a miracle happened. Out of the rocky, stony ground a spring suddenly bubbled up, and its water was as fresh as snow, as sweet as honey, and as white as milk. Thereupon Samuel spoke to the soldiers who came hurrying up, anxious to slake their thirst:

" Ye have murmured and been discontent and have thus sinned against the Lord and your King. Abstain therefore from drinking of this water so as to expiate your fault by your abstinence."

Thus spoke Samuel, but the soldiers paid no heed to the words of the Prophet and disregarded his advice. Three hundred and thirteen men were only found who had strength enough to control themselves and not to drink but just a little out of the hollow of their hands, all the others drinking greedily. When Thalut saw this, he dismissed his army and went out with the small number who had had sufficient control over themselves. Among them were also the six sons of a virtuous man of the name of Isa, his seventh son, by name of David, having remained at home to attend to his father. Saul

[1] *Pirke de Rabbi Eliezer*, Ch. 17; see also *Yalkut, Samuel,* § 154; *Midrash Samuel,* 28; *Jebamoth,* 78b; *Jerushalmi Kiddushin,* IV, I, 65b–c; *Taanith* III, 3, 66c; *Numer. Rabba,* 8, 4.

set his army in array, but none of his men dared advance to fight in single combat the giant Djalut, the King of the Philistines. Thereupon Isa sent also his seventh son to the battlefield to take provisions to his brethren and to inquire after their welfare. The boy was not dressed as a warrior but like a simple shepherd, carrying his pouch and a staff in his hand. On his way he suddenly heard the voice of a stone that was calling to him, and thus it spoke: " Pick me up and take me with thee, for I am the stone wherewith the Prophet Abraham had once driven away Satan." David stooped, picked up the stone, and placed it in his pouch. When he had taken a few paces, another stone addressed him, and thus it spoke: " Pick me up and take me with thee, for I am the stone on which the foot of the angel Gabriel once rested when he caused a fountain to be opened in the desert for Ishmael, the son of Hagar." Once more the boy stooped down, and picking up the speaking stone placed it in his pouch.

And when he had taken a few more paces he heard the voice of the third stone, and thus it spoke: " Pick me up, for I am the very stone wherewith Jacob once strove against the angel whom his brother Esau had sent against him." For the third time David stooped down and picked up the stone.

When he reached the army, he heard the voice of a herald, making the following proclamation: " He who will kill the giant Djalut shall marry Thalut's daughter and become his successor upon the throne."

David tried to persuade his brethren to wrestle with the giant, not on account of the promised reward, but so as to wipe out the shame and disgrace thus cast upon the name of the Israelites. As his brothers, however, lacked the courage to meet the enemy in single combat, he went himself to Thalut and offered to fight the giant.

Saul's Jealousy of the Young Hero

Now Thalut grew very jealous of the young and now popular hero, and although he had promised to give him his daughter to wife, he refused to do so until David had brought him a hundred more heads of giants. And the greater David's heroism, the more intense Thalut's jealousy grew, for the boy's praise was in everybody's mouth.

One day Thalut came to visit his daughter in her husband's absence, and thus spoke to her: " Introduce me to-night into thy husband's chamber so that I can slay him with my own hand."

When his wife informed him of the promise she had been compelled to give her father, David calmly bade her be comforted, and do as she had promised: " The God of my Fathers," said he, " will deliver me from the sword of thy father and make his weapon harmless, even as he made harmless the knife of Abraham when he raised it to slaughter Ishmael." Thereupon David went into his smithy, where he fashioned for himself a suit of chain mail that was to cover his whole body. This suit of chain mail was as fine and thin as hair, and fitted his body as if it had been made of wool; it also resisted the thrust of every weapon.

David went to bed and slept, but was awakened at midnight when his father-in-law began to stab him in his sleep. He awoke, and wresting the sword from Thalut's hands broke it as if it had been a piece of cake.

David thereupon escaped and was pursued by his father-in-law. One night Thalut and his soldiers lodged in a cave. David was in another near by, but his pursuers knew it not. In the middle of the night he carried off the seal-ring of the King and also his sword and his banner and went forth out of the cave, which had a double issue. On the following morning he appeared on the top of a mountain, opposite the camp of the

Israelites. Girt with the King's long sword and waving the royal banner, he stretched out his hand so that all could perceive the royal seal-ring on his finger. Great was Thalut's astonishment, and he admired not only David's pluck and courage but also his generosity. His jealousy and envy abated, and he reconciled himself with his son-in-law. Henceforth they lived in peace and unity until Thalut was killed in the battle against the Philistines.[1]

The story of the Witch of Endor and the death of Saul is related as follows in Mohammedan tradition:

When Saul went out in pursuit of David, the future King of Israel, the wise and learned men of Israel came and reproached the King for the sin he was committing in trying to kill the anointed of the Lord. Thereupon Saul waxed wroth and slew them. Of all the people who had interfered and remonstrated with the King only one escaped and remained alive, and she was a wise woman. The vizier had not only spared her life but also taken her into his house, where she henceforth lived.

Now it happened that some time afterwards King Saul had a dream wherein he was reproached for the sin he had committed in slaying the wise men of Israel. When he awoke in the morning, he was full of grief and remorse. He went to his vizier and thus he spoke:

" I have put to death all the wise men in Israel and now I am full of remorse and would fain atone for my crime. Has none of the wise men escaped so that I might ask counsel and learn how to expiate my sin?"

Thereupon the vizier made reply: " There remains only one, and she is a woman."

" Bring her to me," said Saul.

And when the wise woman was brought into the presence of the King, the latter said unto her: " I am greatly troubled

[1] Weil, *Biblische Legenden der Muselmänner*, pp. 200–7.

in my mind and I want thee to tell me how I could best make atonement for my crime."

To this the wise woman made reply: " Take me to the tomb of a prophet where I will pray. Perchance God will permit him to speak and let thee know His will."

Thereupon Saul led her to the tomb of the Prophet Samuel, where the wise woman prayed.

And suddenly the voice of Samuel coming from the sepulchre was heard, and thus he spoke: " Let the King and his sons go down to the city of the giants and there they shall fall."

Saul then called his twelve sons and related unto them what had occurred. They all declared themselves ready to go to the city of the giants. They fought valiantly and fell all in one day.[1]

Tabari relates the story of the Witch of Endor somewhat differently. Saul had caused all the wise men of Israel to be put to death, and only one woman had escaped because she knew the Ineffable name of God. Thereupon Saul commanded a giant to kill this woman, but the giant had pity on her and let her escape. Later on, however, Saul repented of his sin and wept and lamented. Every night he went out to the graves where lay the victims he had slain, and thus he spoke: " I conjure you, in the name of God, if you know a way how I can expiate my crime, tell me."

And one night a voice from the grave answered him, and thus it spoke: " O Thalut, is it not enough that thou didst put an end to our lives that thou must come now and worry us when we are dead?"

When Thalut heard these words he was sorely grieved, and the giant, who had pity on him, inquired after the cause of his suffering.

" Dost thou know," said Thalut, " any wise man in the

---

[1] Weil, *Biblische Legenden der Muselmänner*, pp, 200–7.

land who could tell me how I can expiate my sin and thus obtain the forgiveness of the Lord?"

To this the giant made answer: " Dost thou know, O King, to whom thou art to be compared? To the King who had caused all the cocks to be killed. One day, being on a journey, he reached a town and heard a cock crow. Considering the cock's chant as a bad omen, he gave instructions for all the cocks in the town to be killed. When it was time for him to go to bed, he ordered his servant to wake him up with the crowing of the cock, but his servant replied: " All the cocks have been killed and there is none left to crow. Thou, Thalut, hast killed all the wise men in Israel, and there is none whom thou canst consult."

When he saw, however, how grieved Thalut was, he said: " There is one wise woman in the land whose life I did spare."

Thalut visited the wise woman, and she led him to the grave of Joshua the son of Nun. He came out of his grave and asked: " What has happened? Has the day of resurrection come?"

" No," replied the woman, " but Thalut wants to know how he could expiate his crime?"

" Let him resign his power," answered Joshua the son of Nun, " and go out with his sons and fight until they all fall in battle in the defence of the true faith."

Thalut informed his sons of what had occurred, and they were all ready to go out and seek death on the battlefield.[1]

---

[1] Tabari, I, p. 324; Grünbaum, *loc. cit.*, pp. 186–7.

CHAPTER II
The Birth of the Shepherd

David before his birth—Three hours only allotted to him—Adam's gift—The piety of Jesse—Ruth, the ancestress of David—Nazbath, the mother of David—Jesse and his beautiful slave—The wife's ruse—David's life in the desert—Tender care of young lambs—The sleeping rhinoceros —David's vow to build the Temple—The visit of Samuel—The red-haired youngster—The anointment of David—Miraculous tall stature— The flowing horn—The honey jars—David's cleverness—The gold pieces in the honey jars—The thief detected—The blaspheming giant—Orpah, the sister-in-law of Ruth—Forty steps—Saul's armour—Goliath's in-coherent speech—Uriah's request—The promised wife—Why Goliath fell face downwards—The descendants of the clans of Perez and Zerah— David pursued—The advantages of lunacy—Ahish, King of Gath—The wasp and the water-bottle.

KING DAVID—HIS BIRTH AND YOUTH

Long before his birth David is supposed to have played an important rôle, for the whole world, according to Jewish legendary lore, is said to have been created only for the sake and merits of David. He was the goal and purpose of creation, for his Psalms give expression to the complete development of the human soul. Three hours, says a Midrash,[1] were only allotted to David when he was born, and he would have died immediately had not Adam made him a present of 70 years. His ancestors are compared in Midrashic lore with worthless sand wherein a king on his travels had once lost a precious jewel from his crown.[2] David's father, however, Jesse, forms an exception, for he is said to have been one of

[1] *Yalkut*, I, § 41; see also Vol. I of this work.　　[2] *Genesis Rabba*, 39.

the four men who were absolutely without sin. The other three were Benjamin, the son of Jacob, Amram, the father of Moses, and Kilab, the son of David. Had not the Almighty ordained, in consequence of the fall of Adam, that all men must die, the Angel of Death would never have had any power over these four pious men.

Among David's ancestresses are mentioned Thamar, the daughter-in-law of Judah, Miriam, the sister of Moses,[1] and Ruth, the Moabite. She was called Ruth because she had a great happiness to count among her descendants David, who was destined to offer unto the Lord his songs and praises.[2] David's mother's name was Nazbath, the daughter of Adiel, although he was at first supposed to have been the son of a slave.[3]

It happened as follows: In spite of his great piety, Jesse was not quite free from temptation. He possessed a beautiful slave upon whom he had cast his eyes, and one day he made up his mind to set the slave free and marry her. He would have carried out his design, had not his wife frustrated it. Nazbath disguised herself as the slave, and was thus married to her husband for the second time. The fruit of this union was David, and hence his words: " Behold, I was shapen in wickedness and in sin did my mother conceive me " (*Psalms*, li, 5).

Although Jesse afterwards discovered the deception, he esteemed David but lightly, and the supposed son of a slave was not educated with the other sons. David was sent to tend the sheep and was practically the servant of his brethren. When Samuel came to anoint one of the sons of Jesse as King of Israel, the father brought before the Prophet his twelve sons except David, the despised boy who was accustomed to do the menial work and to pasture the sheep. He was twenty-eight when Samuel appeared upon the scene and anointed the

---

[1] *Sotah*, 11b.   [2] *Berachoth*, 7b.   [3] *Yalkut Makhiri*, ed. Buber, II, 214.

lad as King of Israel. Hitherto David had led a life of hardship
in the desert. Here the future King of Israel had grown
accustomed to a life of privation, but he also developed his
physical strength and had many an opportunity to give proofs
both of his nobility of character and his courage. Like Moses,
when he tended the flocks of his father-in-law Jethro, David
treated the sheep entrusted to him with such loving care and
such tenderness that the Lord said: " David tends his father's
sheep with gentleness and loving care and therefore he shall
one day be the shepherd of my flock Israel." [1] David used to
separate the sheep from the young lambs. At first he led the
young lambs and let them feed on the tender grass and the
heads of the herbs, then he guided the older sheep to feed on
the less juicy grass, and finally he led the strong sturdy young
rams and let them devour the tough roots and weeds.[2]

More than once the future King of Israel had an opportunity to show his physical strength and courage in the wilderness where he passed almost his entire existence. He is supposed to have killed in one day three lions and two bears.[3]
One story, which also shows David's anxiety to build a temple
to the Lord, runs as follows:

One day David was wandering in the desert, seeking
pasture for his flock, when he suddenly came upon a reem
(rhinoceros) asleep. David, unaware that it was a reem, took
the gigantic animal for a big mountain and began to climb it,
driving his flock up its back for the purpose of letting it feed
on the grass which he supposed would grow on the mountain.
Suddenly the rhinoceros (reem) awoke from his sleep and
stood up. David was lifted up high into the air, up to the
sky. Courageous though he was, the lad was seized with
terror. He vowed then to the Lord that if God would save his
life and bring him safely to the ground, he would build a

---

[1] *Exodus Rabba*, 2, 2; *Midrash Tehillim*, 78, 70.   [2] *Exodus Rabba*, 2.
[3] *Midrash Samuel*. 20, 5.

temple as high as the horns of the reem upon which he was
being lifted up, namely, one hundred cubits. David's vow was
heard, and the Lord sent a lion upon the scene. When the
reem beheld the lion he was awestruck, for all the animals,
even the biggest, are afraid of this king of all the beasts. The
reem at once lay down, and David could have descended with
his flock as fast as possible, but he was afraid of the lion. What
did the Lord do? He sent a deer which the lion immediately
pursued, so that David was saved both from the reem and the
lion.[1] David would have kept his promise and built the
temple of the Lord as he had vowed, but it was the Lord who
would not suffer him to do so.

Soon this lonely life of a shepherd in the desert was to
come to an end, for the supposed son of a slave was to be
anointed King of Israel by Samuel, the prophet of the Lord
and kingmaker. Originally David's eldest brother Eliab, had
been destined to become King, but on account of his violent
nature and his frequent ill-treatment of his brother David he
was not deemed worthy. That was the reason why Samuel
committed an error and assumed that God's choice had fallen
upon Eliab. David was red-haired, and when, at the request
of the Prophet, the despised son of a slave was fetched from the
field, Samuel, on beholding his red hair, was taken aback and
said: " He will shed blood even as Esau did." But the Lord
replied unto Samuel: " Fear not, for David will shed blood
only with the consent of the supreme tribunal, the Sanhedrin,
i.e. he will execute those whom the latter will have sentenced
to death." [2]

Thereupon Samuel proceeded to anoint David. He had
already tried to pour oil upon the heads of David's brothers,
but every time the oil remained in the vessel and would not
come forth. Scarcely, however, did he hold the vessel over
David's head, when the oil began to flow freely and of its own

[1] *Midrash Tehillim*, 22, 28.　　　[2] *Genesis Rabba*, 63, 8.

accord from the horn, which, nevertheless, remained as full as before.

Great was the astonishment of all present when they saw that the despised son of the slave was destined to become King in Israel. It was then that David's mother, Nazbath, came forward and related how she had frustrated her husband's intention and taken the place of the beautiful slave, and that David was consequently her own son.[1]

David was very small and short of stature, but as soon as Samuel had poured the Holy Oil over him he became very tall. It is said that when he later on went out to fight the giant Goliath and put on Saul's armour, it fitted him perfectly, although King Saul was a head and shoulder taller than every man in Israel.[2]

Soon after his anointment David came to the court of King Saul. The latter had already had occasion one day to make the acquaintance of the lad and to admire his cleverness under the following circumstances:

THE MONEY AND THE HONEY JARS

There was a certain man in the days of King Saul, the King of Israel, who had a very beautiful and fascinating wife. He also possessed great wealth. He was very old and felt that the time was drawing near when he would have to depart from this world. Now the governor of the town had cast his eyes upon the young woman and wanted to take her as his concubine. The young woman refused to listen to the governor's proposal, and was consequently in great fear. She therefore took all the gold she possessed, placed it in jars, and poured on the top of it a quantity of honey. Thereupon she went to a friend of her husband, and in the presence of witnesses besought him to take care of these jars of honey until her

---

[1] *Yalkut Makhiri, ibid.*
[2] *Yalkut Makhiri, ibid.*; *Midrash Tanchuma*, ed. Buber, III, 84.

return. The woman then left the country so as to escape the wrath of the governor. Now one day the friend to whom the jars containing the gold had been entrusted married his son and required some honey for the banquet. He accordingly sent his servant to open one of the jars in his keeping and to take a little honey. Great was the servant's surprise when, on opening one jar, he discovered the gold underneath the honey. He informed his master of his discovery, and the latter examined all the other jars. They were full of gold. The man did not hesitate to abstract the gold, and on the following day he procured a quantity of honey and filled all the jars.

Some time afterwards the governor of the town died, and the woman returned to her home. She immediately claimed the jars wherein she had concealed the gold, but great was her amazement and distress when she found all the gold gone and the jars filled with honey. She went to the judge and complained of the theft of her fortune, but the judge asked her whether she could bring any witnesses or produce some other evidence to prove the theft committed by her friend.

" Alas," replied the woman, " no one knew of the gold concealed in the jars."

" Then I cannot help thee," said the judge, " and I can only advise thee to appeal to King Saul. He may be able to render thee justice."

The woman betook herself to the royal palace and begged the King to help her in her distress. But neither the King nor his councillors dared give judgment in favour of the poor woman, as her friend persistently denied having received any gold from her, and his faithlessness could not be proved. Thus the poor woman left the royal palace sorely grieved. On her way she met young David, the future King of Israel, who was a child then and playing with his companions. When he noticed the dejection of the woman and learned the cause of her distress, David thus said to her: " Go and desire the

King to allow me to deal with this matter, and I promise thee
that I will prove the truth."

Thereupon the woman returned to King Saul, and thus
she spoke to him: " My Lord, I have met a clever boy who
maintains that he can prove the truth of my assertions. I desire thee, O King, in the name of justice, to let that boy deal
with the matter."

Saul gave his permission, and when young David was
brought into his presence, he authorized him to deal with the
matter and to prove if he could that the woman had spoken
the truth.

" With the help of God," said David, " I will try to let
the truth prevail." Thereupon he had the honey jars wherein
the woman had concealed her fortune brought, and caused
them to be emptied completely and then broken in the presence of the accused and all the court. And lo, one or two gold
pieces were found to have stuck to the bottom and the inner
side of the jars. In his greed and eagerness to refill the jars
with honey and thus hide his theft, the dishonest friend had
overlooked the gold pieces adhering to the jars. He had to
admit his guilt, and was ordered to restore her fortune to the
woman he had cheated.[1]

DAVID AND GOLIATH

Soon afterwards David was called upon to meet the giant
Goliath whom he slew in battle. Goliath was the son of
Orpah, the Moabite, the sister-in-law of Ruth, who was the
ancestress of David. For forty days this giant was allowed
to come and jeer at the children of Israel because his mother
Orpah had accompanied her mother-in-law Naomi forty
steps.[2]

[1] Jellineck, *Beth-Hamidrash*, IV, pp. 150–1; *Hibbur Maassiot*; Wünsche, *Aus Israel's Lehrhallen*, II, pp, 22–24; cf. *Monatsschrift*, XXII, pp. 121–2; *Hebraische Bibliographie*, XVIII, p. 40.   [2] See Rosner, *David's Leben u. Character*.

Thereupon Jesse, David's father, said unto his son: " Now is the time for thee, my son, to redeem the pledge once given by thy ancestor Judah, the son of Jacob, who had pledged himself for the safety of Benjamin, the ancestor of Saul." [1]

Saul himself being unable to go out and fight with Goliath, David obeyed his father and went out to wrestle with the giant. In spite of the attractive and alluring promises of the King, none of the Israelites was willing to go out and encounter the terrible giant, whilst the King himself, hero though he was, was prevented by his malady from fighting Goliath. David therefore obeyed his father and declared his willingness to meet the giant in single combat.

Saul now offered the lad his armour, and though David was only of slight build and Saul very tall, the armour fitted the young hero perfectly. [2]   Saul at once recognized that the boy had been chosen by the Lord for the encounter with the giant, but he nevertheless grew pale for jealousy. David, noticing it, at once asked the King to allow him to fight the giant in his ordinary shepherd's array. On his way five stones came to meet him on their own accord, and all five turned into one stone when David touched them. [3]

David was full of misgiving when he began to move towards the redoubtable giant, but when he heard the latter blaspheming Israel, his fear disappeared completely. [4]   When he came face to face with his foe, David noticed that confusion had come over Goliath and that he was terror struck. [5]   Goliath was so confused that he uttered foolish words that had no sense: " I will cast thy flesh to the cattle of the fields."

" He seems to have lost his senses," thought David, " for he is talking foolishly, as if cattle ate flesh."

Goliath had cause for confusion and fear, for he suddenly felt that he was rooted to the ground and could not move.

[1] *Midrash Tanchuma*, section *Vayigash*.   [2] *Midrash Tanchuma*, section *Emor*.
[3] See Rosner, *loc. cit.*   [4] *Midrash Tehillin*, 36, 2.   [5] *Midrash Samuel*, 21, 3.

Two hundred and forty-eight chains enchained the limbs of the giant's body.[1]

David was now sure of victory. Throwing a pebble, he struck the giant on his forehead. The latter fell to the ground face downwards and not on his back, for two reasons. It was first for the sake of David, so that he should not have to walk a long way to cut off the head of the giant. Another reason why Goliath fell face downwards was because he was wearing the image of the idol Dagon on his breast, and the latter thus came to shame.[2]

David now approached and tried to cut off the head of Goliath, but he did not know how to remove his armours. At that moment Uriah the Hittite came up and offered to show David how Goliath's armours were fastened at his heels.

" I will help thee," said Uriah, " but promise me that thou wilt assist me in finding a wife among the daughters of Israel." David promised, and Uriah showed him how the armour was fastened by bands across the giant's feet. The Lord, however, was not pleased with David because he had not hesitated to promise the hand of a Jewess to the Hittite. " I will give him her who had been destined to be thy own wife," said the Lord. And thus Bath-Sheba, who had been pre-destined from the day of creation to be the wife of David married Uriah, and later on was the cause of David's sin.[3] His victory over Goliath made David famous, and his praises were sung in Israel. Saul grew even more jealous. He knew that the boy was of the tribe of Judah, but he caused inquiries to be made whether he was of the clan of Perez or Zerah, because he was aware that the descendants of Perez were destined to be kings in Israel.[4]

David's enemy, Doeg, informed King Saul that David

[1] *Midrash Samuel*, 21, 3; *Pesikta de Rab Kahana*, Piska, 27.
[2] *Midrash Tehillim*, 18, 32; *Midrash Shir Hashirim Rabba*, 4, 4.
[3] *Alshech*, I, Samuel, 17, 50.
[4] *Jebamot*, 76b–77a; *Midrash Ruth Rabba*, 4, 4; *Midrash Samuel*, 22.

practically had no right at all to be considered a member of the Jewish community, for he was a descendant of the Moabitess Ruth.[1] Soon after he had defeated Goliath David was compelled to flee from the court of Saul on account of the King's jealousy. Saul had promised David as a reward of his great victory over Goliath the hand of his daughter, but he tried to break his promise. David fled to Samuel, and even in his days of storm and stress assiduously studied the Law and glorified the Lord with his praises. During his wanderings he received more than one lesson in humility, and found out the wisdom of God and acknowledged His just rule and guidance of the World.

Thus one day David said unto God: "All that Thou hast created is beautiful, and wisdom is more beautiful than anything in the World. Lunacy, however, Thou shouldst not have created, for it is useless in the World and has no place in the plan of Thy harmonious and beautiful Universe. Is it beautiful or does it serve any purpose to see some lunatic running through the streets, tearing his garments and being pursued by mocking children and a hooting mob?"

Thus spoke David, to which the Lord replied: "Thou dost not approve of lunacy which I have created, but the day will soon come when thou thyself wilt take recourse to it and find it useful. Thou wilt supplicate me to afflict thee with madness."

Now it soon happened that David, fleeing from Saul, came to Ahish, King of the Philistines, who dwelt in Gath. The brothers of Goliath, whom David had killed in battle and whose sword he still carried, were in King Ahish's bodyguard. "Our Lord and King," said the brothers of Goliath, "the earth is still wet with the blood of our brother slain by David, and we therefore demand that his murderer, who is now in Gath, be executed as he well deserves." But King

[1] *Jebamot*, 76b–77a; *Midrash Ruth Rabba*, 4, 4; *Midrash Samuel*, 22.

Ahish took David's defence and tried to save his life: " He has killed your brother," said the King, " in open battle. Moreover, it was Goliath who had challenged the Jews to combat, and he was slain according to the conditions of an open and honest combat."

Thus spoke Ahish, who was a pious heathen and wished to save David's life, but the brothers of Goliath replied: " If such be the case, then according to those conditions of the combat thou shouldst now give up thy throne to David and let us be his servants." David's position was desperate, and he was in great distress. He therefore prayed to the Lord to let him appear in the eyes of King Ahish as if he had been afflicted with lunacy. The Lord granted his prayer and lent him strength to appear a madman in the eyes of the King. David now went about in the streets of Gath and wrote upon the doors: " King Ahish owes me one hundred myriads and his wife fifty." Now it happened that both Ahish's wife and his daughter were insane and caused a terrible tumult in the palace within, whilst David did likewise in front of the royal palace. And it was on account of this that the King exclaimed: " Do I lack madmen that ye have brought this fellow here?" Thus David was saved from death, thanks to his pretence of lunacy, and he admitted that even madness served some purpose and was not out of place in the harmony of creation. He composed Psalm 34, where he began his praise with the words: " I will bless the Lord at all times." His son Solomon said afterwards: " Everything hath He beautifully created in its proper time." [1]

One day, when he was being pursued by King Saul, David, having surprised his enemies while they were asleep, made up his mind to carry off Abner's water-flask, which was standing between this giant's feet. Now Abner's knees were at first drawn, and David could pass beneath them quite easily.

[1] *Midrash Tehillim*, 34, 1; cf. Bialik, *Sepher Haaggadah*, Vol. I, pp. 99–100.

Suddenly, however, Abner moved in his sleep, and stretching out his feet pinned down David with his legs as with two solid pillars. In that moment David prayed to the Lord for help, and God sent a wasp to sting Abner. The giant in his sleep once more moved his feet and drew up his knees so that David could escape. This was another instructive lesson for David, who had once doubted the usefulness of wasps and wondered why the Lord had ever created them.[1]

It was when he was being pursued by Saul that David once cut off the skirt of Saul's robe, and for this sin he was afterwards punished. He expiated his fault in his old age, when he found no warmth in his clothes wherewith he wrapped himself.[2]

Long and hot were the pursuits of Saul, and endless the sufferings of David, who had been anointed and destined to succeed Saul upon the throne of Israel. News at last reached David of the tragic death of his enemy. He uttered his famous funeral oration, cursing the mounts of Gilboa, but it is only natural to expect him to have felt some relief at the death of his bitter enemy. The way to the throne now stood open, and David is said to have composed Psalm 18 on that occasion. He was rebuked by the Lord, who reminded him of Saul's many virtues.[3]

---

[1] *Alphabetum Siracidis*, ed. Venice; Bialik, *Sepher Haaggadah*, Vol. I, p. 100,
[2] *Berachoth*, 62b.   [3] Rosner, *David's Leben*, p. 48.

CHAPTER III

The Pious King

The conquest of Jerusalem—The claims of the Jebusites—Abraham's
covenant with the heathen—The brass monuments—Joab and the tall
cypress—In the valley of the giants—The tutelary angel of the Philistines
—The rustling treetops—A scrap of paper and a piece of bronze—The
bridle of a mule—Laban's Mazebot—David's piety—The wonderful harp
—David rebuked by a frog—The power to call down rain—David's coins
—The modesty of the King—The beautiful Bath-Sheba—David is tempted
—Satan in the shape of a bird—The beauty behind the wicker screen—
David's penance—The King afflicted with leprosy—The rebellious son—
The visit to Hebron—The giant Ishbi Benob—David hunting a deer
—The water that turned to blood—The moaning dove—The royal mule
—Abishai and Orpah—The spindle of Orpah—A story in the *Ramayana*—
Rama and the demon Mârica—The ruse of the demon—The rape of Sita—
Stories told in mediæval literature—Joab the son of Zeruya—The capture
of Kinsali—The broken sword—Blood issuing from underneath the gates
—The crown of the Amalekite King—The father and his twelve sons—
The love of a father.

As soon as David had ascended the throne and been recognized as King by the whole nation of Israel, he made up
his mind to subdue the remaining part of the land which the
Israelites had not yet conquered. He also decided to capture
the ancient city of Jerusalem, which was in the possession of
the heathen Jebusites. He advanced with his army against the
heathen possessors of the city which was destined to become
the centre of Israel's greatness and religion. The Jebusites,
however, laughed at David. In the burgh of Zion they felt
quite safe, not only because the city was surrounded by a high
wall, but also because they could appeal to a covenant once
made by Abraham with their ancestors.[1]

---

[1] *Pirke de Rabbi Eliezer*, Ch. 36; see Vol. I of the present work.

When Abraham came to acquire the Cave of Machpelah from the Hittites, the latter consented to sell him the cave only under certain conditions. They insisted that the Patriarch should make a covenant with them according to which his descendants, when they came to conquer Palestine, would never wrest the city from the Jebusites. Thereupon the Jebusites had erected in their market place brass monuments upon which the conditions of the covenant were engraved. To these monuments the Jebusites now pointed when David approached their city.

" You cannot enter our city," the Jebusites said, " before you have destroyed these monuments."

David could, of course, have pointed out that the Jebusites had already attacked the Jews in the time of Joshua, but he determined to buy the city from them.

At first, however, he decided to enter the city so as to show the heathen possessors that he feared neither their power nor their high wall, but respected the promise once given by the Patriarch Abraham. His commander Joab now devised a plan how to enter the city. He took a flourishing tall cypress tree, planted it near the wall, and then bent the tree downwards, giving it to David to hold. Standing on David's head, Joab grasped the tip of the tree, and when it rebounded he sat high above the wall. He jumped into the city and here destroyed the brass monuments. The wall in the meantime miraculously lowered itself and David could enter the city.[1]

Jerusalem was now in his possession, but David wanted to indemnify the Jebusites and offered them 600 shekels, that is, 50 shekels for each of the twelve tribes of Israel.[2] The descendants of the sons of Heth took the money even as their ancestors had accepted the shekels from the Patriarch Abraham for the Cave of Machpelah. Thus Jerusalem was not only captured but bought by David, King of Israel.

[1] *Midrash Tehillim*, 18.   [2] *Pirke de Rabbi Eliezer, ibid.*

David now prepared for battle with the Philistines whom he met in the valley of Rephaim, or the Giants. Now God commanded David not to attack the enemy until he heard the treetops move. The tutelary angel of the Philistines was namely pleading the cause of the nation under his protection, and the Lord decided to pass judgment first on the tutelary angel of the Philistines and then to hand over the nation to David.

The two armies were facing one another, and the distance between them was only four ells. The Israelites were anxious to throw themselves upon the enemy, but David forbade them to move. He even had to make use of his royal authority to refrain his heroes from giving battle. " I will not disobey the will of the Lord," said David, " and I prefer to be killed by the Philistines and die a pious man rather than be victorious and disobedient to the will of the Almighty." Thus spoke David, and lo, suddenly a rustling noise was heard, and the treetops moved. The tutelary angel of the Philistines had been judged, and David was thus commanded by the Lord to attack the enemy. Thereupon the Lord said unto his angels: " Behold the difference between Saul and David." [1]

This was not the only occasion on which David obeyed the will of the Lord before going to war. Moreover, he carefully considered his right to make war and attack the enemy. To break a covenant made by his ancestors, to disregard a scrap of paper, or rather a piece of stone or brass which contained such a covenant, never entered his mind. His jurisconsults, the Sanhedrin, were instructed to investigate the causes of the war and the possible claims of the enemy. Thus before going out to war against the Philistines, David instructed the Sanhedrin to investigate certain claims the enemy had raised. The Philistines pretended that David had no right to wage a war against them because Isaac had once concluded

[1] *Midrash Tehillim*, 27.

a covenant with their King Abimelech, and the nation still possessed a pledge which consisted in the bridle of a mule which the Patriarch had given to the King of the Philistines.

A modern king, Frederick II of Prussia, is supposed to have said: " Let us first take Silesia, we shall easily find a jurisconsult afterwards who will prove our right to it." David, according to Jewish legend, acted in a different manner. He instructed the Sanhedrin carefully to investigate the claims of the Philistines. The Court decided that the claim of this nation was unfounded. Isaac had indeed concluded an alliance with Abimelech, but the present-day Philistines were in no way the descendants of the ancient inhabitants of the country. They had come to Palestine at a later date, immigrating from Caphtor.[1]

A somewhat similar claim to an alliance was raised by the Aramaeans. This nation pretended that David had no right to wage war against them because the Patriarch Jacob had once concluded a treaty with Laban, and they pointed to those *Mazebot* once erected as a sign and in memory of the alliance between the countries of Aram and Canaan. Again David consulted the Sanhedrin, and the latter declared that the Aramaeans themselves were the first to break the ancient covenant, for did they not make war against Israel in the days of Moses and Joshua? [2]

DAVID'S PIETY

David was not only a hero and a great ruler, but also a pious man, a poet, and a Psalmist. He judged his people by day and occupied himself with affairs of State, devoting the nights to study and prayer, and tasting but little sleep. " Sixty winks " of sleep did Israel's King enjoy, and the alarm-clock which awakened him was worthy of the poet and Psalmist.

[1] *Pirke de Rabbi Eliezer*, Ch. 36; *Midrash Tehillim*, 60. [2] *Ibid.*

He had hung up a wonderful harp over his head, and the strings of that harp had been made of the gut of that ram which Abraham had once sacrificed on Mount Moriah. At midnight the cool night breeze blowing from the north through the open window whispered and stirred the strings of the royal harp, and they began to vibrate, giving forth sweet and harmonious sounds, and immediately the King arose and began to study and to sing his Psalms. Once only did the royal singer forget his modesty and boast that no creature praised the Lord as much as he did. Immediately a croaking frog appeared and informed David that it had uttered more praises to the Creator than he ever did. It was then that David sang Psalms 119 and 57 (119, 62; 57, 9).[1]

It is said that David's piety was so great that he had the power to call down the rain, the tempest, and the hail. These things were formerly stored up in heaven, but to David, on account of his great piety, was granted the power to make them descend on the earth. David showed his modesty even in the manner in which he had his coins struck. They contained not his own effigy, as is and was the custom of modern and ancient rulers, but the tower of David on one side and a shepherd's pouch on the other.[2]

BATH-SHEBA

Even the sin David had committed when he took to wife the beautiful Bath-Sheba, the widow of Uriah the Hittite, is explained in Haggadic lore as a punishment sent to him for his self-confidence and his boast that he had the power to resist temptation, even like the three Patriarchs.

One day David himself besought the Lord to lead him into temptation. " Lord of the Universe," he prayed, " why

[1] Berachoth, 3b; Midrash Tehillim, 22, 8; 37, 4; Midrash Ruth, 6, 1; Succah, 26b; Pirke de Rabbi Eliezer, Ch. 21; Yalkut, II, § 889; Sotah, 10b; cf. Lewner, Kol Aggadoth, Vol. III, pp. 265-268. [2] Genesis Rabba, 39.

art Thou called the God of Abraham, Isaac, and Jacob, and not the God of David?"

" Because," replied the Creator, " I have proved these pious men, but thee I have not yet proved."

" Then try me, too, O Lord," prayed David. God granted his request, and even warned him beforehand, a privilege never vouchsafed to the Patriarchs, that he would be tempted and tried by a woman.

One day Satan appeared in the disguise of a bird, and David shot an arrow at the bird. It had perched on a beehive or wicker screen behind which the beautiful Bath-Sheba was combing her long tresses. The shot, instead of hitting the bird, threw over the wicker screen, and the King suddenly beheld the dazzling beauty of Bath-Sheba. David fell in love with her and took her to wife. In legendary lore, however, it is explained that the royal lover never really committed any sin in marrying Bath-Sheba. Uriah the Hittite had left for the wars and, as it was customary, had given his wife a bill of divorce.[1]

Whatever his sin, David repented of it and strove to expiate it. He did penance for twenty-two years, and accepted with pious resignation and even joy the punishments and sorrows the Lord sent him.[2] It is said that David was afflicted with leprosy for six months and was cast out and separated from his people, his court, and even the Sanhedrin.[3]

The greatest blow to David was perhaps the rebellion of his son Absalom. David's friends reproached him for having married a captive of war, the woman who bore him Absalom, the rebellious son. The latter had cunningly obtained from his father a written permission to select two distinguished men who would accompany him on his visit to Hebron. Thereupon he travelled all over Palestine, showing his father's letter in every town, and thus induced two of the most distinguished

[1] *Sanhedrin, 107a; Sabbath, 56a.* [2] *Tana debe Eliahu Rabba,* II. [3] *Sanhedrin, 107a.*

and influential men to accompany him. He thus succeeded in
gathering two hundred men round him whom his faithful
followers tried to win over to his cause during a banquet he
offered them at Hebron.[1]

DAVID AND ISHBI BENOB

David repented of his sins, and he gladly accepted the
numerous sufferings that were sent upon him, but his sins
were not so easily forgiven. He was responsible for the murder
of the priests of Nob, and for the death of many others who
had perished through him (or been punished by him).

One day the Lord said unto him: " Choose now, what
dost thou prefer, to see thy posterity destroyed or to fall into
the hands of the enemy." And David replied: " Lord of the
Universe, deliver me into the hands of my enemy, but let not
my house be doomed to destruction."

Now it happened that war had again broken out between
Israel and the Philistines.

One day David went out hunting when Satan appeared to
him in the disguise of a deer. David chased the animal and was
thus enticed into the land of the enemy. He was suddenly
recognized by Ishbi Benob, a brother of the giant Goliath,
who exclaimed: " Here is the man who has slain my brother;
he is now in my power, and I will take my revenge." Thereupon Ishbi Benob seized King David, chained him, and cast
him down and laid a wine-press upon him. David might have
been crushed and life squeezed out of him, but a miracle
happened which saved his life. God caused the earth underneath the prisoner to soften and sink so that it yielded to the
weight of David's body, and the King was saved from death.
All this happened on a Sabbath eve. At this moment Abishai,
the son of Zeruyah, was just preparing for the incoming

[1] *Sanhedrin*, 107a; *Jerushalmi, Sotah*, I, 5; *Midrash Tanchuma*, section *Vayetze*, 17.

Sabbath and was washing his head in four basins of water.
Suddenly he perceived drops of blood in the water. Raising
up his head, he beheld a dove, and was startled by the moaning and plaining of the bird. "The dove," thought Abishai,
" is the symbol of the people of Israel, and I presume that this
bird has come to apprise me that the King is in danger." Thereupon Abishai hurried to the royal palace and searched for the
King. Not finding David at home, he made up his mind to
mount the swiftest animal he could find and hurry out in search
of the King. Now the swiftest animal at Abishai's disposal
was the royal mule, the one David himself was wont to ride.
Abishai, however, hesitated to mount the royal mule without
an express permission of the doctors learned in the law. He
knew that the law forbade the subject to ride the King's horse,
mount his throne, or grasp his sceptre.[1] This, however, was
a case of emergency, and time was pressing.

Abishai therefore went to the sages and obtained their
permission. On account of the impending danger, the sages
permitted him to avail himself of the mule used by the King.
Abishai now mounted the animal and swiftly rode out into
the desert. A miracle, however, happened, and the earth flew
under him. He had scarcely left Jerusalem when he already
found himself in the land of the Philistines and in front of
Ishbi's house. Here Abishai met Orpah, the mother of the
giant, who was sitting without the door spinning. The mother
of the giant, on perceiving the new arrival, broke her thread
and flung the spindle at him with intent to kill him. Abishai
picked up the spindle and hurled it at Orpah with such force
that it struck her on her brow and killed her.

When Ishbi saw what had happened, he said unto himself:
" Now there are two of them here and they will kill me." Thereupon he drew David from under the wine-press and, hurling
him up in the air, held his lance up in the hope that David would

<hr />

[1] *Sanhedrin, 22a.*

fall upon it and be transfixed. Abishai, however, quickly uttered the Ineffable name of God, which had the effect of arresting David in his fall and keeping him suspended between Heaven and Earth. Thereupon Abishai questioned David as to how he had come to be in such a sore plight, and the King acquainted his cousin with the question the Lord had asked him and with the answer he himself had made. Abishai, however, persuaded the King to change his mind. This courtier, had he lived centuries later, would have approved of the famous saying: *Après nous le déluge.*

" What dost thou care," said Abishai to his royal master, " what happens to thy descendants? Let them sell wax if they like, as long as thou art left in peace! Follow my advice and reverse thy prayer, plead for thyself rather, and let thy descendants take care of themselves."

David was persuaded, and the two now joined their prayers and pleaded to the Lord to avert David's doom and to save him from the hands of the Philistine. Thereupon Abishai once more spoke the Ineffable name, and David gradually came down to earth at some distance from the lance of the giant. The two now at first swiftly ran away from the giant, but suddenly changing their minds offered resistance. When they reminded Ishbi of his mother's death, his strength and courage forsook him and he was slain by David and Abishai.[1]

This story is told in a different version in another place, where it is given as an illustration of the words of the Prophet: " Let not the strong boast of his strength." (*Jeremiah*, 9, 22.) David was namely beginning to be proud of his strength, for it is said that he could transfix 800 men with one throw of his spear. The Lord wanted to show him that without divine assistance he was a weak, helpless mortal.[2]

There is a story in the *Ramayana* which closely resembles

---

[1] *Sanhedrin*, 95a; cf, Lewner, *l.c.* 286–291.
[2] Jellinek, *Beth-Hamidrash*, IV, p. 140; VI, pp. 106–108; *Midrash Tanchuma*, section *Vayetze*; *Midrash Tehillim*, 18, 30.

this Talmudical legend of David and Ishbi Benob. Rama was living in the forest of Dandaka together with the beautiful Sita and his brother Lakshmana. Single-handed he had destroyed fourteen thousand giants and demons who were infesting the forest where he had chosen his abode. Now Ravana, King of the Rakshasas, heard of the massacre of his people, and was also informed of Sita's supernatural beauty. To wreak revenge on Rama he decided to carry off Sita, and for that purpose sent to the forest one of his faithful serving spirits, the demon Mârica. The latter assumed a disguise and appeared to Rama as a deer, dazzling like gold.

When Sita beheld the glorious animal, she expressed the desire to possess its brilliant fur and to spread it on her couch. Rama thereupon left Sita with his brother whilst he himself went out in pursuit of the deer. The disguised demon enticed Rama to the very outskirts of the forest. Rama at last loosed an arrow, and Mârica was hit. But even whilst feeling himself on the point of death the demon remained faithful to his King, and by a ruse tried to help him. He uttered a terrible cry, shouting: " It is I, Rama, help, my brother!"

Sita heard the cry and, thinking that Rama was in danger of death, dispatched Lakshmana to her husband. Thereupon Ravana, who had been lying in wait, availed himself of the absence of the two heroes, and captured Sita.

The situation is, of course, different in the Talmudical legend and in the tale in the *Ramayana*, but in both it is a demon in the disguise of a deer who is enticing the hunter, leading him into danger. Are we entitled to conclude that the Talmudical legend is of Indian origin and that the Rabbis of the Talmud had received the story from Persian sources? [1]

In addition, however, to the demon assuming the disguise of a deer and enticing the hunter, the above legend also contains another motive, namely that of the water changing into

[1] *Revue des Études Juives*, II, p. 302.

blood which is supposed to have informed Abishai that David was in distress. This motive is found not only in an Egyptian legend of the fourteenth century B.C., but also in a Serbian tale; in the famous mediæval French novel *Histoire d'Olivier de Castille et d'Artus d'Algarbe*, where the water, as a sign of danger, turns black; in a Russian popular tale,[1] and in many other European folk-tales.[2]

There are numerous examples in folk-lore where a metal object is changing colour at the moment the person who is dear to us is in danger or distress. We find it in the Talmud in the case of the friends of Job who knew of his distress because they had each a crown on which were engraven the portraits of the other three friends. When one of them was in danger, the aspect of his portrait was suddenly changed.[3] We find this trait in a story of *Thousand and One Nights* (the story of the two sisters who were jealous of the younger sister), in a tale of the *Pentameron*, and in the French novel *Floire et Blanchefleur*.[4]

We see no reason whatever why the Talmudical legend should have been borrowed from a Persian source. It must be borne in mind that the tale is an interpretation, as the majority of Talmudical legends are, of the Biblical passage *II Sam.* 21, 16–17, " and Ishbi Benob who was of the descendants of Harapha ". It is quite possible that the Talmudical legend is an adaptation from the Persian, but then it has exercised its influence (as we have pointed out in the Introduction to Vol. I) upon mediæval folk-lore.

---

[1] A. Rambaud, *La Russie épique*, p. 378.
[2] Cosquin, *Contes populaires de Lorraine*, Vol. I, pp. lxv, ff; *Revue des Études Juives*, XVII, p. 204.
[3] *Baba Batra*, 16b.
[4] Cosquin, *loc. cit.*; Israël Lévi, in *Revue des Études Juives*, XVII, 204.

Joab the Son of Zeruya. The Capture of Kinsali

One of David's most famous chieftains was the hero Joab, whose achievements in the field were very great. The occasion on which he gave proof of his heroism in the most remarkable manner was when he captured single-handed the Amalekite capital Kinsali.

In the days of David, King of Israel, it happened that Joab, the son of Zeruya, betook himself to Kinsali, the Amalekite capital, which he wanted to take. The children of Israel laid siege to the town. When six months had elapsed, the heroes assembled, and thus they spoke unto Joab, their general.

" We can no longer remain here, for it is such a long time since we left our villages, and it is high time that we returned to our homes, our wives, and our children."

Thereupon Joab said to them: " If ye return home the King will be displeased, and moreover, all the other nations will hear of this and will be greatly encouraged to unite and make war against us. I now propose unto ye to make a sling and to hurl me into the city."

Thereupon Joab took 1000 pieces of silver and his sword, and he was hurled into the city. Before leaving his men he thus spoke to them: " Wait another forty days, and when ye see blood flow from underneath the gates of the city then know ye that I am still alive, otherwise ye may conclude that I am dead and ye can return to your houses."

Thus Joab was cast into the city, and he fell into the courtyard of a widow who also had a married daughter. The young woman, on going out into the courtyard, found Joab lying there in a faint. She called her mother and her husband, and the three brought him into the house, where they revived him. When he had regained consciousness, they asked him who he was and how he had come into the courtyard.

" I am an Amalekite," said Joab, " and was taken prisoner
by the Israelites. They brought me into the presence of their
King, who ordered his soldiers to hurl me into this city. I beg
you, therefore, to spare my life." Thereupon he handed them
ten silver pieces, and they received him kindly and gave him
hospitality.

Joab remained in the house for ten days and then asked
permission to go out into the town.

" Thou canst not go out," said his hosts, " in thy present
apparel." They gave him an Amalekite garb, and he went out
into the town.

There were 140 squares in the town, one larger than the
other, and each had two entrances. Joab immediately went
to an armourer and, showing him his broken sword, asked the
Amalekite to forge him another like the weapon he had broken.
When the armourer saw Joab's broken sword he was amazed,
for he had never seen such a weapon in all his life. He forged
a new sword, but Joab snapped it in two, and he did likewise
with the second sword. The third sword the armourer had
fashioned Joab shook but did not break. Grasping the sword,
he asked the armourer whom he ought to slay with it, to which
the latter unhesitatingly replied: " Joab, the general of the
King of Israel."

" Let us suppose that I am he," said Joab, and then added:
" Look behind thee." The smith turned his head, and Joab
ran him through and threw aside his body. Thereupon he
went out into one of the squares and killed 500 warriors, and
none of them remained alive. He sheathed his sword and returned to the house where he had found hospitality.

In the meantime the rumour had spread in the town that
Ashmedai, King of the demons, had slain 500 warriors. When
his hosts inquired of Joab whether he had heard the rumour,
he said that he had not heard anything about it. Once more
Joab took out some money and dispensed it among his hosts.

On the following day he went out for the second time, slew another 500 Amalekites, and returned to his lodgings. As his hand was tired from so much action and his sword clave to it, he asked his young hostess to bring him some warm water to wash his hand and to take the sword out of it.

"Thou eatest and drinkest with us," cried the young woman, "and yet thou slayest our warriors." He immediately slew the woman, afraid lest she betray him. His hand became immediately free, and he once more sallied forth. He heard a herald proclaiming that the King had commanded that anybody who sheltered a guest in his house should bring the stranger immediately. Joab slew the herald and did likewise to everyone whom he met.

Thereupon he opened the gates of the city and blood issued forth. When the Israelites, who had mourned Joab as dead and made up their minds to return to their homes, saw the blood they knew that their general was alive, and they cried out with one accord: "Hear, O Israel, the Eternal is our God, the Eternal is One."

Thereupon Joab mounted upon the tower, so that the children of Israel could see him, and called aloud: "The Lord will not forget His people for the sake of His great name, and ye, Israelites, assault the city and capture it."

They slew all the inhabitants and destroyed the heathen temples. The Amalekite King, however, whom Joab had left alive, he brought before David. And he took the crown which was of pure gold and set in with a wonderful gem from the head of the heathen King and placed it upon that of David, the King of Israel.[1]

[1] Jellinek, *Beth-Hamidrash*, V, pp. 146–148.

The Father who would not Sell his Son

Although a warrior, a blunt soldier, Joab was not disinclined to study and even to argue with David on moral questions. Now when he heard the King utter the words, " Like as a father pitieth his children, so the Lord pitieth them that fear him ", he felt rather surprised, and thus he spoke unto himself: " Should the love of a father for his child be used for the comparison and not the love of a mother for her child? Is it not the mother who loves the child more, who is looking after it and is taking care of it? How can my royal master utter such words? I will keep my eyes open, observe the conduct and behaviour of the people, and endeavour to find out whether the words of David are really true to fact."

And Joab roamed about in the land of Israel. On one of his journeys he came to a place where he happened to meet an old man who was rather poor but had twelve children. All day long the old man toiled hard to support his twelve children, and when evening came he bought with the money he had earned a loaf of bread, and thus he supported his family with his scanty earnings. Though he was old and feeble, none of his children had to work, for the father supported them and worked for them. When the man came home in the evening, it was his habit to cut his loaf into fourteen parts, two for himself and his wife, and twelve for his twelve children.

When Joab saw this man and the hard life he was compelled to lead, he said unto himself: " I will try my first experiment with this man." Thereupon he approached the man when he was about to begin his work in the field, and thus he spoke to him: " How strange is thy conduct! Thou art an old man and yet dost thou work hard in order to support thy children. Would it not be more just if thy children were to work for thee and support thee in thine old age? Anyhow, I propose unto thee to sell one of thy children to the King, my royal master. Thou wilt thus have one less to support, whilst the money thou wilt realize thou canst apply to the support of thy other children."

Thus spoke Joab, but the old man angrily rejected the proposition. No, he would not sell any of his children.

Joab now decided to approach the mother and to make the same proposal to her. He visited her in the absence of her husband and thus spoke to her: " Thou and thy husband are both old and ye have brought up twelve children, and whilst ye are working they are living on the labour of your hands and your daily toil." Thus spoke Joab, to which the woman replied: " What can we do? Such is the way of the world that parents work for and take care of their children."

" That may be true," replied Joab, " but I wish to lessen your burden, and I therefore offer thee a hundred gold pieces if thou wilt sell me one of thy sons. The money will be enough for you to end your days in peace and plenty."

The woman soon yielded to his persuasions, but she was afraid of her husband. " If my husband," she said, " becomes aware of the fact that I have sold one of our sons, he will surely kill me."

" He will not miss one son out of so many," said Joab, " but should he do so, then I will give thee back thy son."

The woman accepted the offer, took the hundred gold pieces, and sold one of her sons. When the old man returned home in the evening, he cut his bread, as was his daily custom, into fourteen portions, and when he saw that one piece of bread had remained, he missed one of his children. He inquired after the missing child, and insisted so long until the woman told him the truth. " I have sold the child," said the mother, " to the stranger who called here before, and here are the hundred gold pieces he gave me."

When the father heard what had occurred, he was greatly grieved and would take neither food nor drink. Impatiently he waited for the next morning, when he immediately set out to find Joab and to claim his child. He took with him the hundred gold pieces and a weapon, firmly decided to return the money to the stranger, but to slay him should he refuse to give up the child.

Joab was in the meantime waiting on the road to see what would happen. When the old man beheld Joab he angrily exclaimed: " Here is thy money, and give me back my child."

" Thy wife sold me thy son," replied Joab, " and she had a right to do so." But the father waxed very wroth and threateningly said: " I will not parley with thee; if thou wilt return my child it is well, otherwise I will fight thee to the death and either kill thee or be killed myself." Joab smiled and finally surrendered the child to the loving father.

" David was right," he exclaimed, " when he uttered his words: ' Like as a father pitieth his children, so the Lord pitieth them that fear him '. He did not say ' Like as a mother pitieth her children ', for here have I met a mother who was ready to sell one of her sons, although she had not to work for the child's maintenance. The father, on the contrary, who has to support the twelve children, was ready to lay down his life rather than part with one of them." [1]

---

[1] Jellinek, *loc. cit.*, V, pp. 52–53; cf. pp. xxii–xxiv, and VI, pp. xvi–xvii; *Ozar Midrashim*, I, pp. 213*a*–214*a*; Bin Gorion, *loc. cit.*, Vol. III, pp. 87–90.

CHAPTER IV

The Dead Lion, or King David
after his Death

The death of a king—The measure of his days—David's request—The
Lord's refusal—David destined to die on a Saturday—The angel of death
and the study of the Torah—The angel's ruse—The noise in the garden
—The broken stairs—The removal of the corpse—The barking dogs—
Solomon's perplexity—The decision of the Sanhedrin—A living dog is
better than a dead lion—David is still alive—Messiah the son of David—
The messianic banquet—The cup of blessing—The royal tomb—The pious
washerwoman—Her miraculous escape—The sword of the pasha—The
kadi's advice—The Rabbi of Jerusalem—The pious beadle—What he saw
in the royal tomb.

THE DEATH OF A KING

A Living Dog is better than a Dead Lion

David had frequently prayed to the Lord " to inform him as
to his end, and the measure of his days " (*Psalms*, 39, 4), that is,
to tell him when his life would run out. The Lord, however,
refused to grant David's prayer, for it was an inalterable decree
that such information be hidden from man, and no man (with
the exception of Hezekiah) was to foreknow his end. David
thereupon begged to be informed on what day of the week
his life would come to an end, and it was revealed to him that
this would happen on a Sabbath.

" Lord of the Universe," prayed David, " let the day of
my death be postponed for one day, and may I be permitted

40

to die on the Sunday following." This request was not vouch-safed unto him. "The reign of Solomon," said the Lord, "will begin on that Saturday, the day of thy death, and no reign should overlap even by one moment the reign of another."

Thereupon David besought the Lord to permit him to die on the Friday, the day before. Once more the Lord denied his request. God delighted in the study of the Law, rather than in holocausts. "One day," said the Lord, "spent by thee in the study of the Torah is better than a thousand burnt offerings which thy son Solomon will bring upon the altar in the Temple" (*Psalms*, 84, 10).

Now the angel of death has no power over a man when he is engaged upon the study of the Torah. Henceforth David spent every Sabbath in the study of the Torah, never per-mitting himself any pause. He thus hoped to foil the angel of death. When David's life had actually run out and the angel of death presented himself to take the pious king's soul, he was greatly embarrassed, for David never for a moment interrupted his study.

Weary of waiting, the angel of death at last had resort to a ruse. There was a garden behind the royal palace, and the angel of death went and shook one of the trees, making a tre-mendous noise. Greatly astonished, David rose up and went out to ascertain the cause of the strange noise. He interrupted his study for a moment and descended a stairway leading into the garden. This was an opportunity which the angel of death immediately seized. One of the steps gave way, and David fell down and was killed.

Now the body of David was exposed to the scorching sun, and Solomon doubted whether he could remove it on the Sabbath. The dogs, too, had not been fed the day before and were barking fiercely. Solomon therefore sent word to the Sanhedrin and asked the assembly's advice.

"My father is dead," said Solomon, "and exposed to the
scorching sun, and the dogs have not been fed and are growing
fierce. What can I do in the matter without desecrating the
Sabbath?" Promptly came the decision of the Sanhedrin:
"Put a loaf of bread or a child upon the body of thy father
and then remove it, so that it will appear as if the loaf or the
child were *really* moved. As for the dogs, cut a carcass and
throw it before them, for it is permitted to profane the Sabbath
for the purpose of feeding a living creature."

When Solomon heard this decision of the Sanhedrin, he
exclaimed: "A living dog is better than a dead lion." [1]

According to another version, the day on which David
died was both a Sabbath and the first day of Pentecost. As
the body of the dead King could not be moved, Solomon,
who had sway of beasts and birds, summoned the eagles
and commanded them to guard the body of his father with
their wings. [2]

David, however, the King of Israel, is supposed to be still
alive. His death was merely a removal from his earthly scene
of action. He dwells in Paradise among the elect, his brilliant
crown upon his head. [3] He is the ancestor of the Redeemer
who will put an end to Israel's suffering and who is referred
to as "Messiah, the son of David".

According to several Haggadic passages in the Talmud, it
is not one of his descendants but King David himself who will
be the Messiah. He will reappear and assume the rule over
Israel. He ruled in the past and he will rule in the future, in
this world and in the world to come. [4]

King David enjoys great distinction among the elect and
the just who dwell in Paradise. According to Talmudic
legend, a great distinction and honour will be vouchsafed unto

[1] *Sabbath*, 30a–b.   [2] *Ruth Rabba*, I, 17; cf. Lewner, *l.c.* Vol. III, pp. 303–305.
[3] Jellinek, *Beth-Hamidrash*, V, p. 168; VI, pp. 25–26.
[4] *Midrash Tehillim*, 5, 4; 18, 27; 57, 3; *Midrash Samuel*, 19, 6; see also A. Rosner,
David's Leben, 1908, p. iii.

him on the day of the Last Judgment. On the day on which the Lord will have redeemed His people and accomplished His loving kindness to the seed of Isaac, He will make a banquet for the righteous. The throne of David will be placed by the side of the Throne of Glory. At the end of the banquet a blessing will have to be said over a cup of wine. This cup will be offered at first to the Patriarch Abraham. Abraham, however, will decline the honour: " I am not worthy," he will say, " to pronounce the blessing over the cup of wine, because I begot Ishmael whose descendants do not walk in the ways of the Lord."

The cup of blessing will then be offered to Isaac, but he, too, will decline the honour. " I am not worthy to pronounce the blessing," he will say, " because I am the father of Esau." Jacob, too, will refuse to say the blessing because he had married two sisters simultaneously, which the Torah afterwards prohibited.

" Moses," the Lord will say, " speak thou the blessing over the cup of wine," but he who led the Israelites out of bondage will decline the honour. " I am not worthy of it," he will say, " since I was not counted worthy to enter the Holy Land."

Joshua, too, to whom the cup will be offered, will refuse the honour on the ground that he was not deemed worthy to have a son. The cup will then be offered unto David, who will accept the honour of saying the blessing.

" I will pronounce the blessing," the King of Israel will say, " and I will not decline the honour. I will take the cup of salvation and call upon the Name of the Lord." [1]

---

[1] *Pesachim*, 119b.

THE ROYAL TOMB

Many wonderful stories are told in post-Talmudical literature of the tomb of David and the miracles which happened in connection with it. The two following tales are a good example.

THE PIOUS WASHERWOMAN

There once lived in Jerusalem a righteous woman who had lost her husband and children. She was earning her living by the toil of her hands, washing the clothes of her neighbours. Among her customers was also the keeper of the tomb of David, peace be upon him.

One day when she brought to this man his linen, white as snow, he thus spoke unto her: " Thou art a good and pious woman, and my soul is yearning to give thee a great joy. Thou wouldst no doubt be happy to visit the tomb of the King, which no Jew has hitherto been allowed to enter."

" I should indeed be most happy," replied the woman, " to be deemed worthy of such an honour."

" Then come with me," said the keeper of the tomb. He led her to a gate which he bade her pass, but scarcely had she entered the passage when he closed and locked the gate, leaving the poor woman alone in the darkness. Thereupon he ran to the *kadi* and informed him that a Jewess had had the audacity to enter the tomb of David, and that as soon as he had noticed it he had immediately locked the gate.

When the kadi heard this he was greatly incensed, and exclaimed: " By the Prophet, this woman deserves death. Lead her out, and she will be condemned to be burnt alive."

The poor woman, in the meantime, realized the fact that she had been betrayed by the keeper and that her life was in danger. She fell upon her knees and prayed to the Lord to have pity on her for the sake of His servant David. As she was thus weeping and praying, a great light suddenly rent the darkness of the tomb, and she beheld a white-haired old man with a shining and benevolent countenance. Taking the trembling woman by the hand, he led her through tortuous and winding subterranean passages until they reached the open. Thereupon the old man said to her: " Run swiftly to thy house, and there start thy work at the wash-tub without confiding to anyone what has occurred." The woman opened her mouth to thank the wonderful old man, but he had already vanished.

In the meantime the kadi, accompanied by his officials, arrived before the gate of the tomb, and orders were given to seize the woman and lead her to the place of execution. In vain, however, did the kadi and his servants search the tomb, for no trace of the woman was to be found. Greatly astonished, the kadi accused the keeper of having mocked him, but the latter swore by the Prophet that the woman had really entered the tomb. The kadi thereupon sent his servants to the home of the washerwoman, and the messengers soon returned informing their master that they had found the accused in front of her washing-tub.

The keeper was now accused of perjury, and by the order of the kadi he was seized and burnt. The pious washerwoman never divulged to anyone the miracle which had happened to her in the tomb of David. On her deathbed only she acquainted the community of Jerusalem with her secret.[1]

THE SWORD OF THE PASHA

Another miraculous story about the tomb of David runs as follows: It happened one day that a pasha, standing in front of the tomb of David and looking through a window of the mausoleum, let fall his sword. The weapon, ornamented with

[1] *Maasse Nissim*, § 3; see *Midr. Abot*, 44*b*; Bin Gorion, *Der Born Judas*, Vol. V, pp. 63–66.

pearls and diamonds, dropped into the interior of the cave. The pasha was anxious to recover his sword, and an Ishmaelite, or Mohammedan, was lowered on a cord through the window. When the man was drawn up again he was dead. A second, a third, and a fourth Mohammedan met with the same fate.

The pasha declared that he was determined to have his sword, even if all the inhabitants of Jerusalem were to perish in the search after it.

Thereupon the kadi approached, and thus he spoke: " My Lord, may it please unto thee to spare the lives of the faithful and to listen to the advice of thy servant. Send thy messenger to the house of the Jewish Rabbi, the Haham Basha, and command him to send one of his co-religionists to be lowered into the tomb. King David is of the Jewish race, and he will not harm any one of the children of Israel."

Thus spoke the kadi, and the pasha acted upon his advice. He informed the Rabbi of Jerusalem that should he refuse to send one of his community to fetch the weapon, all the Jews of Jerusalem would suffer.

Great was the distress of the Rabbi when he saw himself placed between the alternative of either desecrating the tomb of King David or of letting his people suffer. For three days he and his community fasted and prayed at the grave of Rachel, and on the fourth day he decided to cast lots as to who should dare descend into the tomb of David. The beadle of the Synagogue, a pious and righteous man, was designated as the messenger. He accepted the mission, purified his soul, and made ready for the perilous descent. In an attitude of prayer, with tearful eyes, he betook himself to the mausoleum containing the royal tombs of the Kings of Israel. He was lowered down through the window, and both Jews and Mohammedans breathlessly waited for the result. After a while, a feeble voice was heard calling from the tomb: " Draw me up."

Soon the beadle, deathly pale, but holding the pasha's

THE RECOVERY OF THE PASHA'S SWORD

sword in his trembling hand, came up. The people present fell upon their faces and exclaimed, " Blessed be the Lord, the God of Israel," and the Jews of Jerusalem manifested great joy. The beadle refused to reveal to anyone what he had seen in the tomb. He told the Rabbi, however, that when he entered the tomb he saw a great light, and then a venerable old man suddenly stood before him and handed him the sword he had come to fetch.[1]

---

[1] *Maasse Nissim*, § 2; see Bin Gorion, *loc. cit.*, Vol. V, pp. 61–63.

CHAPTER V
King Solomon's Judgments

Solomon's prayer—The heavenly gift—Wisdom instead of gold—The true son—The faithless servant—A finger cut off from the dead body—The blood test—The blood and the bone—A man and his three sons—The legitimate heir—The sons shoot an arrow at the dead body of their father—The rightful heir—The King and the Gaon Saadya—A story from Barbazan's *Fabliaux*—A story from the *Gesta Romanorum*—The sons beating at the father's grave—The superstition attached to blood—Talmud and mediæval folk-lore—The blood accusation—Hartland on the bond of blood—The three travellers and the theft of gold—Solomon tells a story—The maiden who plighted her troth—The honest robber—A story told by Campbell—The farmer and his three sons—The two-headed man—Seven that are eight—Ashmedai and King Solomon—The claim of the two-headed heir—Hot water and wine poured over the two-headed man—Solomon's judgment.

Solomon's Prayer

The Lord appeared to Solomon in Gibeon in a dream by night and said unto him: " Ask what I should give unto thee;" and Solomon thought in his heart: " What shall I ask from the Lord? Gold and silver? Power over my enemies? The Lord will surely grant my request, but then I will only be like the other Kings of the earth. I will therefore ask some gift besides which everything else is as nought." And he asked from the Lord to bestow upon him wisdom and understanding which will enable him to distinguish between right and wrong and help him to judge the children of Israel. And when the Lord saw that Solomon did not ask for wisdom so that it might enable him to make war and conquer many lands, but for the purpose of judging the children of Israel with justice and equity, He granted his request.[1] Solomon was greater in wisdom than the wisest men before him and after him. He gave many proofs of his early wisdom, as the following stories told of the famous King will show.

THE TRUE SON

A certain man who lived in the days of King David had acquired great wealth and had vast possessions and slaves. He had only one son, to whom he gave much gold and merchandise, and sent him to distant lands to traffic and do business. The son boarded a ship and sailed to Africa, where he prospered exceedingly. In the meantime his father had died and left all his gold and his possessions in the hands of one of his servants. The latter now began to ill-treat all the other servants so that they all ran away. The servant now appropriated unto himself all the gold and possessions his master had left, and began to behave as if he were the rightful heir and owner of the vast wealth. After a lapse of time the son returned from distant lands, and when he heard that his father was dead he wished to come into his inheritance. But the servant beat him and drove him out of the house.

" I am the rightful son and heir," he cried, " and thou art only a lying slave who wishes to take the place of his master." In his despair the rightful son went to King David and submitted the matter to him.

" Hast thou any witnesses who could prove that thou art the son of the deceased and his rightful heir?" asked King David.

" I have been away for many years," replied the son, " and all the people who knew me are dead. I have no witnesses who could prove my identity."

[1] *Midrash Tanchuma*, section *Houkat*; see Lewner, *Kol Aggadoth*, Vol. III. p. 307, No. 304.

When King David heard these words, he said: " If thou canst not produce any witnesses then I cannot give judgment in thy favour."

The cries and lamentations of the son deprived of his rightful inheritance availed him not until Solomon, who was then only a child, came to his rescue. The young Prince called the son aside and thus said unto him: " Go thou again before the King and ask him to pronounce judgment in thy favour, but if he be perplexed, beg him to allow me to deal with the matter, for I can bring it to a just end."

The man followed Solomon's advice, and King David consented and allowed his son to act as judge. Solomon now called the servant who had usurped the place of his master and asked him whether he knew the place where his father was buried.

" I do," replied the usurper.

" Then go and cut off one of his fingers and bring it to me," said Solomon.

The usurper did as he was bidden. When the finger of the dead man was brought, Solomon commanded both the rightful son and the pretender to cut their flesh and let their blood run into separate vessels. He then commanded that the dead man's finger be dipped into the blood of the servant. This was done, but the blood had no effect upon the dead bone, and it remained as white as if the blood had been water. The finger was then dipped into the blood of the son, and lo, the bone was at once dyed red, having sucked in all the blood.

" He is the son of the deceased," said Solomon, " and the rightful owner of his wealth." Lifting up the dead man's finger, he said: " See that this bone and this blood are related, for this man is flesh of the flesh and bone of the bone of the deceased. He has proved himself to be the son and rightful owner, and the other is only an usurper." Solomon accordingly gave judgment in favour of the son.[1]

Another version of this story runs as follows:

A certain man had three sons, but entertained some doubts as to their being all legitimates and in reality his sons. He believed, moreover, that only one of the three sons was his. What did he do? When his time to die came near, he made a will, in which he bequeathed all his money to him who was his legitimate son. After their father's death, the three sons naturally began to quarrel among themselves, each maintaining that he and not the others was the legitimate son and entitled to the inheritance. As they could not agree, they at last determined to go to King Solomon and to submit the matter to him.

As no witnesses could be produced in favour of any of the sons able to prove that he and not the others was the legitimate son, King Solomon ordered the corpse of the dead man to be disinterred and brought into his presence. He thereupon commanded his servants to tie the corpse to a tree. Turning to the three sons, he thus addressed them:

" It is impossible to say which of you is the legitimate son and the rightful heir to the wealth your father has left, and I have therefore decided to give the inheritance to him who will have proved the best shot of the three. Take ye, therefore, your bows and arrows and loose an arrow at the corpse of your father."

The first son immediately took up his bow and aiming at his father's corpse pierced his hand, whilst the second shot it through the forehead. When it was the turn of the third son to shoot, he at first took up his bow and prepared to follow the example of his brothers, but suddenly he realized what an impious act he was about to commit. Casting his bow and

---

[1] Jellinek, *Beth-Hamidrash*, IV, pp. 145–146; Wünsche, *Aus Israel's Lehrhallen*, Vol. II, pp. 13–14; *Hibbur Hamaassiot Vehamidrashot*, ed. Venice; Bin Gorion, *Der Born Judas*, Vol. III, p. 61; *Hebr. Bibliographie*, XVIII, p. 39.

arrow to the ground, he exclaimed: " I prefer to give up my claim to my father's inheritance rather than treat his body in such an unfilial manner unworthy of his son."

" Thou art indeed the deceased man's son," cried the King, " for thou alone hast shown thy filial affection and respect for thy deceased parent. By his will, thou art therefore the heir of his wealth." [1]

This tale is told differently in the *Sepher Hassidim*, where it runs as follows:

It happened in the days of the Gaon Saadya ben Joseph the wise. There was a man who went on a journey, leaving at home his wife in a state of pregnancy. He had taken with him much wealth and was accompanied by his servant. Now it happened that the master suddenly died, leaving a considerable amount of property behind. The slave now appropriated all the wealth and passed himself off as the deceased man's son and rightful heir. In the meantime the son to whom the widow of the deceased had given birth grew up, and when he learned of his father's death he went to the slave and claimed his property. The usurper, however, had in the meantime established high connections and was related to the mighty in the land, so that the rightful heir was afraid to press his claim lest he lose it and come to harm besides. He therefore went to the Gaon Saadya, to whom he told the entire story.

" My advice," said the Gaon, " is that thou seek redress from the King."

This the son accordingly did. The King now sent for the Gaon and asked him to give judgment in the matter. Thereupon the Gaon gave orders for both the son and the slave to be bled and their blood collected in separate vessels. He then caused some bones to be brought from the disinterred body of the deceased merchant. He dipped the bone of the dead man first into the blood of the slave, but the blood was not absorbed

[1] *Revue des Études Juives*, Vol. XI, p. 7.

by the bone; he then dipped the bone into the blood of the son, and at once the blood was absorbed by the bone, for the two were one body and flesh. Thereupon the Gaon restored the property to the rightful heir.[1]

THE JUDGMENT OF SOLOMON, OR THE TRUE HEIR

This incident, in a naturally different version, is told by Barbazan in his *Fabliaux*, under the title of *Le Jugement de Solomon*. The story runs as follows:

After the death of their father, two princes quarrelled about the inheritance. Solomon, who was King of Christendom, was appealed to and gave judgment. He ordered the father's corpse to be disinterred and fastened to an upright stake. He then declared that he of the two brothers who would drive his spear farthest into the body should be declared the right heir. The elder brother immediately seized his spear and struck home, but the young brother refused to commit an impious act and mangle the corpse of his father.

" I prefer to lose all my share in my father's inheritance," he said, " rather than dishonour the body of my father." He was declared the rightful heir by consent of all the Barons and put into possession of the principality. Thus by resorting to the test of natural affection, Solomon managed to solve the difficulty.[2]

In the *Gesta Romanorum* the story is somewhat similar to that related in the Midrash. It is told of the sons of a King, and the judgment is pronounced by a knight of the late King.

There was once a certain King who had a beloved but not loving wife. He also had four sons, only one of whom was legitimate. After the King's death, the sons quarrelled about the succession, and at last decided to refer the matter to an

---

[1] *Sepher Hassidim*, ed. Bologna, § 232. See also Salzberger, *Die Salomon Sage in der semitischen Literatur.*

[2] Barbazan, *Fabliaux*, Paris, 1808, Vol. II, p. 440; cf. Kemble, *The Dialogue of Solomon and Saturn*, 1848, p. 106.

honourable knight of the late King. The knight bade them
draw out the body of their father from his sepulchre and set
it upright as a mark for their arrows.

" Whosoever of you," he declared, " will succeed in trans-
fixing the heart of your father shall succeed to the throne and
be King."

The four sons agreed. Three of them took up their bows
and drove their arrows, one wounding the father's hand, the
second sending his arrow into his father's head, whilst the third
nearly pierced the father's heart. The fourth son, however,
refused to drive an arrow into the dead king's body, and would
rather give up his claim to the kingdom than commit an impious act. He was therefore declared to be the true son and
proclaimed King.[1]

Very little attention seems to have been attached to a
legend in the Talmud where the following incident is told:

One day a man overheard his wife conversing with her
daughter and boasting that although she had ten sons only one
of them was by her husband. What did the man do? He left
a will wherein he bequeathed all his property to one son, the
one that was his legitimate child. As no name was mentioned,
the sons naturally quarrelled among themselves, each pre-
tending that he was the legitimate son. At last the sons decided
to put the matter before Rabbi Benaiah and ask him to arbitrate.

" As you do not know to whom your father intended to
bequeath his property, you will be well advised to go and beat
at your father's grave until he rises up and tells you whom he
meant to be his heir."

Although somewhat puzzled, the sons went and did as the
Rabbi had advised them to. One son only refused to beat
at his father's grave and show such marked unfilial behaviour. He preferred to lose the property rather than show
disrespect to his father's grave, and because he alone of the

---

[1] *Gesta Romanorum*, ed. Graesse, No. 45.

ten brothers had shown respect for his father's memory and affection for his dead parent, the Rabbi decided that he was the rightful owner, and that it was to him that his father had bequeathed the property.[1]

The blood-test story related of Solomon is, in our opinion, of a purely Jewish origin.

There are many superstitions among the Jews connected with blood, blood having always been considered as an object of sacred and religious awe, and nothing is more preposterous than the ritual blood-accusation raised against the Jews from time to time.

The Bible already considers the blood to be the seat of the soul, and the Talmud considerably intensifies the commands and prohibition against partaking of blood. In folk-lore blood plays a prominent part, and it is employed not only for the binding of compacts and sealing of kingships, but also for various superstitions as well as judicial purposes.[2]

It has been proved by Hermann Strack that the Jews have never practised the blood-rite, and that the sacred awe they had for blood prevented them from the practice of the blood-rite, but also from covenanting by blood and applying it for the purposes in vogue among other nations. There are, however, many superstitions among the Jews connected with the power of blood, some of which, although they may be traced to the Talmud, did not originate among the Jews. One of these superstitions is the accusing power of blood, which has given rise to many superstitions and folk-tales. We read in the Talmud [3] that the blood of the Prophet Zechariah, whom the Jews had killed, could never be stilled, and continued to flow even when Nebuchadnezzar had killed many innocents and caused their blood to mingle with that of the Prophet.

---

[1] Hershon, *A Talmudical Miscellany* p. 142, § 29; *Revue des Études Juives*, Vol. XXXIII, pp. 233–234; see also Clouston, *Popular Tales*, Vol. I, p. 14.

[2] Cf. P. Cassel, *Die Symbolik des Blutes und der Arme Heinrich von Hartmann von der Ane*, Berlin, 1882; H. C. Trumbull, *The Blood Covenant*, Philadelphia, 1893.

[3] See Hershon, *loc. cit.*, 110, 275, 276.

It is upon this story that is based the legend of John the Baptist, who is supposed to wander through the world, his blood boiling and bubbling, and of the miracle of St. Januarius.[1]

Another passage in the Talmud relates that when Cain had killed his brother Abel, the earth refused to absorb the blood of the victim until the assassin had been punished.[2]

Now, although the Jews, as a rule, are opposed to any covenanting by blood, and considered the so-called ordeals and trials such as the ordeal of water as a heathen custom, they seem to have believed during the Middle Ages in the trial by blood. Some superstitions and ceremonies ascribed to the Jews are pure inventions, whilst others did not in any case originate among the Jews. Curiously enough, the Jews seem to have shared the belief in the accusing power of blood, namely, that the blood of a murdered man is crying aloud for vengeance, and when the murderer is touching the inanimate body the blood will begin to flow afresh. Thus mediæval Jewish writers, such as the author of the famous *Sepher Hassidim*, by Joseph Hahn (1630), and even Manasseh ben Israel (1604–1657), write that the body of a murdered man will break out bleeding afresh whenever the murderer comes near it, or if it is approached with a knife.[3] This popular belief gave rise to several Jewish folk-tales, one of which clusters round Solomon and which has been related above.

It is this old superstition of discovering blood kinship by means of the blood itself which attributed the story to King Solomon and afterwards to the Gaon Saadya.[4] The story is quoted by Strack from the *Sepher Hassidim*, and is also referred to by Hartland.

" The bond of blood," writes Hartland, " has always proved stronger than any other force that can sway human

---

[1] Grünbaum, *Neue Beiträge*, pp. 237–240. [2] *Gittin*, 57b.
[3] See *Sepher Hassidim;* Manasseh ben Israel, *Nishmat Chayim*, Amsterdam, 1651, III, 3.
[4] *Sepher Hassidim*, ed. Bologna, 1538, § 232; see H. Strack, *Der Blutaberglaube*, 1891, p. 37; cf. Steinschreider, *Hebraische Bibliographie*, XIII, p. 134; *Germania*, No. XVIII, pp. 363, 365.

nature, until it encounters the overmastering energy of one of
the great world religions, or becomes distracted and spent
amid the complexities of modern life. Weakened as it is in
Europe nowadays, it is yet not entirely dissipated. Its claims
are put forth more timidly but they are still within certain
limits respected. To the utmost of those limits they are still
efficient instruments in the hands of the poet, the playwright
and the novelist,—and not only on the moral side, where we are
accustomed to appeals founded upon kinship, but also upon
what I may call the physical side. The involuntary recognition
of the same blood is a convention not yet wholly discarded
by the writers who thus aim at affecting our emotions." [1]

The Three Travellers and the Theft of Gold

On another occasion Solomon gave proof of great wisdom
by detecting a clever thief, compelling him to confess his guilt.

In the days of Solomon it happened that three youths were
travelling together on the eve of Sabbath. Not wishing to
carry any money about them on the day of rest, they said to
each other: " Let us go and conceal our gold in one place,"
and this they accordingly did.

In the middle of the night one of the three travellers arose,
stole all the gold, and concealed it in another place. On the
night following the Sabbath the three travellers went to the
place where they had concealed the gold, but, to their great
surprise, found that it had gone. They accused each other of
the thefts, saying one to the other: " Thou hast stolen it."
They finally went to King Solomon and laid the matter before
him, each accusing the other two of the theft.

King Solomon then said: " To-morrow will I decide the
matter and give judgment." But he was greatly embarrassed
and perplexed, thinking within himself: " If I do not elucidate
the truth and decide the matter, my people will say that

[1] Hartland, *The Legend of Perseus*, Vol. II, p. 423.

Solomon's wisdom has been overrated, and they will laugh
at me."

What did he do? He sat and pondered and thought of
means how to make the thief confess the truth. " If I command them to take an oath, two of them will have sworn for
no purpose, whilst the thief will have committed perjury.
I must therefore try and ensnare them in their own talk and
answers."

When the three travellers appeared before him on the
following morning, the King thus addressed them: " I have
heard of ye that ye are great merchants, wise men, and capable
judges of affairs. I would therefore ask your opinion on a
matter which has been submitted to me by a king of Rome.
It happened thus: There dwelt in a certain place in his kingdom a youth and a maiden. They lived in one house and from
their earliest childhood had loved each other. One day the
youth said to the maiden: ' If I can manage to be betrothed to
thee before a certain day, then it is well, otherwise promise
me that thou wilt not marry any other man unless I have
given my consent.' The maiden promised him to do so,
and they confirmed their agreement with an oath. After a
time, the maiden was betrothed to another man, but when
the bridegroom wished to marry her and take her to wife, she
told him of the agreement she had made with her friend, and
the oath she had sworn.

" ' I cannot be thy wife,' she said, ' unless my friend give
his consent.'

" When her betrothed heard these words, he said: ' Let us
go to this man and ask him to set thee free.'

" They accordingly took much gold and silver, and went to
the house of the friend and begged him to set the maiden free.

" ' I have been faithful to my oath,' said the maiden, ' and
I have now come to ask thee to set me free and consent to
my marrying this man.'

" When the friend of her early childhood heard these words, he said unto the maiden: ' Since thou hast been faithful to thy oath and hast kept our agreement, I will not stand in the way of thy happiness and I set thee free. Go ye both in peace and be happy, but I will take no gold for setting thee free.' So the maiden departed with her betrothed.

" On their way homewards, they were attacked by robbers. One of the brigands, an old man, took all the gold and silver they carried and all the jewels of the maiden, and also wished to take her to wife against her will and without her consent.

" ' I beg thee,' said the maiden, ' to wait a little until I have acquainted thee with my history.' Thereupon she told him all that happened.

" ' If this man, my friend, who is a youth, has acted so nobly, curbed his passion and refused to take my gold, thou, who art an old man, and venerable, shouldst be God-fearing, curb thy passion, and let me go in peace with my betrothed.'

" When the old robber heard these words, he took them to heart and said: ' I am old and will soon die, and will not commit such a wicked deed.' He had pity on the maiden, gave her back all her gold and silver and jewels, and let her go in peace with her betrothed.'

" This," continued King Solomon, " is the matter submitted to me by the King of Rome. He has asked me how to decide and to tell him who of all these people has acted most nobly. Tell me now your opinion and declare which was the most praiseworthy." Thus spoke King Solomon.

Thereupon the first of the travellers said: " I praise the betrothed who had respected the oath of the maiden and would not marry her until she had been set free." The second traveller answered: " No, I praise the maiden who had been faithful to the oath she had sworn."

" And what sayest thou?" asked the King, turning to the third traveller.

" I praise them both," replied the man, " but I think that the first young man, though he acted nobly, is a fool to have refused to take the gold offered to him."

When King Solomon heard his reply, he said:

" If thy thoughts turn to the gold which thou hast *not* seen, and thou art prompted to call the youth a fool because he refused to accept what was offered to him, how much more must thou have coveted the gold which thou *didst* see. Now thou art the thief and hast stolen the gold of thy travelling companions."

Thereupon the King ordered him to be bound and put in prison, and he confessed the truth and indicated the place where he had concealed the gold he had stolen. And the people saw that the wisdom of God was in Solomon, and no one ever dared to put forth his hand and take what did not belong to him.[1]

Another version of this tale runs somewhat differently:

When King Solomon asked the three travellers to tell him whom they considered to be the most praiseworthy, the first man answered that he praised the maiden, whilst the second was of the opinion that the betrothed was the most praiseworthy; the third man, however, answered: " I praise the old robber, he had the maiden in his power, and he also possessed himself of her gold and silver and jewels. It was quite noble of him to let the maiden go in peace and not compel her to become his wife, but there was no need for him to return also her gold. He is therefore the most praiseworthy of the three.[2]

There is a similar tale in *Thousand and One Nights*, told of the Sultan Akshid, and another in the Persian *Tutti Nameh*. The contents of the latter are briefly as follows:

---

[1] *Hibbur Yafeh*, p. 38a–b.

[2] *Hibbur Hamaassiot-ve-Hamidrashot*, ed. Venice; Jellinek, *Beth-Hamidrash*, Vol. I, p. 86; Wünsche, *Midrash Ruth Rabba Anhang*, p. 81; *Hebr. Bibliographie*, XVIII, p. 40; cf. Benfey, *Orient and Occident*, II, p. 316; Grünbaum, *Neue Beiträge*, p. 236.

A husbandman once discovered a precious stone in his field the like of which no man had ever seen before. No one could tell him the value of the stone, and his friends advised him to offer the gem as a present to the Sultan of Rum.

"No one," said the peasant's friends, "will be able to pay thee the money the precious stone is worth; besides, should the king hear of thy find, he will take the gem away from thee by force. On the other hand, the Sultan of Rum will reward thee richly for the present thou wilt bring him."

The peasant acted upon this advice and set out on his journey. On the road he met three travellers with whom he struck up an acquaintance and continued his journey in their company. They stopped the night at a wayside inn and during the night, when the peasant, tired from tramping all day, was fast asleep, the travellers, who had learned of the existence of the precious stone, stole it. When the peasant awoke in the morning he missed the gem, but thought it wiser to say nothing about it, lest the thieves take his life.

On reaching the capital of the realm of Rum, he immediately sent a petition to the Sultan wherein he accused his fellow-travellers of the theft. The Sultan summoned the accused into his presence and commanded them to restore the jewel, but the thieves protested their innocence and swore that they had never seen the stone. As the peasant could not prove his accusation, the Sultan was greatly perplexed, for he was anxious to let justice prevail—without punishing the innocent.

Now the Sultan had a daughter whose name was Mihr-i-Shah-Banoh, and whose beauty was only equalled by her wisdom and intelligence. When she learned the cause of her father's evident perplexity she craved permission to deal with the matter. The Sultan readily granted her request. Thereupon the princess betook herself to the house where the thieves were lodging and thus she spoke to them:

"My august father was on the point of committing an

injustice, for, without further proof, he was about to punish you
for a theft you have never committed. I have made inquiries
and learned that the ' garment of your honesty has never been
soiled by such a crime, nor has the breath of theft dimmed the
brightness of your innocence '. But as ye are travelled men
and no doubt have gathered much wisdom on your journeys,
it will give me pleasure to see ye often in my home and learn
wisdom from such men as ye." Highly flattered, the thieves
consented to visit the princess and to tell her their experiences.
One day she asked them to solve a riddle for her, and told
them the following story:

" There was once a beautiful maid, the daughter of a very
wealthy merchant at Damascus. One day Dilefruz, such was
the name of the damsel, saw a wonderful rose in her father's
garden and asked her maidservants to fetch it for her. The
maidservants were unable to pluck the rose, and in her im-
patience Dilefruz promised to grant any wish to whomsoever
would bring her the beautiful rose. The gardener heard her
words and swiftly ran and brought the rose to his mistress.

" ' What is thy request?' asked the happy Dilefruz.

" ' My desire ', replied the gardener, ' is that on the eve
of thy marriage thou comest to see me here.' The maiden
consented to keep her promise.

" Soon afterwards her father found a husband for her and
on the eve of her marriage she told him of the promise she
had given to the gardener. ' Thou must keep thy word,' said
her affianced husband; ' go and visit the gardener, but beware
of sin.'

" Arrayed in costly garments and decked out with jewels,
Dilefruz hurried to the abode of the gardener. On her way
she was attacked by a wolf, but when she told him her story
he let her go. A robber, springing from the thicket, then
fell upon her, but he, too, had compassion on her and allowed
her to continue on her way without taking any of her jewels.

When she reached the abode of the gardener, the young man was overjoyed to see his mistress. Praising her loyalty and faithfulness to her given word, he assured her that his intentions were pure. Thereupon he led her back to her husband.

" ' Such ', continued Princess Mihr-i-Shah, ' is the story of the beautiful maid of Damascus. And now, ye who are men of great experience, tell me, who in your opinion acted most nobly: the husband, the wolf, the robber, or the gardener?"

The travellers, without any hesitation, replied that all the four were big fools to let go a prize they actually had in their possession. When the princess heard these words she knew that they were guilty of the theft of the precious gem, even as the peasant had accused them. Thereupon the Sultan put the three travellers in prison and they were compelled to confess their guilt and to produce the stolen gem.[1]

A similar tale is told by Campbell of a farmer and his three sons.

THE INHERITANCE

There was once a farmer who was well off. He had three sons. When his time to die came, he called his three sons and informed them that in a certain drawer he had left a sum of gold. "This," he said, "ye will divide fairly and honestly amongst ye."

After his death, the sons went to seek for the gold, but found the drawer empty, for one of the sons had stolen the money.

" There has perhaps never been any money in this drawer," said the brother who had stolen it."

" No," replied the others, " our father never told a lie, and wherever the money is now, it surely was in this drawer."

Thereupon they went to an old man who had been a great friend of their father, and asked for his advice.

---

[1] *Tutti Nameh*, German translation by G. Rosen, Leipzig, 1858, Vol. II, pp. 243–258.

" Abide with me," said the old man, " and I will think this matter over." And so the three brothers stayed with him for ten days. When ten days had passed, he sent for the three young lads and made them sit down beside him and told them the following story:

" There was once a young lad, and he was poor; he took love for the daughter of a rich neighbour, and she took love for him. But because he was so poor, there could be no wedding. So at last they pledged themselves to each other, and the young man went away and stayed in his own house. After a time there came another suitor, and because he was well off, the girl's father made her promise to marry him, and after a time they were married. But when the bridegroom came to her, he found her weeping and wailing; and he said: ' What ails thee?' When she told him that she was pledged to another man, he told her to dress herself and to follow him. He took her upon his horse and brought her to the other man, where he left her.

" When the other man got up and fetched a light and saw the bride, he asked her who had brought her. She told him that her husband had done this because she had told him of their pledge. When the man heard these words, he took the horse, rode to the priest, and brought him to the house, and before the priest he loosed the woman from the pledge she had given, and gave her a line of writing that she was free.

" So the bride rode away, but in a thick forest, which she had to cross on her journey homewards, she was stopped and seized by three robbers.

" ' Let me go,' she said, ' let me go; the man I was pledged to has let me go. Here are ten pounds in gold, take them and let me go,' and she told them her story. One of the robbers, who was of a better nature, had compassion on her and took her home, refusing to take even a penny from her.

" ' Take thou the money,' she said, but the robber replied:

' I will not take a penny.' The other two robbers, however, said: ' Give us the money,' and they took the ten pounds. The disinterested robber brought her home, where she showed to her husband the line of writing the other had given her." This is the story which the old man told the three sons.

"Now," said he, "which of all these do you think did best?"

So the eldest said: " I think the man that sent the woman to him to whom she was pledged was the honest, generous man; he did well."

The second said: " Yes, but the man to whom she was pledged, did still better when he sent her to her husband."

The youngest said: " I do not know myself, but perhaps the wisest of all were the robbers who got the money."

Then the old man rose up and said: " Thou hast thy father's gold and silver. I know your father never told a lie, and thou hast stolen the money." [1]

THE TWO-HEADED MAN, OR SEVEN THAT ARE EIGHT

One day Ashmedai, King of the demons, came to King Solomon, and thus he spoke: " Art thou of whom it is said that he is the wisest of all men?"

" So it is," replied the King. Ashmedai then said: " If thou wilt allow me, I can show thee something the like of which thou hast never seen."

" Be it so," said the King.

Thereupon Ashmedai stretched out his hand, and from the entrails of the earth he brought forth a man with two heads and four eyes. Fear and terror seized the King at this sight, and he said: " Bring him into my own apartment." He then sent for Benaiah, the son of Jehoiada, who immediately appeared in the royal presence.

[1] J. F. Campbell, *Popular Tales of the West Highlands*, 1890, Vol. II, pp. 24–27. No. 29.

" Dost thou believe," asked the King, " that there are men living under us in the entrails of the earth?"

" By the life of my soul, my Lord King," replied Benaiah, " if I know it. But I have heard it said by Achitophel, thy father's counsellor and teacher, that there are indeed men living under us."

" What wilt thou say now," replied Solomon, " if I show thee one of these men?"

" How canst thou do such a thing?" asked Benaiah, " and bring up one of these men from the depth of the earth which is at a distance of five hundred years' journey, and the distance between our earth and the next is again a five hundred years' journey?"

Thereupon Solomon commanded that the two-headed man be brought into his presence. When Benaiah saw this inhabitant of another planet, he fell upon his face and said: " Blessed be Thou Eternal, our God, King of the Universe, who hast preserved me alive to this day."

Thereupon he asked the man: " Whose son art thou?"

" I am the son of men," replied the two-headed one, " and of the descendants of Cain."

" Where dost thou dwell?" Benaiah continued.

" In an inhabited world," replied the man.

" Are there sun and moon in your world?"

" Yes. We also plough, and reap, and possess sheep and other cattle."

" And on which side does the sun rise in your world?" queried Benaiah.

" It rises in the West and sets in the East."

" Do ye pray?" asked Benaiah.

" So we do," the two-headed one made answer.

" And what prayer do ye utter?"

" How manifold are Thy works, O Lord; in wisdom hast Thou made them all " (*Psalms*, civ, 24).

" If thou wilt," said Benaiah, " we will send thee back to thine own land."

" May it please ye to send me back to my own land." replied the man.

King Solomon thereupon summoned Ashmedai and commanded him to bring the man back to his own country. To this Ashmedai answered: " That I cannot do, O King; I cannot bring this man home."

When the man saw his position, he married a wife and settled. He had seven sons by his wife, six of whom resembled the mother, whilst the seventh was like his father, for he had two heads. The stranger now bought land, ploughed and reaped, and soon became a wealthy man, one of the rich in the land. Many years passed and the man died, leaving his possessions to his sons. Now the six sons who were like their mother said among themselves: " We are seven brethren and will divide our father's property into seven equal parts." The son, however, who had two heads said: " We are eight, for I am entitled to two portions of our father's inheritance."

So all the sons went to King Solomon, and thus they said to him: " Our Lord the King, we are seven, but our brother here, he with two heads, pretends that we are eight. He desires us to divide our father's inheritance into eight parts, and he himself claims two portions." When Solomon heard this matter it was somewhat hidden from him. He therefore summoned the Sanhedrin, and said to the members of this Court: " What say ye to this matter?"

Now the members of the Sanhedrin thought within themselves: " If we say that the man with two heads is one and is entitled only to one portion, the King will perhaps say that he is two and should consequently receive two portions." So they kept silent.

Thereupon Solomon said: " To-morrow will I give judgment."

At midnight he went into the Temple and stood in prayer before the Lord.

" Lord of the Universe," he prayed, " when Thou didst manifest Thyself unto me at Gibeon, Thou didst say unto me, 'Ask whatever thy heart doth desire,' and I asked neither silver nor gold but wisdom, so as to be able to judge Thy people."

And the Lord hearkened unto Solomon's prayer and assured him that on the morrow He would send him wisdom.

The next morning the King summoned the Court of the Sanhedrin, and when all the members were assembled he said to them: " Let now the man with the two heads come before me." The two-headed man was accordingly brought in. The King then said: " If the one head knows what I am doing to the other, then the man is one person, but otherwise he is two persons."

Thereupon he commanded to bring him hot water, old wine, and linen cloths. When the hot water, old wine, and linen cloths were brought, Solomon ordered the two-headed man to be laid upon his face and blindfolded, and then he poured out the hot water and old wine on *one* head. The man called out: " My Lord King! We die, we die, we are only *one* person and not two."

" Did ye not say," replied the King, " that ye were two?"

When the Israelites saw the wisdom of the King and his judgment, they were filled with wonder, but they also trembled before him and feared him. Therefore it is written: And he was wiser than all men.[1]

---

[1] Jellinek, *loc. cit.*, IV, pp. 151, 152; *Hibbur Maassiot*. Wünsche, *Aus Israel's Lehrhallen*, Vol. II, pp. 24–26; cf. *Hebraische Bibliographie*, XVIII, 61; *Revue des Études Juives*, XLV, pp. 305–308; see Bin Gorion, *loc. cit.*, Vol. III, p. 73; Bialik, *loc. cit.*, Vol. I, p. 103.

CHAPTER VI

Solomon's Wisdom, or Solomon and the Animals and Birds

One man in a thousand—Solomon and the Sanhedrin—The upright man and his beautiful wife—The offer of the king—The sleeping wife and her babes—The kind-hearted husband—The beautiful woman—The temptation—The tin sword—The treachery of woman—The indignant husband—In the presence of the King—The dead men and their shrouds —Solomon and the King of Egypt—The artists who were destined to die within the year—Solomon's wisdom—His letter to the King of Egypt— The quarrel of the organs of the body—The King of Persia and his physician —The milk of a lioness—Benaiah's ruse—The physician's dream—The superiority of the tongue—The three brothers—Solomon's three counsels —The success of the youngest brother—The false accusation—His condemnation and escape—The man and the snake—The jug of milk and the snake's promise—The cock's advice—The language of birds and animals —The ox and the ass—The laughing husband—The curious wife—The grief of the dog—The cock's advice—The game of chess—The cheating of Benaiah—The two thieves—The ruse of Solomon.

ONE MAN IN A THOUSAND HAVE I FOUND

Solomon had a thousand wives, and Oriental potentate that he was, his opinion of them was not very high. He uttered many wise sayings containing severe criticisms of women, whom he was wont to accuse of falsehood, inconstancy, and treachery. In this connection the following story is told, where the King is said to have convinced his court of the truth of his psychological analysis.

One day the members of the Sanhedrin asked King Solomon to explain unto them the meaning of his words: " One man among a thousand have I found; but a woman among all those I have not found " (*Ecclesiastes*, vii, 28).

"Are there not," argued the members of the Sanhedrin, "many women in the world who are faithful and worthy?"

"I will prove to you," replied the King, "that my words are true."

Thereupon he commanded his servants to seek out in the land a man who was upright and righteous, and who had a beautiful wife who was apparently as upright and righteous as her husband. The servants of King Solomon sought all over the land and informed their master that they had indeed found such a man who was upright and righteous and who also had a very beautiful wife.

"Bring the man before me," commanded the King.

When the man appeared in the royal presence, Solomon thus addressed him: "I have heard of thy righteousness and uprightness and thy understanding, and I desire to honour thee and to make thee great. I will give thee my daughter to wife and raise thee above all the princes of my realm."

The man said: "Who am I that I should marry the daughter of my master the King?" But the King replied: "Thy modesty only shows thy worth and thy wisdom. If thou wilt therefore slay thy wife to-night and bring me her head, to-morrow I will do as I have said. I will give thee my daughter to wife and make thee great."

When the man heard these words, he replied: "I will do as the King doth command me." Thereupon he went home, but he was sore grieved and thought in his heart: "How can I slay my wife who is so beautiful, upright, and righteous, and is the mother of my little children."

When his wife saw how sad he was, she asked him: "Why art thou so downcast and so troubled?"

"My heart is afflicted with sorrow," he replied.

She placed before him food and drink, but he could neither eat nor drink, and she ate and drank herself, and went to bed with her little children and soon fell asleep.

The man sat deep in thought, greatly troubled, and thought within himself: "How can I commit such a crime and sin before God?" and he made up his mind to despise the honour and the gifts the King had promised him. But once more he remembered the King's words and thought within himself: "If I slay her I shall become the King's son-in-law, rich and honoured." He took his sword and approached his wife, but when he saw her sleeping with her children, one child on her breast and the other in her arms, he let his sword fall from his hands and said: "How can I slay my wife and children and lose my portion in the next world? The Lord rebuke thee, Satan," he added. He returned his sword to its sheath and went and sat down. But evil thoughts once more crowded his brain, and the tempter stirred ambition in his heart. Thereupon he once more drew his sword and approached the bed upon which lay his wife and her children. He found that her hair had fallen over the child that lay at her breast, covering it, and it touched his heart, and he was overcome with pity.

"No," he cried, "I cannot do such a deed. I despise all the honours the King has promised me, and even the hand of his daughter, for they are like nought." Thereupon he sheathed his sword once more and lay down upon his bed.

On the following morning there came the messengers of the King and said: "Come with us before the King, for he waiteth for thee."

When the man was brought into the King's presence, Solomon said unto him:

"Where is the head of thy wife which thou didst promise to bring me? What hast thou done?"

"May it please unto the King," said the man, "to have pity on me and not to ask me to do such a deed."

Thereupon he related unto the King all that happened.

"Twice," he said, "during the night, I made an attempt

to obey the King's command. Twice did I draw my sword and approach the bed upon which lay my wife and children, but overcome with pity I could not find it in my heart to slay her. I pray the King not to be wroth with me."

Thus spoke the man, and King Solomon smiled. Turning to the members of the Sanhedrin, he said: " One man among a thousand have I found." To the man he said: " Go thou home; I did desire to honour thee, but thou didst not know how to avail thyself of the opportunity."

The man, however, went home happy and content.

When thirty days had elapsed, Solomon sent again his servants and summoned the wife into his presence. When the woman was brought before him, he said unto her: " I have heard of thy beauty and of thy wisdom, and I have a great desire to take thee to wife. I will set thee above all my wives and exalt thee above all my Kingdom, I will deck thee with gold and array thee in royal garments and place a golden crown upon thy head."

When the woman heard these words, she bowed low and said: "My Lord the King, I am thine, and thou canst do with me as thou pleasest."

" I cannot, however, marry thee," continued the King, " as long as thou hast a husband and he stands between us. Go thou, therefore, home and slay thy husband, and thou wilt be free. I will then take thee to wife and exalt thee above all in the Kingdom."

" I will do as the King doth command," replied the woman, " and to-morrow I will bring to my Lord the King the head of my husband."

Thus spoke the woman, ready to do the bidding of the King. And the King thought in his heart: " If I do not prevent this woman, she will certainly have no pity upon her husband and shed innocent blood. I will therefore give her a sword which can do no harm." And he had a sword of tin brought to him and gave it to the woman, saying unto her: " Take this sharp sword and slay thy husband with it. Strike once with it and thou wilt cut his neck."

The woman took the sword, not knowing that it was made of tin, hid it in her garments, and returned to her house.

When the husband came home in the evening, she hastened to meet him, kissed and hugged him, and placed food and drink before him. She gave him wine to drink, and he drank until he was intoxicated and fell down into a deep sleep. Thereupon the woman drew the sword which the King had given her and struck at her husband's neck with it. The sword, however, only bent, and the husband awoke from his sleep. When he saw his wife standing before him with a bent sword in her hand, as if ready to slay him, he waxed very wroth and said: " Who gave thee this sword, and why didst thou intend to slay me? Tell me the truth and hide nothing from me, for otherwise I will cut thee into little pieces."

Greatly embarrassed and ashamed, the woman confessed the truth and related all that had occurred, and how the King had given her the sword to slay her husband with it.

In the morning the messengers of the King came and brought the man and his wife before Solomon and the Sanhedrin. When the King saw them he broke out into loud laughter and said: " Tell me what hath befallen ye during the night?" And the man related what had occurred.

" My Lord King," he said, " when I awoke in the night, I saw my wife standing before me with this tin sword in her hand. Had not the sword been made of tin, she would surely have killed me and had no pity on me even as I had pity on her."

" I knew," said the King, " that thy wife would have had no pity on thee, therefore I gave her this sword of tin so as to prevent her from shedding innocent blood."

And when the members of the Sanhedrin heard this, they admitted that Solomon's words were true when he said: " One man among a thousand have I found; but a woman among all those have I not found." [1]

THE DEAD MEN AND THEIR SHROUDS

Many a time did Solomon have occasion to impress foreign rulers with his wisdom, which was greater even than that of the Egyptians renowned for their manifold knowledge. When the Lord had commanded Solomon to build the temple, the King wrote to Pharaoh, King of Egypt, and asked him for help. " Send me, I beg of you," he wrote to the King of Egypt, " master-artisans and artists who can do all the work I require, and stipulate their fees, which I will gladly pay."

Pharaoh thereupon sent for his astrologers and commanded them to determine which among his artists were destined to die within the year. The astrologers did as they had been commanded by their royal master. Thereupon Pharaoh took all the men destined to die within a year and sent them to Jerusalem.

" Here are the men," he wrote, " that thou dost require."

But when King Solomon looked at the artists from Egypt, he at once knew that their days were numbered, and that Egypt's King had played a trick upon him. He therefore commanded his servants to provide every one of the Egyptians with a shroud and a coffin, and to send them back to their native country. To Pharaoh he sent word:

" Is it because thou hast no graves or shrouds in Egypt that thou didst send the men to me? I return them to thee with their coffins and shrouds, and in future there is really no need for thee to send the men themselves to the land of the Hebrews to be measured for shrouds and coffins. You have

[1] *Hibbur Yafeh*, pp. 14a–15a; Jellinek, *Beth-Hamidrash*, IV, pp. 146–148; Wünsche, *Aus Israel's Lehrhallen*, Vol. II, pp. 16–19.

only to send their measurements, and all they require will be forwarded."

And when the King of Egypt read these words he was greatly astonished and exclaimed: " Verily, the wisdom of the Lord is dwelling in Solomon, King of Israel." [1]

THE QUARREL OF THE ORGANS OF THE BODY

On another occasion it was the King of Persia who turned to Solomon for advice.

There was once a King of Persia who fell very ill, suffering from consumption. The physicians who were treating him told him that there was only one way to save the King. His disease could be cured only by the milk of a lioness, and the King would surely become well again if he were to drink such milk. Thereupon the King of Persia sent his physician to King Solomon, who was reputed for his great wisdom, and begged him to help him obtain lion's milk.

Solomon sent for his faithful chancellor Benaiah and gave him instructions to obtain lion's milk. Benaiah knew a lion's den in the neighbourhood of Jerusalem, and thither he repaired with his servants, taking with them ten young kids. Every day he threw a young kid to the lioness, and each time he came a little nearer to the den, until on the tenth day he became quite familiar with the beast and could play with her. Thereupon he came quite close to her, touched her udders, and then drew some milk. He returned to Solomon and handed the lioness's milk to the foreign physician, who went away well content to have succeeded in his errand. On his way back to his native land of Persia, the physician fell asleep and dreamed that the organs of his body were quarrelling among themselves. The feet said that had they not carried him to King Solomon he would never have been able to obtain the

[1] *Numer. Rabba,* 19.

lioness's milk. The hands argued that had not Benaiah's hands touched the udders of the beast there would not have been any milk. The mouth and the eyes, in their turn, pretended that the greatest credit in procuring the remedy for the King of Persia belonged to them.

Thereupon the tongue said: " You are all wrong; the greatest share of credit belongs to me, for had there been no language you would all have been useless." The other organs, however, upbraided the tongue and said: " How durst thou compare thyself to us, and much more pretend that thy own contribution to the service which has just been rendered is superior to ours? Thou art only flesh without bone, and thou dost dwell in darkness." The tongue thereupon replied: " To-day even ye shall know that I am your master."

The physician awoke from his sleep and remembered his dream. When he appeared in presence of his royal master, he thus spoke to him: " Here is the dog's milk which I have obtained for your Majesty; drink it." Greatly enraged, the King gave orders for his physician to be hanged. When he was being led to the place of execution, all the members and organs of the condemned man's body began to tremble violently. Thereupon the tongue thus addressed all the other limbs:

" I told ye that without me you were all useless; now will ye admit my superiority and acknowledge me as your master if I promise to save ye even now from death?"

The organs of the body readily promised, and the physician's tongue spoke to the executioner, requesting him to lead him once more before the King. Brought into the presence of his royal master, the physician asked him why he had ordered him to be hanged.

" Because," said the King, " thou didst not obey my instruction, and didst bring me dog's milk instead of that of a lioness."

" And what does it matter if it is a remedy and will cure

thee of thy disease? Besides, we often call a lioness a bitch. I beg now your Majesty to drink of the milk I have brought."

The King granted the physician's request, drank of the milk, and soon recovered. He thereupon set the physician free and dismissed him in peace.

The members and organs of the body then said to the tongue: " Now we see that thou art really master over all the organs of the human body, and we readily acknowledge thee as such."

Therefore Solomon said: " Death and life are in the power of the tongue " (*Proverbs*, xviii, 21).[1]

THE THREE BROTHERS

The fame of Solomon's wisdom spread far and wide, and from all parts of the world men came to his court to learn wisdom from the King of Israel.

One day three brothers came to King Solomon to learn from him wisdom and instruction in the Law.

" Abide with me," said the King, " and serve me, and I will teach ye as ye desire." He appointed them as officers in his court, and they spent thirteen years with him. At the end of that time one of the brothers said to the others: " What have we done? It is thirteen years now since we left our houses and all that belongs to us and came hither to learn wisdom and to study the Law. We have served the King faithfully, but he has taught us nothing. Come, let us take leave of him and return to our homes."

Thereupon they appeared before the King, and thus they spoke:

" Thirteen years have now passed, O King, since we quitted our houses and came to thee to study the Law and

[1] *Midrash Tehillim*, 39; *Sepher Hamaassiot*, pp. 38b–39a; cf. *Monatsschrift*, Vol. XXXIX, pp. 107–110.

learn wisdom. Grant us now thy permission to return to our homes and to our families."

On hearing this, King Solomon commanded his treasurer to bring three hundred pieces of gold, and thus he spoke to the brothers: " Choose whatever ye prefer. Either will I give unto each of ye three wise counsels or a hundred pieces of gold." They consulted with one another, chose the gold, and departed.

When they had gone a little way on their journey, a distance of four *mils* from the town, the youngest of the brothers suddenly said: " What have we done? Was it for the sake of gold that we came hither or for the purpose of learning wisdom from the King? If ye are willing to listen to my advice and be guided by me, I propose that we return the gold to the King and rather learn wisdom from Solomon and good counsel instead."

Thus spoke the youngest, but his brothers replied: " If thou art anxious to restore the gold to the King and learn wisdom instead, do as thou pleasest. We, however, are not going to retrace our steps and acquire wise counsel for gold."

Thereupon the youngest of the three brothers returned to King Solomon, and thus he spoke: " My Lord! I did not come to thy court for the sake of gold, and I beg thee to take it back and teach me wisdom and wise counsel instead."

" My son," said the King, " I will take back the pieces of gold and give thee three wise counsels instead.

" Whenever thou hast occasion to go on a journey, start with dawn and be careful to go to rest ere sunset. That is the first counsel. Whenever thou comest to a river in flood, beware of crossing it, but wait until the waters have subsided and the river has returned to its bed. That is the second counsel. Never entrust a secret to a woman, be she even thine own wife. That is the third counsel."

Thus spoke the King. The disciple took his leave, mounted

his horse, and departed, hastening after his brothers. When he had caught up with them, they asked him: " And what hast thou learned from the King?" " The wisdom I have acquired," replied the youngest brother, " I have acquired for myself."

After riding for nine hours, the travellers came to a beautiful spot which seemed to be suitable for rest.

" Methinks," said the youngest brother, he who had learned wisdom from King Solomon, " that this spot is excellent and well suited for camping. We can pass the night here, for here we have trees and water and grass for our horses. If ye are willing, let us remain here overnight and repose, and to-morrow morning at dawn, if God spares our lives, we will set out again on our journey."

" Thou art a fool!" replied the others. " It seems to us that since thou hast restored the gold to King Solomon, so as to acquire wisdom instead, thou hast no wisdom whatever but folly. We can travel at least another eight miles ere night falls, and thou dost counsel us to camp here for the night."

" Do as ye please," replied the youngest brother. " As for me, I am not going to stir from this spot but abide here alone."

Thereupon the two elder brothers continued their journey, the youngest remaining behind. He cut down wood and made a fire, and also built a booth to shelter himself and his beast. He let his horse graze until night fell, then gave it barley and also took his own meal, whereupon he made ready to go to rest.

The other two brothers had in the meantime continued their journey until night had fallen. In vain, however, did they look for wood and water for themselves and pasture for their beasts. Then a snowstorm arose and snow began to fall heavily. Many wanderers succumbed to the bitter cold, but the young man who had remained behind suffered neither from the snow nor from the cold, because he was sheltered in the booth he had built unto himself. He also had fire, food, and drink.

With the break of day the young man arose, made ready for the journey, mounted his horse, and hastened after his brothers. He did not search long for them, but found them on the road frozen to death. When he saw his brothers lying dead, he threw himself upon them weeping aloud. Thereupon he took the gold which his brothers had with them, buried their bodies, and continued on his journey. The sun had in the meantime risen high, shining warmly; it caused the snow to melt and the rivers to swell. When the young man came to a river, the latter was in flood, and the traveller refrained from crossing it. He dismounted and prepared to wait until the waters had subsided.

Whilst he was walking up and down on the bank, he saw two servants of King Solomon approach, leading two animals laden with gold. They asked him: " Why art thou not crossing the river?" He replied: " Because I am waiting until the waters subside." The servants of King Solomon were not afraid of the high water. They made an attempt to cross the river, were carried away by the flood, and perished. The young man, however, who had patiently waited until the waters had subsided, crossed the river in safety. He took with him the gold which the servants of the King were carrying and returned to his home.

Now the wives of his brothers came to see him on his return, and inquired after their husbands. " They have remained behind to learn wisdom," replied the young man. He then began to purchase fields and vineyards, to build houses, and to acquire many possessions.

One day his wife said unto him: " My Lord, tell me, whence hast thou this gold?" On hearing this question, he waxed very wroth and began to beat her. He said: " Never ask again this question, and try not to discover the secret."

His wife, nevertheless, did not abate in her curiosity, and wearied him so often with her question that at last he told her all. One day, when he was hotly disputing with his wife, she cried out aloud and said: " Thou hast not only slain thy two brothers, but now thou wouldst slay me too." When his sisters-in-law heard these words and learned of the death of their husbands, they hastened to King Solomon and accused the young man of having murdered his brothers. The King thereupon commanded that the accused be brought into his presence, and he sentenced him to death.

When the condemned man was being led to the place of execution, he said to the soldiers accompanying him: " I beg you to grant my last request; lead me once more into the presence of the King that I may once more speak and relate unto him the true story."

When he found himself in the presence of the King, the condemned man fell upon his face, and thus he spoke: " My Lord the King, I am one of the three brothers who once came to thee to learn wisdom and who served thee thirteen years. I am the youngest of the three who alone, as thou wilt remember, O King, came to restore the gold pieces unto thee so as to acquire wise counsel instead. It seems, however, that the wisdom I have acquired has proved my misfortune."

The King immediately recognized the truth, and thus he said: " Fear not, the gold thou hast taken from thy brothers and from my servants is thine, and the wisdom which thou hast acquired has saved thee from death and from these women. Now go in peace."

And in this hour King Solomon said: " How much better is it to get wisdom than gold " (*Proverbs*, xvi, 16).[1]

---

[1] Jellinek, *loc. cit.*, Vol. IV, pp. 148–150; Lewner, *l.c.* 349–354; Wünsche, *loc. cit.*, pp. 19–21; *Hebr. Bibliographie*, XVIII, pp. 39–40; cf. *Revue des Études Juives*, Vol. XI, pp. 224–228.

The Man and the Snake

One day a man carrying a jug of milk in his hand was crossing a field. Suddenly he perceived a snake wailing and lamenting for thirst.

"Why art thou wailing so pitifully?" the man asked the snake, to which the latter replied:

"I am wailing because I am tortured with thirst. And what art thou carrying in that jug?" the snake further asked.

"It is milk that I have in the jug," replied the man.

Thereupon the snake begged the man to let it drink of the milk. "If thou wilt let me drink of the milk, I will show unto thee a place where a great treasure lies hidden." The man was moved to pity, and gave the milk to the snake to slake its thirst. Thereupon the snake led the man to a place where a great rock was lying.

"Here, underneath this rock," said the snake, "a big treasure is hidden." The man rolled aside the rock, found the treasure, and prepared to carry it home, when suddenly the snake sprang up and coiled itself round its benefactor's neck.

"And what is the meaning of this?" asked the man, greatly frightened.

"It means," replied the snake, "that I am going to kill thee because thou art taking away all my wealth."

"Well," said the man, "I suggest that we put our case before King Solomon, and let him judge who of us is right and who is wrong."

The snake consented, and the two betook themselves before King Solomon. When they had explained the case, the King asked of the snake: "What is it that thou dost demand of the man?"

"I want to kill him," was the snake's answer, "because

Scripture commands me to do it, for it says: ' And thou shalt bruise the heel of man '." [1]

" Thou art quite right," said the King, " but first of all release thy hold of the man. You are both now standing before the judge, and before judgment has been given none of the litigants should hold fast the other party and thus enjoy an advantage."

The snake obeyed, released its hold upon the man, and uncoiling itself from the latter's neck glided down.

Thereupon King Solomon said unto the snake: " Now explain thy case and what it is thou dost want of the man." The snake repeated its words: " I want to kill this man because Scripture commands me to do it."

Thereupon Solomon turned to the man and said: " And thee, too, the Lord commanded ' to bruise the head of the snake '; [2] why dost thou not do it?" The man immediately raised his foot and crushed the snake's head. [3]

The King's Disciple and Friend, or the Cock's Advice

King Solomon had a friend and disciple who lived in a distant land and annually came to visit the King and to learn wisdom from him. Before his friend departed home, the King was in the habit of bestowing some gifts upon him and giving him also presents to carry home for his family. One day the friend brought Solomon some precious gift, and when he was about to depart the King wanted to give him some costly present. The man, however, refused the gift, and thus he spoke:

" My Lord and Master, I have no desire for wealth and riches. Thanks to the Almighty and to thy generosity, I have all that a man might desire, and I want nothing. If I have,

---

[1] *Genesis*, iii, 15.   [2] *Ibid.*
[3] *Midrash Tehillim*; see Bialik, *loc. cit.*, Vol. I, pp. 104-105; Cf. Grünbaum, *Neue Beiträge zur semitischen Sagenkunde*, p. 236.

however, found favour in thine eyes, bestow another gift upon me and teach me the language of birds and animals."

Thereupon King Solomon said unto his friend: " I will not refuse thy request and teach thee the language of the birds and animals, but I must warn thee that such a knowledge is not without great danger and that it must remain a dead secret. Shouldst thou one day reveal to others what thou hearest from some animal, then thou wilt surely die; no expiation will save thee from death." Thus spoke King Solomon, but his friend, nevertheless, insisted upon his request.

" If I can only acquire a part of thy wisdom, I will do as thou dost advise me." And when the King saw how anxious his friend was to learn the language of birds and animals, he granted his request and instructed him in the art. The man then went home full of joy.

Now it happened one day that this man and his wife were sitting in front of their house when the ox was brought home from the field. The animal was attached to a crib full of fodder and placed side by side with the ass that had remained at home all that day, as it had given itself out to be sick. And the friend of King Solomon, who now understood the language of animals, overheard the ass address the ox as follows:

" Friend, how dost thou fare in this house?"

" Alas, friend," the ox replied, " by day and night I know nothing but hard toil and labour." Then the ass said:

" I am well disposed towards thee, wishing thee relief and rest, and I can give thee good advice how to get rid of thy misery and hard work."

" Brother," said the ox, " thou hast pity on me; may thy heart always be with me. I will obey thy words and follow thy advice implicitly."

Thereupon the ass said: " Heaven alone knows that I am speaking in the sincerity of my heart and the purity of my thoughts; my advice is that thou shalt devour neither straw

nor fodder this night. When our master notices that thou hast
not eaten anything, he will conclude that thou art sick and
relieve thee from burdensome work and painful toil. Thou
wilt then enjoy a good rest like me."

Thus spoke the ass, and his words pleased the ox very
much. He followed the advice of his companion and touched
neither straw nor fodder. Before dawn the master, who had
overheard the conversation, went down to the stable, and he
saw how the ass was devouring the fodder belonging to the
ox, whilst the latter was asleep. Remembering the conversation he had overheard and understanding now the ruse of
the ass, he laughed aloud. His wife heard him and wondered
greatly what it was that had made her husband suddenly
burst out into loud laughter. When he re-entered the house,
she insisted upon knowing the reason of his merry outburst.

" Oh, it was nothing," replied the husband evasively; " I
just remembered a ludicrous incident which once happened
to me, and I could not help laughing out aloud." On the
following morning the master of the house instructed the
stable-boy to relieve the ox from work on that day. " The
ox," he said, " shall do no work to-day; harness the ass instead, and let him do to-day the work for himself and the ox."
In the evening the ass returned to the stable tired and exhausted.

" Brother," asked the ox, " hast thou heard the heartless
children of man speak concerning me?" To which the ass
promptly replied: " I heard our master saying that should
the ox continue to abstain from fodder then he would have
him slaughtered and use his flesh as food."

When the ox heard these words he was greatly frightened,
and like a lion upon his prey he threw himself upon his manger
full of fodder. He never lifted his head until he had devoured
his fodder to the last mouthful. The master, who had again
overheard the conversation between the two animals, burst

out into loud uproarious laughter, and his wife, who heard him, insisted upon knowing the cause of his merriment.

" Yesterday," she said, " you laughed aloud, and I thought it was by accident. Now you have again been moved to an uproarious laughter for no evident reason, no stranger being present to have given you cause for merriment. You are no doubt laughing at me, perceiving something ridiculous and ludicrous in my person. I swear that I will not allow you to come near me until you will have revealed unto me the reason of your merriment."

Thereupon the husband, who loved his wife dearly, begged and implored her not to insist upon knowing the cause of his laughter.

" Be quiet, my dear," he said, " do not urge me, for I am not allowed to reveal the secret unto thee." The woman, however, remained obstinate.

" I have taken an oath," she replied, " not to live with thee, and thou shalt not behold my face again until thou hast told me the truth."

" I know that if I reveal the secret unto thee," said her husband, " I will suffer death."

" And I know," retorted the woman, " that I will not partake of either food or drink, but sooner die unless thou dost tell me the truth."

Thereupon the man said: " I am ready to sacrifice my life and give my soul rather than see thee suffer; I prefer death than life without thee, for what is my life without thee?" He loved her so devotedly that he was willing to lose his life, and made up his mind to tell her his secret.

" Now," he said, addressing his wife, " I will go and put my house in order, and then I will tell thee all thou dost wish to know."

Now the unhappy man had a dog who was very grieved when he became aware of the fate that awaited his master.

"YOU ARE NO DOUBT LAUGHING AT ME"

Sadly did the faithful beast run about all over the house, refusing to touch some bread and meat that had been put before him.

Thereupon the cock came along and appropriated the bread and meat which the dog had disdained to touch, and he and his wife joyfully and with great predilection devoured it. The dog was shocked at the conduct of the cock and waxed very wroth.

" Thou heartless, impious fellow," he barked, " how great is thy greed and how insignificant thy modesty. Thy master is hovering between life and death like a poor miserable sinner, and thou gorgest thyself and doest thee well in his own house."

Thereupon the cock made reply: " Well, is it my fault that thy master is such a fool, lacking understanding? Look at me, I have ten wives, and I rule over them; none of them would dare do anything that is contrary to my wish. Thy master has only one companion, and even her he is unable to command, control, and punish!" And aloud the cock shouted: " Is there any greater evil than that of being caught in the meshes of one's wife? Now prick thine ears, my friend dog, and learn wisdom from the mouth of a cock!"

" Then what ought my master to do? how is he to treat his wife?"

" Do, treat?" said the cock contemptuously; " let thy master simply take up a stick and belabour his wife with it properly. I warrant thee, friend dog, that the lady will scream and beg for mercy, and never again will she dare worry her husband and induce him to reveal his secrets unto her."

Now the master of the house, who was preparing to die, had overheard the conversation, and found the words of the cock wise.

He followed his advice and thus escaped destruction. There is a similar story in the *Tutti Nameh*.[1]

[1] *Ben Hamelech ve-Hanazir*, pp. 71b–73a; see Bin Gorion, *loc. cit.*, pp. 105–109; Lewner, *loc. cit.*, Vol. III, pp. 362–370; cf. Meinhof, *Afrikanische Märchen*, p. 81. *Tutti Nameh*, Vol. II, pp. 236–241

The Court of Solomon. A Game of Chess

Among the courtiers of King Solomon the most famous was Benaiah ben Jehoiada. Now King Solomon's most favourite pastime was a game of chess. One day he was playing with his chancellor Benaiah, and the latter was, as usually, on the point of losing, for no one was a match for Solomon in the game of chess. Suddenly a noise of a street fight between two drunken men made the King look up and then approach the window to see what was the matter. Benaiah availed himself of the absence of the King to remove one of the latter's chess-men, and the King consequently lost the game. Solomon did not at first notice the absence of one of his chess-men, and Benaiah, who was always in the habit of being the loser, won the game.

The King was both annoyed and surprised that he had lost his game, and tried to find out where he had made a mistake. Replacing the chess-men just as they had been when he had left the table, he began to play the game over again. He found out that one of the chess-men was missing, and soon came to the conclusion that the chancellor had removed a figure.

"He cheated me," thought the King, "when I was looking out of the window. Now I am not going to tell him openly that he had dealt dishonestly with me and thus put him to shame, but arrange it in such a way that he will be compelled to confess the truth of his own free will." Some time afterwards the King found an opportunity how to elicit the truth from his chancellor.

One day Solomon was leaning out of the window of his palace and noticed two suspicious individuals, carrying sacks on their shoulders, passing in front of the palace and whispering between themselves. An idea at once occurred to him. Disguising himself as one of the royal servants, he hurried down into the street, where he joined the two suspicious individuals. He had rightly guessed that the two were out to commit some act of burglary, and he now proposed unto them to rob the royal palace. " Greeting unto you, my friends," said the King, " I, too, am one of your profession, and my fingers have learned the art of burglary. Look, here is the key to the royal apartments where the King's treasures are hidden. I have planned the robbery, but dare not undertake it alone. If you are willing, then come with me and together we will carry away precious booty."

Thus spoke the King, and the two thieves, suspecting no guile, readily accepted his proposal.

" We are quite ready to follow thee," they said; " show us the way and we will soon do the job."

They decided to wait till midnight, when the palace would be wrapt in darkness and all its inmates asleep. Thereupon Solomon took his companions to the palace, and leading them through several rooms full of valuables brought them to a chamber which contained many precious stones and gems.

" Take as much as you like," said the King, " and whilst you two are filling your pockets, I will go out and keep watch lest we be surprised and taken unawares." Thereupon Solomon went out and locked the door behind him. He then put on his royal garments and roused his servants."

" There are thieves in my treasure house," he said; " catch them and take them into custody, let none of them escape." The thieves were accordingly caught and secured.

The next morning Solomon convened his supreme tribunal of justice presided over by Benaiah.

" Tell me," said the King, " ye truth-loving and learned judges, what punishment deserves the thief who has been caught in the act of robbing the King?" When Benaiah heard these words he began to tremble, for he felt sure that the King had invented the story of the two thieves whom his servants had apprehended, and had only used it for the purpose of punishing him for having dealt dishonestly with his royal master.

"The King," thought the chancellor, "has surely found out that I had cheated him at the game of chess, and he will have me convicted and condemned as a thief. If I keep silent and wait until the sentence is pronounced, I will be doubly disgraced. It is better, therefore, for me to confess and to beg my master's forgiveness."

Thereupon Benaiah fell at the feet of the King, confessed his guilt, and begged his royal master's pardon.

"I am the thief, your gracious Majesty," said Benaiah, "for at our last game of chess I stole one of the chess-men and thus won the game. I frankly confess my guilt and humbly beg your Majesty's pardon."

Solomon heard his chancellor's confession, and smilingly replied: "Do not worry, my friend, I harbour no evil thoughts against thee, for I have long forgotten the incident and readily forgiven thee for having dealt dishonestly with me. I assure thee, my friend, that to-day I have convened the supreme tribunal in order to judge two delinquents, for two thieves have really broken into my treasury this night, and have been caught in the act of robbing me. Now, gentlemen judges, pronounce your sentence."

The tribunal examined the case and condemned the two thieves to death. Solomon, however, was greatly pleased to have thus compelled Benaiah to confess his guilt. His chancellor's confession thus confirmed his supposition that Benaiah had cheated him, and that he had in reality not lost the game.[1]

[1] Jellinek, *Beth-Hamidrash*, Vol. VI, pp. 124–126.

CHAPTER VII

Solomon's Wisdom (*Continued*)

The charitable woman—The three loaves of bread—The shipwrecked stranger—The hungry prisoner—The empty sack—The gust of wind—The woman's complaint—The wealthy merchants—The leak in the boat—The miracle—The merchants' vow and prayer—Seven thousand gold pieces—The leaking vessel—The sack of flour—The Lord never forsakes those who walk in His ways—The borrowed egg—The promise of the borrower—The revenue derived from an egg—Solomon's advice—Boiled beans—The surprised soldiers—Boiled beans and boiled eggs.

The Charitable Woman

In the days of King Solomon, peace be upon him, there lived a charitable woman who was always ready to do good. Although not rich herself, she constantly gave away of her possessions to others. Every day she baked three loaves of bread, two of which she distributed among the poor, keeping the third loaf for herself. One day a stranger knocked at her door, and thus he spoke: " I was sailing in a vessel with all my possessions when a storm arose and broke my craft. All my companions and the pilot perished and I alone escaped, thrown on the shore by the waves. I am tired and exhausted, as I have not tasted any food for three days."

When the charitable woman heard these words, she immediately fetched one of the loaves she had baked and offered it to the hungry stranger. Thereupon she sat down and prepared to consume the second loaf herself, when another stranger appeared on her threshold. " My dear lady," he said, " I was kept a prisoner by enemies but managed to escape three days ago. I have not tasted any food ever since, and I implore thee to have pity on me and give me a piece of bread so that I may appease my hunger and not die." The woman immediately handed the stranger the second loaf and praised the Lord, who had afforded her the opportunity of bestowing charity upon the needy and the hungry.

Thereupon she produced the third loaf and prepared to make a meal, when a third beggar suddenly appeared and asked for bread. " On the road," said he, " I was caught by robbers, but I escaped into the forest. For three days I have lived on roots and herbs, and I have forgotten the taste of bread. Have pity on me and give me some to appease the pangs of my hunger."

Unhesitatingly the charitable woman offered him the third loaf, leaving none for herself. Thereupon she said unto herself: " I will see whether I can find some more flour in the sack and bake another loaf for myself. The sack, however, was quite empty, and the woman went out into the fields to gather a few grains of wheat. She collected a handful of grains, carried them to the mill, and had them ground to flour. Carrying her small sack upon her head, she was walking home when suddenly a gust of wind came from the sea and snatching the small sack, hurled it away into the distance. The woman's hopes were thus frustrated, and she remained without bread for the day. Bitterly did she cry, exclaiming in her despair: " Lord of the Universe! What sin have I committed that I should thus be punished?"

She went to King Solomon to complain of her misfortune. On that day the High Council had been convened by the King of Israel, and the woman thus addressed the members of the Sanhedrin:

" Ye judges in Israel, tell me why hath the Lord punished me thus that I, who have given of my substance to the hungry, am compelled to suffer the pangs of hunger myself?"

Whilst she was thus speaking, three merchants who had landed from their boat entered the judgment hall. " Our Lord and King," said the merchants, " take these seven thousand gold pieces and distribute them among the noble and deserving poor." Said King Solomon: " What has happened to ye that ye are so willingly giving away in charity so much gold?"

Thereupon the merchants told their story: " We were sailing in our vessel, which was laden with costly merchandise, and were already approaching the shore, when we suddenly noticed that the boat had a leak. We looked round for something to stop the hole but found nothing suitable. The boat was about to sink, and we seemed to be doomed to drown with all our belongings. In our dire distress we prayed to the Lord, and thus we said: " Lord of the Universe! If we reach the shore safely then we will give away to the poor the tenth part of the costly merchandise which we are carrying in our vessel. Thereupon we fell upon our faces and in silent prayer awaited a miracle or death. And so great was our distress that our senses were troubled, and we never noticed that our vessel had in the meantime safely reached the shore. Thereupon we calculated the value of our merchandise and found that the tenth part of it was exactly seven thousand gold pieces. This money, faithful to our vow, we have now brought to thee, and beg thee to distribute it among the poor."

Thereupon Solomon, the wise King of Israel, asked the merchants: " Know ye the exact spot where your vessel did leak, and did ye notice how the hole was stopped?" to which the merchants replied: " This we know not, for in our joy and our anxiety to come here we never investigated the matter."

" Then go and examine your vessel," said the King, who had already guessed the truth. The merchants went away and soon returned with a small sack of flour.

" This sack," they said, " had, unbeknown to us, stopped the hole in our vessel."

Turning to the pious and charitable woman, Solomon asked: " Dost thou recognize this sack of flour?"

" I do," replied the woman; " it is the very sack I was carrying on my head when the gust of wind snatched it away and hurled it into the distance."

Thereupon King Solomon said: " The seven thousand gold pieces are thine; it is for thy sake that the Lord wrought this miracle. The Lord never forsakes those who walk in His ways." Thus spoke King Solomon, and the members of the High Council and all present admired the wisdom of the King of Israel.[1]

THE BORROWED EGG

One day the servants of David were partaking of a meal, and boiled eggs were served unto them. One of the boys, being more hungry than the others, had quickly eaten up his portion, and when his friends began to take their food he felt rather ashamed to see his plate empty. He therefore said unto his neighbour at table: " Lend me one of thy eggs."

" I will gladly do it," said his comrade, " if thou wilt promise me before witnesses that whenever I ask thee for the egg thou wilt return it to me together with the full amount it would have yielded to me during the time that will have elapsed." The boy accepted the bargain and promised before all present to fulfil the conditions.

A long time had passed, when the lender asked for repayment. " Thou hast lent me an egg," said the borrower, " and I will return thee another." But the lender asked for a large sum of money, which he pretended the egg would have brought him in during the time. They went to King David and submitted their case to him. Before the gate of the royal palace the youths met the boy Solomon, who was in the habit of asking all the litigants coming to see his father after the nature

[1] *Maassim Tobim*, § 13; see also Bin Gorion, *Der Born Judas*, Vol. III, pp. 67–70.

of their respective cases. When the two boys appeared, Solomon asked them to acquaint him with their case, and they did so. Thereupon Solomon said: " Submit your case to my father and then tell me what judgment he has given."

The litigants went before the King, and the plaintiff brought his witnesses, who confirmed his story of the bargain. He claimed from the borrower the entire amount which the egg would have brought him in during the time since he had lent it. Thereupon King David said to the borrower: " Thou must pay thy debt."

" Your Majesty," replied the youth, " I do not know how much the amount is."

The lender now explained to King David how much he claimed. " In the course of one year," he said, " the egg would have produced a chicken, next year this chicken would have given birth to eighteen other chickens, and in the third year these would have given birth each to another eighteen chickens, and so on. He thus claimed for the one egg he had lent an enormous sum, the equivalent of hundreds of chickens. The borrower of the egg left the hall of justice greatly distressed.

At the gate of the royal mansion Solomon once more addressed the two litigants, inquiring what judgment his father had given. " I am compelled," replied the borrower of the egg, " to pay an enormous sum which my friend, as he pretends, could have realized from the egg he had once lent me." Thereupon young Solomon said: " Listen unto me and I will give thee good advice."

" Long mayest thou live," replied the poor youth.

Said Solomon: " Go thou out into the fields and busy thyself at a ploughed plot of ground—where the regiments of the King are daily passing by. When thou dost perceive the warriors coming along, take a handful of boiled beans and throw them upon the ground. Should they ask thee what thou art doing, then say: ' I am sowing boiled beans.' And when they mock thee and ask: ' Who has ever heard of boiled beans bringing forth any fruit?' then reply: ' And who has heard of a boiled egg bringing forth a chicken?' "

The boy did as Solomon had advised him to. When the soldiers inquired what he was doing, he replied that he was sowing boiled beans. " Who has ever heard of such a thing?" asked the astonished soldiers, " that a boiled thing should take root and bring forth fruit?"

" And who has ever heard of a boiled egg producing a chicken?" retorted the boy.

Every regiment that passed asked the same question and received the same answer. The news of the strange conduct of the boy at last reached King David, who immediately summoned him into his presence.

" Who was it that advised thee to act as thou didst?" asked the King.

" It was my own idea," replied the boy.

" No," said the King, " I recognize the hand of Solomon in it." Thereupon the youth confessed the truth and admitted that it was indeed Solomon who had commanded him to act as he had done. David now summoned his son Solomon and asked him to give judgment in the case.

" How can the boy," asked the Prince, " be responsible for things which cannot be looked upon as really existing? An egg boiled in hot water can never be considered as a potential chicken."

David admitted the justice of Solomon's words and ordered the youth to pay his friend the value of one egg and not more.[1]

[1] *Revue des Études Juives*, XXXV, pp. 65–67, §¶IX; see also *Ozar Midrashim*, I, pp. 347–348; cf. Bin Gorion, *loc. cit.*, pp. 64–67.

CHAPTER VIII

The Magic Carpet and the Mysterious Palace

The magic carpet—The four princes—The travel in the air—A morning meal at Damascus and an evening meal in Media—Solomon's boast—Rukh's retort—In the valley of the ants—The black ant—Solomon's question and the ant's answers—The ant rebukes the King—The mysterious palace—The three old eagles—The entrance to the palace—The four doors—The inscriptions—The idol—The tablet on its neck—The mysterious writing—Solomon's trouble—The young man from the wilderness—Sheddad, son of Od—King over ten thousand provinces—Nothing remains but a good name.

IN THE VALLEY OF THE ANTS, OR A LESSON IN HUMILITY

This is what happened in the days of Solomon, King of Israel. When the Holy One gave Solomon, the son of David, the Kingdom of Israel, and made him the ruler over all sorts of wild and tame animals, over man and all the creatures in the world, over the beasts in the field and the birds in the air, in a word, over all the creatures that the Lord had created, He also gave him a great carpet to sit upon.

This carpet was made of yellow-green silk, interwoven with fine gold and embroidered with all sorts of images. It was sixty mils in length and sixty mils in breadth. Solomon had also four princes to serve him: one prince was of the sons of men, the other of the demons, the third of the wild beasts, and the fourth of the birds. The prince of the sons of men was Asaf, the son of Berechiah, the prince who was of the demons was Ramirath, whilst the two princes who were of the wild beasts and the birds were a lion and an eagle respectively. When he travelled, Solomon only did so upon the wings of the wind, and he would have his morning meal in Damascus and his evening meal in Media, that is in the East and in the West.

Now it happened one day that Solomon was boasting himself and saying: " There is none like me in the world, for the Lord hath given me wisdom and understanding, knowledge and intelligence, and hath made me ruler over all His creatures." Immediately the wind moved away and 40,000 men fell off from the carpet. When Solomon saw this, he cried to the wind and said: "Return, Rukh! Rukh! I command thee to return." Then the wind replied: " If thou, O Solomon, wilt return to thy God and not boast thyself any more, then will I return to thee!" And in that hour Solomon was put to shame by the words of the wind.

One day, whilst travelling on his carpet and on the wings of the wind, Solomon was passing over a valley in which there were ants. He suddenly heard the voice of a black ant saying to the other ants: " Go into your houses, lest the hosts of King Solomon crush you."

When King Solomon heard these words, he grew very angry and at once commanded the wind to descend upon the earth. The wind obeyed, and King Solomon sent for the ants and said unto them: " Which of you said: ' Go into your houses, lest the hosts of King Solomon crush you?' " And the black ant that had spoken answered and said: " It was I who had thus spoken to my companions."

" Why didst thou speak thus?" asked King Solomon.

" Because," replied the ant, " I feared that they might feel inclined to go out and look upon thy hosts, and would thus interrupt their praises with which they constantly praise the Lord, and then the anger of the Holy One might be kindled against us and He would destroy us."

Thereupon King Solomon asked: "Why didst thou alone speak amongst all the ants thy companions?"

"Because," replied the black ant, "I am their queen."

"And what is thy name?" asked King Solomon.

"Machshamah is my name," replied the ant.

Then Solomon said to the ant: "I wish to ask thee a question."

She answered: "It is not fitting that he who is asking questions should be on high, whilst the one that is being asked should be below."

Solomon lifted the ant up to him, but she again said: "It is not fitting that the one who asks should be seated on his throne, whilst the one who is being asked should be standing on the ground; take me, therefore, into thy hand, and I will answer thee."

Thereupon Solomon took the ant into his hand, but she remained facing him and said: "Now ask thy question."

"Is there in the world anyone greater than I?" he asked.

"There is," said the ant.

"Who is it?" asked Solomon.

"It is I," replied the ant.

"And how art thou greater than I?" asked Solomon, greatly astonished.

"Because," said the ant, "had I not been greater than thou, then the Lord would not have sent thee to me to take me into thy hand."

When Solomon heard these words of the ant, his anger was kindled, and he cast her down upon the ground.

"Ant," he cried, "knowest thou not who I am? I am Solomon, son of King David, peace be upon him."

But the ant said: "Dost thou know that thou art sprung from a vile and evil-smelling clot and shouldst not boast thyself?"

In that hour Solomon fell on his face, and was ashamed

on account of the words of the ant. Turning to the wind, he commanded: " Lift up the carpet and let us go." When the wind lifted up the carpet, the ant cried after Solomon: " Go, but do not forget the name of the Lord, and do not boast thyself exceedingly." [1]

The Mysterious Palace

The wind now set itself into motion, rising higher and higher, and lifted up Solomon between heaven and earth, where he passed ten days and ten nights. One day the King perceived from a distance a lofty palace built of fine gold. " I have never seen anything in the world like this lofty palace," said Solomon to his princes. In that hour Solomon said to the wind: " Descend." The wind immediately obeyed, and Solomon and his prince Asaf, the son of Berechiah, went forth and walked round and round the palace, and the scent of the herbage wafted into their nostrils was like the scent of Paradise. As they could not, however, discover any entrance or gate by which to enter the palace, they wondered greatly at this and asked themselves how they could enter the palace.

While they were thus engaged, the prince of the demons approached, and thus he spoke: " My Lord, why art thou so troubled?"

" I am troubled," replied Solomon, " on account of this palace which has no gate, and I do not know how to enter it or what to do." But the prince of the demons said: " My Lord the King! I will at once command the demons to mount upon the roof of the palace, where they will perhaps find something, a man or a bird, or some other living creature."

Solomon at once commanded the demons to hasten and mount up to the roof of the palace and to see whether they could find aught. The demons obeyed and mounted up to the roof of the palace, but they soon descended again and said:

[1] Jellinek, *loc. cit.*, Vol. V, pp. 22–26; see also *Ozar Hamidrashim*, II. pp. 534–536.

" Our Lord! We have seen no man on the roof of the palace, only a great bird, an eagle, sitting upon his young ones."

Thus spoke the demons, and Solomon at once called the prince of the demons and commanded him to bring the eagle to him. The vulture went immediately, and brought the eagle to King Solomon, upon whom be peace.

Thereupon the eagle opened his mouth in songs and praises to the Holy One, the King over all the Kings of Kings, and then he saluted King Solomon.

" What is thy name?" asked Solomon.

" Alanad," answered the eagle.

" And how old art thou?" asked the King.

" Seven hundred years," replied the eagle.

" Hast thou ever seen, or known, or heard," asked Solomon, " that this palace had an entrance or a gate?"

" By thy life, my lord the King," replied the eagle, " and by the life of thy head, I know it not; but I have a brother who is older than myself by two hundred years; he has knowledge and understanding, and he dwells in the second storey."

Said Solomon to the vulture: " Take back this eagle to his place and bring me at once his brother who is older than himself." And the vulture at once disappeared and returned after a time to Solomon, bringing with him another eagle greater than the first. The eagle opened his mouth in praises to his Creator and then saluted the King.

" What is thy name?" asked King Solomon.

" Elof is my name," answered the eagle.

" And how old art thou?" asked Solomon.

" Nine hundred years," answered the eagle.

" Dost thou know or hast thou heard that there is an entrance or a gate to this palace?"

" By thy life, my lord the King," answered the eagle, " by thy life and by the life of thy head, I know it not; but I have a brother who is older than myself by four hundred years, and he may know; he has knowledge and understanding, and he lives in the third storey."

Thereupon Solomon said to the prince of the birds: " Take back this eagle to his place and bring me his brother who is older than himself." The prince of the birds obeyed and disappeared. He returned after a time and brought the greatest eagle. He was very old and could not fly, and had to be carried by the birds on their wings, who set him before King Solomon. The eagle at once opened his mouth in praises to the Creator and then saluted the King.

" What is thy name?" asked Solomon.

" Altamar," replied the eagle.

" And how old art thou?"

" Thirteen hundred years."

" Dost thou perhaps know, or hast thou heard, whether this palace has a gate or an entrance?" asked Solomon.

" By thy life, my lord," answered the eagle, " I know it not; but my father told me that once there was an entrance to this palace on the western side. In the course of the number of years that had passed the dust had covered it up. If thou wilt command the wind to blow away the dust that has been heaped up round the house, then the entrance will reappear."

Thereupon Solomon commanded the wind to sweep away the dust which had gathered round the house, and the wind immediately began to blow and swept away all the dust so that the entrance was disclosed. There was a big iron gate, but owing to the lapse of time it looked as though it had been consumed and was mouldering.

There was a lock on it upon which were written the words: " Sons of men, be it known unto ye that for many years we dwelt in this palace in delight and prosperity. When famine came upon us we ground pearls *under the wheat*, but it profited us not, and we therefore left the palace to the eagle and laid us down on the ground. We thus said to the eagles: If any man asks ye concerning this palace, then say unto him: We found it ready built."

There was also written: "No man shall dare enter into this house unless he be a Prophet or a King. If he desires to enter this palace, let him dig on the right side of the entrance, where he will find a chest made of glass; let him break this open and he will find therein the keys. When he will open the entrance gate, he will find a door of gold. Let him open this and enter. He will then find a second door; let him open this and enter. He will then find a third door, and when he will have opened this and entered he will perceive a magnificent building, and therein he will see a hall set with Odem, Pitdah, and Bareket, ruby, topaz, emerald, and pearl (*Exodus*, xxviii, 17). He will also see a room adorned with all kinds of pearls, and also many chambers and courts paved with bricks of silver and gold. Let him then look on the ground, and he will behold the figure of scorpion which is of silver. Let him remove the figure, and he will find a room underground full of pearls without number, and silver and gold. Farther down he will find another door and a lock on it, and upon the door is written: 'The Lord of this palace was once highly honoured and mighty, and even lions and bears dreaded him and trembled before his power and majesty. In prosperity and delight did he dwell in this palace where he sat upon his throne and reigned.'

"His hour to die came, however, upon him, and he was taken away before his due time, and the crown fell from his head. Wanderer, enter into the palace and thou shalt behold wonders."

Solomon then opened the door and entered, and he beheld a third gateway on which was written that the inhabitants of the palace had dwelt in riches and honour, they had died, and the ills of time had passed over them. Their treasures alone had remained after them, but they themselves had departed to their graves, and not a trace of them had remained upon earth.

And Solomon unlocked the gate and found himself in a hall of precious stones, and on the wall was written: " How mighty was I who once dwelt in this palace! I possessed great wealth, how I ate and drank, and what beautiful apparel I did wear! How I was feared and how I, in my turn, had to fear!"

Solomon went farther and entered a beautiful mansion of precious stones which had three exits. On the first door the following lines were written: " Son of man, let fortune never deceive thee; thou, too, wilt waste and wither away and depart from thy place, and lie in the end beneath the ground!"

On the second door the following lines were written: " Be not in a hurry, for small only is thy share; be circumspect, for the world is given from one to another."

On the third gate was written as follows: " Take provision for thy journey, and provide thyself with food while it is yet day, for thou shalt not be left upon earth and the day of thy death is hidden from thee."

Solomon then opened the door, crossed the threshold, and entered. He saw the image of a man in sitting posture, and anyone that looked upon the image would have thought that it was alive, and it was surrounded by numerous idols. And when Solomon went up and drew near, the image quaked and cried aloud: " Help! Come hither, ye sons of Satan, for King Solomon has come to destroy you."

Thus cried the image, and fire and smoke issued forth from its nostrils. Then a tremendous noise arose among the demons who raved and shouted, causing earthquake and thunder.

Then Solomon cried out loudly unto them: " Do ye intend to affright me? Know ye not that I am King Solomon, who reigns over all the creatures that the Almighty has created, and that they are subject unto me? I will chastise ye because ye dare rebel against me."

Thereupon King Solomon uttered the Ineffable name of the Lord, and all the demons immediately became motionless, and none of them could utter a word. The images and idols all fell to the ground, and the sons of Satan fled and threw themselves into the waves of the great sea, that they might not fall into the hands of Solomon, the son of David.

Thereupon Solomon drew near to the image and, putting his hand into its mouth, withdrew a silver tablet. On that tablet all that concerned the palace was written, but Solomon could not read the words. He was greatly grieved at this, and turning to the princes who accompanied him he said: " Ye know how much trouble I have taken in order to reach this image, and now that I am in possession of this tablet, I am unable to read the words engraved upon it!"

And while he was considering the matter and asking himself what to do, he suddenly beheld a young man who had come from the wilderness. The youth came up and, bending low to the King, thus addressed him: " Why art thou so grieved, O King Solomon, son of David?" And Solomon answered: " I am grieved on account of this tablet, because I cannot read the words written on it."

Thereupon the young man said: " Give the tablet to me and I will read it for thee. I was sitting in my place, but when the Lord Almighty saw how grieved thou wast, He sent me to read the writing to thee."

Solomon handed over to the young man the tablet he had taken from the neck of the image, and the youth looked at it and his face expressed surprise, and he began to weep. Thereupon he addressed the King, and thus he spoke: " O Solomon! the writing upon this plate is in the Greek tongue, and that is what it says: ' I Sheddad, son of Ad, reigned over ten thousand provinces, and I rode on ten thousand horses; ten thousand

Kings were subject to me. Ten thousand heroes and warriors have I slain, but in the hour when the Angel of Death came to me I could not withstand him.'

" There is further written as follows: ' Whoever doth read this writing, let him give up troubling greatly about this world, for the destiny and end of all men is to die, and nothing remains of man but his good name.' "

And this is what came over King Solomon in this world.[1]

---

[1] *Ibid.*; see also Lewner, *loc. cit.*, pp. 371-375; see *Miscellany of Hebrew Literature*, ed. by A. Lowy, London, 1877, Vol. II, pp. 135-141.

CHAPTER IX

The Royal Marriage and the
Exiled Princess

The Egyptian princess—Solomon's love for Bathya—The consecration
of the Temple—The royal marriage—Great rejoicings—The angel Michael
inserts a reed in the sea—The power of Rome—The destruction of Jerusalem
—The thousand songs of the Egyptian princess—The wonderful canopy—
The starlike gems—Solomon oversleeps himself—The morning sacrifice—
A mother's rebuke—The exiled princess—The deserted island—The high
tower—The young man from Akko—The strange shelter—The carcass of
an ox and the enormous bird—A ride in the air—The miraculous escape—
The amazed princess—The lovers—The contract written in blood—The
eunuch's discovery—The arrival of the King—Solomon's amazement—It
is vain for mortal man to try and prevent the decrees of Providence.

THE EGYPTIAN PRINCESS

Solomon, who is renowned for his severe criticism of the
fair sex, loved many foreign women. His love affairs were
numerous, but he loved most of all Bathya, the daughter of
Pharaoh Necho, whom he married soon after the death of his
teacher, Shimei ben Gera. The King loved the Egyptian princess more than all the other women, and she, more than all his
wives, made him commit many sins.[1]

Solomon married Bathya on the very day on which the
building of the temple had been completed. Great joy reigned
in Jerusalem, on account of the consecration of the sanctuary,
but in the royal palace there were two joys, and the rejoicing
over the royal marriage and the revelry were greater than the

[1] *Sifré*, ed. Friedmann, p. 86a.

rejoicings of the people over the consecration of the Temple.
All were paying flattery to the King, and he was induced to
forget the fear of God. The Lord thereupon decided then
and there to destroy Jerusalem and the holy Temple.[1]

On that very night on which Solomon took to wife the
Egyptian princess, the angel Michael (according to others it
was Gabriel) came down upon earth and inserted a reed in the
sea. In the course of time earth gathered round the reed, and
a sandbank was formed which became an island. A dense
forest grew on it, and on its site one day Rome was built,
that mighty empire which was destined to cause the destruction
of Jerusalem.[2]

It seems that the Egyptian princess, well versed in allure-
ments and harem tricks, knew how to hold the King in the
power of her many charms. From her native home she had
brought to Palestine a thousand musical instruments, and she
knew a thousand sweet songs. She played and sang to the
King on the nuptial night, and at each song she pronounced
the name of the idol to which the song was dedicated. The
Egyptian woman did more. Above the nuptial couch she
spread out a wonderful canopy studded with gems which
shone and sparkled like so many stars. When Solomon opened
his eyes and wanted to rise, he beheld the starlike gems and,
thinking that it was still night, he continued to sleep. He thus
slept on until the fourth hour, that is, ten o'clock. As the
keys to the Temple were under the King's pillow, the morning
sacrifice could not be offered. The people were greatly distressed, but none dared to go and wake the King. They therefore approached the Queen-mother, Bath-Sheba, who came
and rebuked her son. " People will say," she complained,
" that it is my fault if my son is forsaking the Lord. And yet,
I am not to be blamed. Unlike your father's other wives, I

[1] *Numer. Rabba*, 10, 8; *Midrash Mishle*, 31; *Leviticus Rabba*, 12, 4.
[2] *Sanhedrin*, 21b; *Jerushalmi Aboda Zara*, 1, 2; *Sabbath*, 56b.

never prayed to the Lord to give me a son worthy to reign, but for one who would be pious, learned, and virtuous.[1]

KING SOLOMON AND HIS DAUGHTER

THE PRINCESS AND THE HANDSOME BUT POOR LAD FROM AKKO

King Solomon had a daughter named Kaziah who was of peerless beauty and whom the King loved dearly. Once he read in the stars that his daughter would marry a poor and destitute lad of the children of Israel. Greatly grieved at this, King Solomon made up his mind to prevent the occurrence of such an event, and in order to do so he sent his daughter away from Jerusalem.

He commanded his trusted servants to erect a high tower on one of the distant islands out in the sea, and to this tower he sent his daughter. The builders of the tower and the seamen who brought her to the island were all sworn to secrecy. Seventy eunuchs were thereupon commanded to accumulate provisions for the girl and to guard her in this place of seclusion, and not to allow anyone to penetrate into the tower.

Now it happened that the poor lad who was destined to be the husband of the princess, and who lived with his parents at Akko, had made up his mind to go out into the world in order to earn his living and make his way. Journeying on one cold night, he was surprised by the falling darkness in an open field, and he knew not where to hide himself and find shelter. At last he perceived the torn carcass of an ox, and he crept into it so as to warm himself and pass the night therein. He soon fell asleep in his strange place of shelter.

Now an enormous bird came along and, seeing the carcass of the ox, swooped down, seized it, and carried it off in his talons to some place where he could devour it undisturbed.

[1] *Sanhedrin*, 21b; see Faerber, *König Salomon in der Tradition*, 1902, pp. 49–61.

As fate would have it, the bird bore the dead ox with the youth inside it to the roof of the very tower where the daughter of King Solomon was kept in seclusion. The bird devoured the flesh of the ox and went off.

On the following morning the princess as usual went upon the roof of the tower for a walk, and great was her surprise when she beheld the young man.

" Who art thou?" she asked the youth, not less astonished than herself, " and how comest thou hither upon the roof of this high tower?"

" I am from the town of Akko," replied the lad, " and my name is Reuben."

He thereupon told her all that had occurred and how he had been carried here by an enormous bird.

The princess had compassion on the lad and brought him to her apartment, where she set food and drink before him. Thereupon she conducted him to a room where he could bathe and anoint himself and put on other robes. When he again appeared before the princess, she saw that he was very handsome. She talked to him, and soon discovered that he was not only of marvellous beauty but also very learned.

" Thou canst not leave this high tower," said the princess, " nor wilt thou be able to cross the sea, for no ship ever passes this island. Abide thou, therefore, here until the day when my father will come to fetch me, as he promised me on the day when he sent me hither."

Thus the handsome poor lad of Akko, he who was destined to be the husband of King Solomon's daughter, remained with her upon the island. The princess fell in love with the boy of surpassing beauty, of great learning and intelligence, and she wished to marry him.

One day she asked the lad to take her to wife, and as he, too, was burning in love for her, he was only too happy to yield to her request.

Thereupon they plighted their troth, and the lad took a small knife, opened a vein, and, dipping a quill in his blood, wrote the marriage contract according to the law, taking God and two angels as their witnesses. Thus the princess became the wife of the poor and handsome lad from Akko.

A year elapsed, and the eunuchs discovered the truth. They immediately sent word to King Solomon and acquainted him with the true state of affairs. Greatly astonished, the King decided to visit his daughter and to find out how she could have found a man on that distant island and in spite of all the care he had taken.

He journeyed to the place where his daughter was imprisoned, and marvelled greatly when he heard how the lad had been carried by an enormous bird to the very tower where his daughter dwelt. When Solomon saw the lad, beheld his marvellous beauty, and convinced himself that he was wise and learned, he knew that he was indeed the husband concerning whom he had read in the stars. He now understood that it was vain for mortal man to try and prevent the decrees of Providence. He was also overjoyed to find that the lad was indeed a husband not unworthy of his daughter, and he praised God.[1]

This story, which is referred to by Hartland in his *Legend of Perseus*[2], reminds us of the prince borne by the enchanted horse in the *Arabian Nights*.

[1] Buber, Introduction to *Midrash Tanchuma*; Grünbaum, *loc. cit.*, p. 234; *Salzburger loc cit.*, p. 80.
[2] Pp. 100–101, quoted from Koehler in *Academy*, 21st March, 1891

CHAPTER X

Solomon's Throne and Temple

Solomon's throne—Description of the throne according to Targum
Sheni—The fame of Solomon's throne—The Kings of the nations come to
admire the throne of the King of Israel—The fate of Solomon's throne—
Nebuchadnezzar, Shishak, King of Egypt, Antiochus Epiphanes, and Cyrus
—Ahasuerus, King of Shushan—David tries to build the Temple—The
waters of the deep—The jealousy of Achitophel—His advice—The artisans
who built the Temple—The master and his chaste wife—The talisman—
The glimming coal and the piece of cotton—Solomon's surprise—The
two youths who came to tempt the virtuous woman—Solomon in disguise
—The dish of boiled eggs differently painted—The rebuke of the virtuous
woman—The finding of the Shamir—The gates refuse to open—The
merits of David.

It is said in Scripture that Solomon made a great throne of
ivory and overlaid it with gold. There were six steps to the
throne, with a footstool of gold, which were fastened to the
throne, and steps on either side of the sitting place, and two
lions standing beside the steps: and twelve lions stood there
on the one side and on the other upon the six steps.[1] Legend
is very busy in describing the magnificence and glory of the
King's throne. It is related as follows in the *Second Targum to
Esther*.

One day King Solomon sent for Hiram, the artificer from
Tyre, and thus he spoke unto him: " I know that thou art a great
artificer and very clever, and I have sent for thee so that thou
shouldst make a throne for me which will surpass in magnificence the thrones of all the Kings in the world. And Hiram

---

[1] *1 Kings*, x, 18; *2 Chronicles*, ix, 17.

from Tyre made answer: " If the King will place at my disposal gold and silver and gems and precious stones, I will construct a throne the like of which has never been seen. Thereupon King Solomon gave instructions that his treasure-stores be opened to Hiram. And such was the throne which the artificer from Tyre made for King Solomon. There were six steps, and twelve lions of gold stood upon them and twelve eagles of gold faced them. The right paw of a golden lion was directed towards the left wing of each golden eagle, and the left wing of the golden eagle was towards the right paw of each golden lion. There were seventy-two golden lions and as many golden eagles. The top of the throne where the King's seat was, was round-shaped, and it had six steps. Upon the first step there lay a golden lion and facing it was a golden ox. Upon the second step there crouched a golden wolf and opposite to it was a golden lamb. Upon the third step there was a golden panther and opposite to it lay a golden camel. Upon the fourth step there lay a golden eagle and facing it was a golden peacock. Upon the fifth step lay a golden cat and opposite to it was a golden hen. Upon the sixth step lay a golden hawk and opposite to it was a golden dove. On the top of the throne was a golden dove holding in its claws a golden hawk. There was also a candlestick made of pure gold with its lamps, ashpans, and snuffers. And seven pipes issued from it on which were engraven the images of the seven Patriarchs, the work of a clever artificer. The names of the seven Patriarchs are: Adam, Noah, Shem, Abraham, Isaac, Jacob, and Job. On the other side of the candlestick were seven other pipes upon which were engraven the images of the seven pious and just men of the world, who are: Levi, Kehat, Amram, Moses, Aaron, Eldad, and Medad. A golden jar filled with the purest olive oil stood on the top of the candlestick for the purpose of supplying the lamps in the Holy Temple. Underneath the candlestick was a vessel of pure gold filled with the purest olive

oil, supplying the lamps, and upon it was engraven the image
of Eli the High Priest. And two branches proceeded from the
vessel upon which were portrayed the images of the two sons
of Eli the High Priest, Hophni and Phinehas. Two pipes
proceeded from the two branches, and upon them were again
portrayed the images of two sons of Aaron the High Priest,
Nadab and Abihu. Twenty-four vines of gold were placed
on the upper side of the throne so as to give a shade to the
King.

Whenever Solomon wished to ascend his throne and set his
foot on the first step, the golden ox at once raised him to the
second step, the golden bear to the third step, the golden
panther to the fourth step, and so on until the King reached
the sixth step. Then the golden eagles took him up and seated
him on the throne. Whenever he ascended the throne and
sat down, an eagle came and placed the crown upon his head.
Thereupon a golden dove descended from one pillar and
opened a cabinet. It took out the Holy Law and placed it in
the hands of the King. The throne moved upon wheels and
there was a silver serpent round about the wheels. Wherever
Solomon wished to go the throne moved with him, and rivers
of spices flowed wherever he went. On either side of the
throne sat the elders of Israel to judge the people, and no one
could bear false witness before them. Whenever a man came
before the King and the elders and harboured in his heart
the intention of bearing false witness, he was immediately
denounced. At the approach of the would-be perjurer the
wheels of the throne began to move, the oxen to low, the bears
to growl, and the lions to roar. The panthers yelled, the owls
hooted, and the lambs bleated; the peacocks shrieked, the
cocks crowed, and the cats mewed; the birds chirped, and the
hawks screamed. And terror seized those who intended to
bear false witness so that they were greatly afraid and spoke
the truth. " Let us speak the truth," they said, " and only

the truth, for otherwise the world may be destroyed because of us." [1]

The fame of Solomon's throne spread far and wide among all the Kings of the nations. They gathered themselves together and came to visit Solomon and to see with their own eyes the magnificence of his throne and its wonders.

When they came to Jerusalem and beheld the wonderful throne they were dazzled by its great splendour, and falling to the ground, they prostrated themselves before Solomon in his Glory and did him homage. " Never," exclaimed the Kings of the nations, " have we beheld such a throne, for never has such a throne been made for another King and never will its like be made." They coveted the glorious throne in their hearts and envied the King of Israel.

Solomon's throne was later on taken from Jerusalem and carried to strange lands, but none of the rulers of Babylon, Egypt, or Greece was ever allowed to ascend and sit on the throne of the son of David. When Nebuchadnezzar captured Jerusalem and destroyed the Temple, he took the throne with him and it formed part of his plunder. He carried the throne to Babylon and desired to seat himself upon it, but he was punished for his presumption. Ignorant of the mechanism of the throne and the particular manner in which it could only be ascended, Nebuchadnezzar set his foot upon the first step, and the lion stretched out its paw. Instead, however, of raising the ruler of Babylon to the second step, it smote him upon the left foot, and Nebuchadnezzar was lame for the remainder of his life. Afterwards Alexander the Great brought the throne to Egypt, where Shishak, the Pharaoh of Egypt, admired its beauty and glory. He, too, desired to seat himself upon it, but met with the same fate as did Nebuchadnezzar. The lion, stretching out its paw, wounded him, and he remained lame

---

[1] *Targum Sheni*, ed. M. David, Berlin, 1898, and P. Cassel, Leipzig and Berlin, 1885; see also P. Cassel, *Kaiser u. Königsthrone*, Berlin, 1874; Jellinek, *Beth-Hamidrash*, V, pp. 34 ff; Vol. III, pp. 83 ff; Salzberger, *Salomons Tempelbau u. Thron*, Berlin, 1912, pp. 74-99.

until the end of his days. He was therefore called Pharaoh
Necho, or the lame Pharaoh. Afterwards Antiochus Epiphanes
took the famous throne away from Egypt and put it on board
ship, but a leg of it was broken. The King summoned and
brought together all the artificers and goldsmiths of the world,
but none of them was able to repair the broken leg of Solomon's throne. The throne afterwards came into the hands of
the Persian King Cyrus, who had brought about the downfall
of the Kingdom of Antiochus. And because Cyrus had rebuilt
the Temple of Jerusalem he was rewarded for his noble deed
and was granted the distinction of being allowed to ascend
the throne of Solomon and to seat himself upon it. The throne
was thereafter in the possession of King Ahasuerus, and he sat
on it in Shushan the palace.[1]

THE TEMPLE

David had vowed to build a Temple to the Lord, and he
actually began the work. He instructed the labourers to dig
the foundations, and in the course of their labours they came
down to the waters of the deep. Immediately the waters
surged up tumultuously, threatening to flood Jerusalem and
the whole world as in the days of Noah. Great was the despair
of David, and he turned to Achitophel for advice. Achitophel
was jealous of David and thought to himself: " David will
now be drowned and I shall be King in his place." David,
however, turned to him and said: " Whoever knows how to
stop the waters of the deep and refuses to do it, will one day
throttle himself." Then Achitophel was compelled to tell the
King what to do.

He counselled David to take a stone and engrave upon it
the Ineffable Name, the Tetragrammaton, and set it in the
orifice through which the waters were surging. David followed

---

[1] *Yalkut Esther*, § 1046; Salzberger, *loc. cit.*, pp. 60–62, 64–70; *Midrash Abba Gorion*;
Jellinek, *Beth-Hamidrash*, Vol. I, pp. 1–18; see also chap. XIX of this vol.

Achitophel's advice, and immediately the waters of the deep
subsided, and Jerusalem and the whole world were saved
from the danger that threatened them. In the end Achitophel,
nevertheless, committed suicide by hanging himself.[1] The
digging proceeded, but David was not allowed to build the
Temple on account of his having been a man of blood.[2]
When Solomon ascended the throne of his father David,
he carried on the work and built the Temple of Jerusalem
with the help of Hiram, King of Tyre, Sidon, and Phœnicia.
He also wrote to many kings and princes and asked them
to send him artisans and architects to help in the building
of the Temple.

In connection with the masters and artists who came to
Jerusalem from foreign lands the following story is told,
according to which Solomon had to admit that not all women
were worthless.

The Master and his Faithful Wife

King Solomon had uttered many harsh words concerning
women, of whose faithfulness he had but a poor opinion. Once,
however, he met a true and good woman as is related in the
following story.

When the King was about to build the Temple in Jerusalem, he dispatched messengers to the kings and princes of
other countries and asked them to send to the land of Israel
their cleverest artisans, to whom he promised high remuneration for their work. The kings and princes complied with
Solomon's request and sent their best artisans to Jerusalem.

Now in a certain place there lived a clever master who
always refused to betake himself to another town, even when
high remuneration was offered to him for his work. This
master artisan namely had a very beautiful and charming wife,

---

[1] *Jerushalmi Sanhedrin*, X, 29a; *Succah*, 52b–53a.
[2] G. Salzberger, *Salomons Tempelbau und Thron*, p. 7; *Folklore*, Vol. XVI, p. 422.

and he was afraid to leave her alone lest sinful men come and lead her astray from the path of virtue.

Now when King Solomon's messengers arrived in the town where dwelt the master artisan and his beautiful wife and made known the request of the King of Israel, the Prince of the locality summoned into his presence the master artisan. The latter came and, prostrating himself before his King, said: " What is the command of my Lord to his servant?"

" My command," said the King, " is that thou shouldst immediately travel to Jerusalem and there help to build the Temple for King Solomon. He is a mighty ruler, and I dare not disobey his request."

Greatly perturbed and sad at heart, the master returned to his home. When his wife inquired after the cause of his grief, he told her what had occurred. Thereupon the woman said: " If it is on my account that thou art so grieved, then be of good cheer. I will give thee a talisman, and as long as it remains unchanged thou mayest consider it as a sure sign of my innocence and purity. Obey the command of the King and go to Jerusalem, there to work among the other artisans. Have no fear and be sure that I shall remain pure and faithful unto thee."

In the morning the woman gave her husband a tiny glass bulb which contained a small piece of cotton and a glimming coal. " See," she said, " as long as this piece of cotton does not catch fire, thou mayest be sure that the flame of sinful passion has not entered my heart."

The master attached the glass bulb to a chain which he put round his neck, embraced his wife, and proceeded to Jerusalem. Arrived in the holy city, he offered his services to the King and helped in the building of the Temple. Now King Solomon daily came to visit the artisans to see what progress they were making. Well content, he promised to double their wages. One day he raised his eyes and perceived the strange talisman on the neck of the master. Greatly astonished, he summoned the latter and asked him to explain the meaning of the glass bulb. The master related unto the King what had occurred and how his wife had given him the talisman.

Now what did Solomon do? He summoned two handsome youths and commanded them to travel to the town where the beautiful woman dwelt, to abide in her house and to seduce her. When the youths arrived in the town, they took lodging in the woman's house and made themselves agreeable to her. The woman offered the two strangers hospitality and invited them to dine with her. When night came she took them to a room she had prepared for them. Scarcely, however, had the youths entered the chamber when she locked the door and thus kept them prisoners for a whole month.

Every day King Solomon watched the talisman on the master's neck, but lo! the piece of cotton never caught fire. Greatly astonished, Solomon said in his heart: " I will go myself to that city and try to tempt the woman." Disguising himself as an ordinary traveller and accompanied by two servants, he proceeded on his journey. Arrived in the city where dwelt the chaste woman, he took lodging in her house. The woman, who at once guessed that he was Solomon, received him with great honour and prepared a meal worthy of a king. She offered him many dishes, but the last she placed upon the table contained boiled eggs, every one of which was painted with another colour.

" Taste these eggs, my Lord and King," she said.

" Whom dost thou call King?" asked Solomon, to which the woman replied: " The royal dignity and majesty are visible in thine eyes and upon thy countenance. I am only thy humble handmaiden, and I beg thee to partake of these eggs and to tell me how they taste."

King Solomon ate a little of every egg in the dish and said: " These eggs taste all alike."

" Such is the case with us women," replied the chaste wife of the master; " we are only differently painted. It was not worth thy while to travel such a long distance for the sake of a smooth face. I am thy humble servant and thou canst of course do with me as thou wishest, but know that all earthly desires are vain and sinful."

Thus spoke the charming and chaste woman, and Solomon replied: " Blessed be thou unto the Lord and blessed be thy noble and chaste heart." He asked her to be as a sister to him, gave her a costly gift, and returned to Jerusalem. Here he related unto the master what had occurred and sent him home in peace. He paid him his wages a tenfold and bidding him farewell said: " Go back to thy chaste wife and be happy in the possession of such a jewel." The master returned to his wife, and when she related unto him how she had acted, he kissed her upon the head and honoured and loved her even more than he had done before his departure. Everlasting friendship existed henceforth between the pair and King Solomon.[1]

There is a similar story in *Thousand and One Nights* about the King and the wife of his vizier,[2] and one in the *Tutti Nameh* about the Indian Prince and the wife of the warrior.[3]

The story of the finding of the Shamir which Solomon required for the building of the Temple has been told at length in the first volume of this work.[4] It is said that during the building of the Temple none of the artisans died or even fell sick; none of them ever broke his shovel or pickaxe or lost his shoelaces.[5] When the Temple was at last completed and Solomon wished to bring the ark into the Sanctuary, the gates suddenly refused to open. The King recited twenty-four

---

[1] Isr. bar Sason, *Likkute Maassioth*, Jerusalem, pp. 11b–15a; cf. Bin Gorion, *loc. cit.* pp. 109–113.
[2] *Thousand and One Nights*, 10th Night.
[3] *Tutti Nameh*, German translation by G. Rosen, Leipzig, 1858, Vol. I, pp. 83–87.
[4] Vol. I, pp. 80–86; see also Introduction to Vol. I, pp. xxxvi–xl.
[5] *Pesikta Rabbati*, ed. Friedmann, Wien, 1880; see Salzberger, *Tempelbau*, pp. 17–18.

prayers, but still the gates remained shut until Solomon cried
out, " O Lord, remember the love Thou didst bear unto Thy
servant David," and immediately the gates opened.[1] When
at last the ark was brought into the Temple, all the cedars and
trees in the courtyard of the Lord began to blossom and bear
fruit.[2]

---

[1] *Sanhedrin*, 107b; *Sabbath*, 30a; *Yalkut*, § 698; *Moed Katton*, 9a; cf. Salzberger, *loc. cit.*, p. 22.
[2] *Midrash Tanchuma*, ed. Buber; cf. Salzberger, *ibid.* p. 21.

CHAPTER XI

Solomon and the Queen of Sheba

Solomon master over beasts and birds—The royal guests—The missing hoopoe—The city of Kitor in the East—The wonderful country—The Queen of Sheba—The hoopoe's plan—The letter of King Solomon—The frightened Queen—The royal gifts—The visit of the Queen of Sheba—The beauty of Benaiah—The lion and his lair—The house of glass—The bare legs of the Queen—The riddles of the Queen of Sheba—A tube of cosmetic—Naphtha—Flax—The nineteen riddles—The sawn trunk of a cedar tree.

One day, when Solomon was of good cheer and his heart was gladdened on account of wine, he invited the Kings and princes of the neighbouring countries, and they dwelt in his royal palaces. He thereupon commanded his court-musicians to play upon the cymbals and violins which his father David used to play upon. As he was master over beasts and birds, demons and spirits, he summoned before him the birds of the air, the beasts of the field, the creeping reptiles, the *sheddim*, spirits and ghosts, so as to impress his guests, the Kings of the neighbouring countries, with his greatness. The royal scribes called the beasts and birds by name, and they all came of their own accord, neither bound nor fettered, no human being guiding them. Now it happened that the King was examining the birds but found the hoopoe missing from among them. The bird could nowhere be found, and the King waxed wroth and commanded his servants to find the hoopoe and chastise him. The hoopoe, however, appeared of his own accord, and thus he spoke: " Hearken unto me, O Lord of the World, and may my words find entrance in thine ear. Three months have now elapsed since I took a certain resolution, having first taken counsel with myself. No food have I eaten and no water have I drunk, for I said unto myself: 'I will fly about all over the world and see whether there is a country or a realm which is not subject to my lord the King.' And I have discovered a realm the capital of which is the city of Kitor in the East. The dust in that city is more valuable than gold, and the silver is like mud in the streets. The trees in that land are from the days of creation, and are being watered by the waters from the Garden of Eden. Crowds of men, wearing crowns upon their heads, inhabit that city. They know not the art of war, nor do they know how to use the bow or shoot an arrow. I have also noticed that a woman is ruling over the men in that city of Kitor, and her name is Queen of Sheba. If it now please thee, my lord and King, I shall gird my loins like a hero and fly to the city of Kitor, in the country of Sheba. I shall fetter their Kings with chains and their rulers with iron bands, and I will bring them all before my lord the King."

This plan and advice of the hoopoe pleased the King greatly. The royal scribes were immediately summoned, and a letter was written and bound to the hoopoe's wing. Thereupon the hoopoe rose up and flew skyward. He flew high up among the other birds, who followed him to the city of Kitor, in the land of Sheba. Now it happened that in the morning the Queen of Sheba went forth from her palace to pay worship to the sun, and lo! the birds that had just arrived had darkened the light of the sun. The Queen immediately raised her hand and rent her garment, wondering and greatly perturbed. Then the hoopoe alighted, and she perceived that a letter was tied to his wing. She loosed it and read its contents, and this is what was written in it:

" From me, King Solomon, who sends greeting, peace unto thee, Queen of Sheba, and unto thy nobles! Ye are no doubt aware that the Lord of the Universe has appointed me King over the beasts in the field, the birds in the air, the *sheddim*, spirits and ghosts, and that all the Kings of the East and the West, of the North and the South, are coming to bring me greeting and pay homage unto me. Now if ye will come and pay homage unto me I will honour thee more than I honour all the other Kings who are attending me. But if ye refuse and will not appear before me, salute and pay homage unto me, I shall send out against ye Kings and legions and riders. Ye ask who are these Kings, legions, and riders of King Solomon? Know then that the beasts in the field are my Kings, the birds of the air my riders, the spirits, *sheddim*, and ghosts my legions. They will throttle ye in your beds, the beasts of the field will slay ye in the fields, and the birds of the air will consume your flesh."

And when the Queen of Sheba read these words she once more took hold of her garments and rent them. Thereupon she summoned her elders and princes and said unto them: "Know ye not that King Solomon has written to me?"

But they replied: "We know not King Solomon and care not for his dominion."

The Queen, however, trusted not their words, nor did she incline her ear unto them. She sent word and assembled all the ships in the land and loaded them with presents, the finest wood, pearls, and precious stones. She also sent the King six thousand youths and maidens, born in the same year, in the same month, on the same day, in the same hour—all of the same stature and nature and all of them clad in purple garments. And she wrote a letter which she gave them to bear unto King Solomon, and this is what she wrote: " From the city of Kitor to the land of Israel is a journey of seven years, but I will hasten my journey and be in Jerusalem to visit thee at the end of three years."

At the end of the appointed time the Queen of Sheba

KING SOLOMON AND THE QUEEN OF SHEBA

came to visit Solomon, and when the King heard of her arrival
he sent out Benaiah, the son of Jehoiada, to meet her. He was
of great beauty, and his countenance shone like the dawn of
morn in the sky and like Venus, the bright evening star
that outshines all other stars, and like a rose that is growing
by the waterbrook. When the Queen of Sheba beheld
Benaiah, the son of Jehoiada, she descended from her chariot.
Benaiah asked her why she had left her chariot, and she
made answer:

" Art thou not King Solomon?" to which Benaiah replied:
" I am not King Solomon, but only one of his servants attending him and standing in his presence."

The Queen then turned to her nobles and the princes
accompanying her and said to them: " If you have not seen
the lion, then you may at least behold his lair; if you have not
seen King Solomon, then behold at least the beauty of the man
who is standing in his presence."

Thereupon Benaiah brought the Queen into the presence
of his royal master. Solomon had gone to sit in a house of
glass to receive her, and when the Queen of Sheba approached
she was deceived, thinking that Solomon was sitting in water.
She consequently raised her garments in order to cross the
water, and thus bared her legs so that the King noticed the
hair on her bare feet. Thereupon King Solomon said: " Thy
beauty is the beauty of a woman, but thy hair is the hair of
a man; it is an ornament to a man, but it is ugly in a woman."

THE RIDDLES OF THE QUEEN OF SHEBA

Then the Queen of Sheba addressed King Solomon, and
thus she spoke: " My lord and King, I will put to thee three
riddles, and if thou wilt solve them I will know that thou art
wise indeed, but if not, then I will conclude that thou art like
other mortals.

"What is it?" she said. "A wooden well and an iron bucket; it draws stones but pours out water."

"It is a tube of cosmetic," replied the King.

Said again the Queen of Sheba: "It comes as dust from the earth and dust is its food, it is poured out like water, but it lights the house. What is it?"

"Naphtha," replied the King.

And the Queen further asked: "It walks in front of all things, it raises a loud and bitter wailing and crying; it bends its head like a reed, is the glory of the nobles and the disgrace of the poor, the glory of the dead and the disgrace of the living; it is a delight unto the birds, but a distress unto the fishes. What is it?"

"It is flax," answered the King.[1]

The riddles of the Queen of Sheba are enumerated in the second *Targum to Esther* (I, 2) and in the *Midrash Mishle*, or *Midrash to the Proverbs*.[2] The first source contains the above-mentioned three riddles, whilst the second mentions four.

The Queen's meeting with Solomon is related as follows: The Queen said to him:

"Art thou Solomon of whom I have heard so much?"

"Yes."

Then she asked further: "Wilt thou reply to my questions?" to which Solomon made answer:

"The Lord will lend wisdom."

Then she asked the somewhat unseemly questions for a woman:

"What is it? Seven depart and nine enter; two pour out the draught and one only drinks."

Said he: "Seven are the days of woman's defilement, and nine the months of her pregnancy; two breasts nourish the child, and one drinks."

[1] *Targum Sheni to the Book of Esther*, ed. P. Cassel, Leipzig, 1885; ed. E. David, Berlin, 1898.
[2] *Midrash Mishle*, ed. S. Buber, Vilna, 1893; A. Wünsche, *Midrash Mishle*, Leipzig, 1885.

Said she: " I will ask thee another question. A woman
once said unto her son: Thy father is my father, thy grandfather my husband; thou art my son but I am thy sister."

To which Solomon made answer: " It must surely have
been one of Lot's daughters who thus spoke to her son." [1]

Thereupon she called boys and girls all of the same stature
and wearing the same garb, and said unto the King:
" Distinguish between the males and females."

He immediately beckoned to his eunuchs, and they brought
nuts and roasted ears of corn, which he distributed among
them. The boys, who were not bashful, received them in their
laps, lifting up their dresses; the girls took them in the veils
which served them as headgear. Whereupon King Solomon
said: " These are the boys and these the girls."

She thereupon brought to him a number of boys, some
circumcised and others uncircumcised, and she said to him:
" Distinguish between the circumcised and uncircumcised."

Solomon immediately made a sign to the High Priest and
commanded him to open the ark of the covenant. The persons
who were circumcised immediately bowed their bodies to
half their height, and the radiance of the *skekhinah* shone upon
their countenances, but the uncircumcised ones prostrated
themselves and fell upon their faces.

" These are circumcised," said Solomon, " and these are
uncircumcised."

" Thou art wise indeed," said the Queen of Sheba.[2]

The *Midrash Hachefez*,[3] however, contains nineteen riddles.
The first four coincide, with only a slight difference, with those
given in the *Midrash Mishle*, and we shall therefore only give
here the following fifteen:

5. She put other questions to him and said: " Who is he

---

[1] *Midrash Mishle*; see J. Lightfoot, *Horæ Hebraicæ*, Rotterdam, 1686, II, 527; see also
Yalkut, II, § 1085.
[2] *Midrash Mishle*.
[3] *Midrash Hachefez*, ed. and translated by S. Schechter, *Folklore*, No. 1, pp. 349-358.

who neither was born nor has died?" to which Solomon replied: " It is the Lord of the Universe, blessed be He."

6. She asked again: " What land is that which has seen the sun but once?"

" It is the land on which the waters of creation were gathered and the bottom of the sea on the day when the waters were divided for the Israelites to pass."

7. She asked again: " What is it? An enclosure with ten doors; when one is open, nine are shut, and when nine are open, one is shut."

Said he: " The enclosure is the womb, and the ten doors are the ten orifices of man, namely his eyes, his ears, his nostrils, his mouth, the apertures for the discharge of excreta and urine, and the navel. When the child is still in its mother's womb, the navel is open but all the other apertures are shut, but when the child issues from the womb, the navel is closed and all the other orifices are opened."

8. She further asked: " What is it? It never moves when it is living, but when its head has been cut off it moves."

" It is a ship in the sea (made of trees that have been cut down)."

9. " Who are the three," she asked, " who neither ate, nor did they drink, nor has ever a soul been put into them, and yet they saved three lives from death?"

Said he: " They are the seal, the thread, and the staff (which Judah gave unto Thamar), for they saved the lives of Thamar, Pharez, and Zarah."

10. " What is it?" she asked. " Three entered a cave and five issued from it."

" It is Lot, his two daughters and their two children," said he.

11. " What is it?" she asked again. " The dead lived, the grave moved, and the dead prayed."

Said he: " The dead that lived was Jonah, who lived and prayed, and the grave that moved was the fish."

12. " Who were the three," she further asked, " who ate and drank on the earth, but were never born of male and female?"

Said he: " They were the three angels who came to visit Abraham."

13. " What is it?" she asked. " Four entered a place expecting to die and came forth alive, and two entered a place of life and came forth dead."

Said he: " The four were Daniel, Hananiah, Mishael, and Azariah, and the two were Nadab and Abihu."

14. " Who is he," she asked, " who was born but did not die?"

" Elijah and the Messiah," he replied.

15. " What is it that was never born but to which life was given?"

Said he: " It is the golden calf."

16. " What is it? It is produced from the earth but man produces it, and its food is the fruit of the earth."

" It is a wick," said he.

17. " What is it?" she asked. " A woman was married to two husbands and bore two sons, but all these four had one father."

" It is Thamar," he said, " who was married by Or and Onan and bore two sons, Pharez and Zarah, and the four had one father, Judah."

18. " What is it? A house full of dead; no dead came among them nor any living came forth from them."

" It is Samson and the Philistines."

19. The Queen of Sheba thereupon ordered that the sawn trunk of a cedar tree be brought, and then she asked Solomon to tell her at which end the root had been and at which end the branches.

Solomon ordered the trunk to be cast into the water, and one end sank, whilst the other floated on the surface of the water. Then he said unto her: " The part which sank was the root, and that which floated on the surface was the end containing the branches."

Thereupon the Queen of Sheba said unto Solomon: " Thou dost exceed in wisdom and goodness thy great fame; blessed be thy God." [1]

[1] Cf. Perles, *Zur Rabbinischen Sprach und Sagenkunde*, 1873; Delitzsch, *Iris*, 1889; see also Bialik, *Sepher Haaggadah*, Vol. I, pp. 108–110.

CHAPTER XII

The Beggar King

Solomon's pride—The transgressed commandment—The King has multiplied wives—The complaint of the commandment—The Lord summons Ashmedai—The King in exile—I, Koheleth, *was* King over Israel—The sufferings of Solomon—The two hosts—Solomon's grief and tears—The consolation of the poor man—Better is a dinner of herbs where love is than a stalled ox and hatred therewith—The charitable old woman—Solomon's confession—Naamah, the daughter of the King of Ammon—The exiled monarch and the royal head cook—Solomon as a kitchen boy—The delicious food—The enamoured princess—The anger of the King—The exiled lovers—The fish and the signet-ring—The King of Ammon visits Jerusalem—Solomon introduces his wife—The joy of the parents—The behaviour of Ashmedai—The indignant wife—The amazed Queen-mother—Benaiah and the exiled King—The Sanhedrin fight Ashmedai—The Divine voice.

The incident describing the circumstances under which Solomon was temporarily deprived of his crown and had to wander, an exile in foreign lands, has been related in broad outlines in Vol. I of this work. A more detailed version of the King's exile runs as follows:

Seated upon his magnificent throne and wielding great power over men, beasts, birds, demons, and spirits of the air, Solomon's heart was filled with great pride and presumption.

" No one," he spoke in his heart, " is as wise as I."

In his pride and arrogance he transgressed and broke the commandment which forbids the King to multiply wives unto himself.[1] He took a thousand wives unto himself who led him astray, and he declined from the right way.

---

[1] *Deuteronomy*, xvii, 16, 17.

Thereupon the commandment flew up straight to heaven and thus complained before the Lord: " Lord of the Universe," spoke the commandment which Solomon had trodden down, " is there any law in Thy Holy Torah which is superfluous and for no purpose?"

And the Lord replied: " There is none."

" Ruler of the world," spoke the commandment, " Solomon has transgressed me, for he has taken unto himself seven hundred wives and three hundred concubines, who are leading him astray and making him deviate from the right path. He is treading under foot Thy Holy Law."

The Holy One replied: " Thy claim shall be considered and justice rendered unto thee."

Thereupon the Holy One summoned Ashmedai, prince of the demons, unto His presence, and thus He spoke to him: " Descend immediately into the palace of King Solomon, take the signet-ring from his finger, assume his likeness, and seat thyself upon his throne." The Evil One gladly obeyed the command of the Ruler of the universe and took the place of the King.

Snatching up the King, Ashmedai swallowed him up, then he stretched out his wings, so that one touched heaven and the other the earth, and vomited out the King of Israel in a distant land, four hundred miles away. Ashmedai then gave himself out as King Solomon and took his place, whilst the King himself was far away in a strange country and obliged to beg his bread from door to door. He wandered for many years until he came back to Jerusalem, where he claimed his right to the throne. " I, the preacher, was King over Israel in Jerusalem," he repeated every day, but the members of the Sanhedrin thought that he was mad, and would not believe him.[1]

For three years the exiled King wandered through cities

<hr>

[1] *Gittin*, 68*b*; Jellinek, *Beth-Hamidrash*, Vol. II, pp. 86-87.

and villages from door to door, crying aloud: " I, Koheleth, *was* King over Israel in Jerusalem," but no one would believe him, and he was treated with derision.

" Thou art a fool," they mocked him, " for our King is seated upon his throne in Jerusalem, and thou dost pretend that thou art the King."

Great were the sufferings of the exiled King, who was compelled to beg his daily bread from door to door. One day, during his wanderings, Solomon met a rich man who actually recognized him, but failed to understand the reason of the King's predicament. He invited him to his house, where he prepared a banquet for the dethroned monarch and placed delicious food upon the table. Thereupon the host began to speak of the past glories of the King.

" Dost thou remember," he said, " the deeds thou didst accomplish when thou wast King? Great was the splendour which I once witnessed at thy brilliant court."

These reminiscences made the exiled monarch shed bitter tears, and he left the rich man's house in sorrow and grief.

On the following day Solomon met another acquaintance who was a poor man, and whom the beggar-king implored for alms.

" My Lord," said the poor man, " wilt thou honour me with thy presence in my poor dwelling and partake of my hospitality?"

" Gladly will I come and break bread under thy roof," replied the sorely tried monarch, " but promise me that thou wilt not move me to tears by speaking continually of my past glories and the splendour of my court."

" My Lord," said the host, " I am but a poor man and can offer thee only a meagre meal, but I will assuage thy grief and do my best to console thee."

Thereupon he led the King under his humble roof, where he placed a dish of greens before Israel's exiled King. He consoled, however, the once mighty ruler, and assured him that the Lord would not break the oath He had once sworn to David, and would surely restore his son to his kingdom.

" Such are the ways of the Lord," said the kind host. " He punishes and deals severely with us, but, in due course, He vouchsafes unto us His grace. Whom God loves He punishes, but His punishments are those of a father who loves His children." Thus the host comforted his royal guest, and Solomon left the humble dwelling with hope in his heart. And it was then that the exiled King spoke the wise words: " Better is a dinner of herbs where love is than a stalled ox and hatred therewith." [1]

In the course of his wanderings, which had now lasted three years, Solomon came to the house of an old but charitable woman. Tired and exhausted, the King was sorely grieved, and he wept from even till morn. The kind hostess asked her guest to unburden his heart and to tell her why he was so sore grieved and shedding such bitter tears. To this the wanderer replied:

" I am ashamed to tell thee the cause of my sorrow and the story of my misfortunes, for thou wilt never give credence to my words."

But the woman insisted on his unburdening his heart to her. Thereupon the dethroned monarch said:

" Know then that I, a beggar and a wanderer, am in reality Solomon, King of Israel."

" And how didst thou lose thy kingdom and throne?" asked the woman, and Solomon told her.

" One day," he said, " I was playing with my signet-ring when suddenly the prince of demons appeared, and snatching it from my hand hurled it into the sea."

" This is a strange story thou art telling me," said the

---

[1] *Proverbs*, xv, 17; see *Midrash Mishle*; *Yalkut Shimeoni*, II, § 953; Bialik, *Sepher Haaggadah*, Vol. I, p. 112; Lewner, *Kol Aggadoth*, Vol. III, p. 383–385.

SOLOMON'S SIGNET RING IS RESTORED TO HIM

woman, " but it happens that yesterday I bought a big fish in the market, and when I cut it open I found a ring in its belly. Wilt thou see the ring? Perchance it is thy own signet-ring."

Thus spoke the woman and produced the ring.

When Solomon beheld his ring he immediately recognized it. It sparkled and shed a brilliant light in the room.

Once more the dethroned King wept, but this time they were tears of joy which he shed. The woman put the ring upon Solomon's finger, and immediately an angel appeared and carried the dethroned monarch to the very gates of Jerusalem.[1]

THE EXILED KING AND THE ENAMOURED PRINCESS

The story of the ring is told in a more romantic manner in another source. It relates the miraculous restoration of the ring and the love affair of Solomon and Princess Naamah.

He was a dethroned monarch, exiled and begging from door to door, and she was a beautiful princess, the daughter of a mighty king. Solomon had been wandering in strange lands for three years, when the Lord had pity on him and decided to restore him to his kingdom for the sake of the merits of his father David. And because it had been decreed that the Messiah should issue from Naamah, the Ammonite Princess, Solomon was led to the court of the Princess's father. Thus the wandering beggar-king came to Mesichmem, the capital of the land of Ammon.

One day the exiled monarch, sad and weary, was standing in the street of the capital, when the royal head cook passed by. He was carrying baskets laden with all sorts of food which he had bought in the market for the royal table, and he asked the poor, tattered, strange youth to carry them home for him. As the strange youth had found favour in his eyes, the cook engaged his services, and Solomon helped him in the kitchen.

---

[1] *Midrash Shir-ha Shirim*, ed. Grünhut, III, 7, pp. 29a–30a; see also Grünbaum, *Neue Beiträge*, pp. 222–226.

One day Israel's dethroned King begged the cook to permit him to prepare the royal meal, for he was an expert cook himself. The cook granted his request, and Solomon prepared a sumptuous repast. When the dishes were placed upon the royal table and the ruler of Ammon had tasted the food which Solomon had cooked, the King was greatly surprised.

" Never," said he, " have I tasted such delicious food."

He summoned the head cook and asked him how it happened that the food he had tasted to-day was so excellent. The head cook confessed the truth, and related to the King his meeting with the ragged youth. Ammon's King thereupon summoned Solomon into his presence and appointed him head cook.

Now it happened one day that Naamah, the daughter of the King of Ammon, was looking out of a window of the royal palace and beheld Solomon. She fell violently in love with him and informed her mother that she desired to be wedded to her father's cook.

The astonished Queen waxed very wroth and exclaimed: " In thy father's kingdom there are many noble princes from among whom thou mayest choose a husband. How canst thou, a royal princess, so forget thyself as to think of a union with a mean cook, a menial in thy father's service?"

But the charming and headstrong Princess remained firm. " Him will I marry," she said, " and none other."

Thereupon the Queen informed her royal spouse of their daughter's strange infatuation. Ammon's King waxed very wroth and decided to put the lovers to death sooner than give his consent to such a dishonourable union between his daughter and a poor cook. The Lord, however, did not permit the destruction of Solomon and Princess Naamah, and He softened the heart of the King.

" I will not shed their blood," said Ammon's ruler, " but will cast them out and let them meet their doom." He accord-

ingly summoned his servants and bade them take the Princess
and her lover to the desert.

Now Solomon and Princess Naamah wandered for a long
time in the desert until they reached a town on the seashore.
Weary and exhausted, the exiled King was walking along the
shore when he saw some fishermen offering for sale the fish
they had caught. He bought one fish and brought it to Naamah
to clean and prepare it for their evening meal. Great was the
astonishment of the Princess when she opened the fish and
found within a ring upon which was engraved the Ineffable
Name. Naamah handed the ring to her lover, who immediately
recognized it as his own signet-ring. He slipped it on his
finger, and immediately he was a changed man, no longer a
meek and humble tramp, but a King used to rule and command.

Accompanied by the Ammonite Princess, he wended his
way to Jerusalem, where he defeated and set to flight Ashmedai,
the usurper. He once more placed the royal crown upon his own
head and seated himself upon the throne of his father David.

Thereupon Solomon sent word to the King of Ammon
and invited him and his Queen to Jerusalem. When Ammon's
ruler arrived, Solomon thus addressed him: " Why didst thou
put to death two innocent people, the cook who served thee
and thy own daughter?"

On hearing these words, the King of Ammon was greatly
frightened. He swore that he had never killed the two but
sent them away into the desert, and he did not know what had
become of them.

" Wouldst thou recognize thy daughter's lover?" asked
Solomon.

Ammon's King replied that he would. Solomon smiled
and summoned the Princess, and the latter, arrayed in royal
garments, soon appeared before her amazed parents.

" Know then," said Israel's King, " that I, Solomon, King of

Jerusalem, am the cook who once served thee, and the charming and faithful Naamah, thy daughter, is my lawful wife."

Naamah kissed the hands of her parents, who were overjoyed at her great fortune. Happy and content, they returned to their own country.[1]

In other sources the *dénouement* and the manner in which the exiled King regained his throne is related differently:

In the semblance of King Solomon, Ashmedai had sat on the throne for three years, and during this time he behaved rather strangely. He visited the ladies in the harem during the days of separation, as prescribed by the Law. One day, one of his wives rebuked him and said: " Solomon, why art thou behaving so strangely and so contrary to thy custom?" The demon kept silence, and the woman suddenly exclaimed: " Thou art not Solomon, but some demon in disguise."

Ashmedai thereupon went to Bath - Sheba, the Queen-mother, and made a certain request to her. Greatly surprised, the old Queen cried: " Is it possible that thou my son shouldst make such a request to thine own mother who bore thee? By my life, thou art not my son."

Thereupon Bath-Sheba sent for the chancellor Benaiah and related unto him what had occurred. Benaiah rent his clothes and tore his hair in sign of despair and said: " This cannot be Solomon, the son of David. He is surely Ashmedai in the semblance of the King. The youth who is wandering about in the streets of Jerusalem may be right when he pretends to be the King. He must indeed be the true Solomon."

Thereupon Benaiah sent for the youth who was wandering hither and thither and thus addressed him:

" My son, tell me in truth, who art thou?"

" I am Solomon, son of David and King of Israel," replied the youth.

---

[1] Jellinek, *Beth-Hamidrash*, II, pp. 86–87; *Emek-Hamelech*, ed. Amsterdam; Wünsche, *Aus Israel's Lehrhallen*, II, pp. 9–12; cf. Steinschneider, *Hebräische Bibliographie*, XIII, pp. 57–58.

" And how," Benaiah further questioned, " did it happen that thou didst lose thy throne?"

And the youth replied: " I will tell thee. One day when I was sitting on my throne there suddenly came a great gust of wind which seized me and hurled me away out of my palace. From that day I have been as one bereft of his senses and understanding, and I have been wandering about all over the country."

Then Benaiah, the son of Jehoiada, said: " Canst thou give me some proof that thou art really Solomon, the son of David?"

The exiled King replied: " This I can do. On the day of my coronation my father David placed one of my hands in thine and the other in that of the Prophet Nathan. Then my mother, who stood near, kissed my father's head."

On hearing these words, which Benaiah knew to be true, he immediately summoned the members of the Sanhedrin and instructed them to write the Ineffable Name of the Lord upon pieces of parchment and put it over their hearts.

" We are afraid of Ashmedai," said the members of the Sanhedrin, " because he is wearing over his heart the Name of the Most High."

" Should seventy fear one?" asked Benaiah. " Is not the grace of God with ye?"

Thereupon Benaiah, accompanied by the members of the Sanhedrin, appeared before Ashmedai, and dealt him a blow. He tore the signet-ring from his finger, and was about to kill him when a heavenly voice bade him to desist. " Kill him not," it cried, " for it was the Divine command he had obeyed. Solomon was punished because he had trodden under foot one of My Holy Commandments." Thereupon Benaiah handed his signet-ring to the dethroned monarch, who resumed his crown and was restored to his throne and kingdom.[1]

---

[1] Jellinek, *Beth-Hamidrash*, VI, pp. 106–107; see also Bin Gorion, *Der Born Judas*, Vol. III, p. 291, notes.

CHAPTER XIII

The Dethroned King in Mediæval Lore

Solomon in mediæval legend—The legend of Merlin—Rulers guilty of pride and arrogance—The magnificat of pride—The Emperor Jovinianus—The naked Emperor—The usurper—The distress of Jovinianus—The gate-keeper and the Emperor—The repentant ruler and the hermit—The tutelary angel—*Der hochfertig Keiser*—The *Dit du Magnificat*—*Robert Cycyl*—Der Stricker—Herrand de Wildonie—*Von dem nackten Kaiser*—Giovanni Sercambi—The *Gesta Romanorum* and the *Jerushalmi Talmud*—An Indian tale—King Vikramaditya—The magician Samadra-Pala—The art of divesting oneself of one's own body and entering another—The magician enters the vacated body of the King—King Mukunda of Lilavati and the hunch-back—Demons and angels—The legend of Solomon of purely Jewish origin—Lesson in humility—Solomon and Nebuchadnezzar—The *Historia Scholastica*—The *Disciplina Clericalis*—The version of the Jerusalem *Talmud*—Robert of Cisyle—Longfellow's poem *King Robert of Sicily*.

We shall deal in a subsequent chapter with the Solomon legends in Mohammedan traditions and in mediæval and popular European lore. In all these traditions the name of Solomon has been retained, and all the legends cluster round the King of Israel, although he is often represented as a follower of the true faith or as a good Christian. There are, however, many mediæval legends where the name of Solomon has been entirely omitted, but which are nevertheless based upon a Solomon legend as it is related in Talmud and Midrash. With regard, for instance, to the tale of Merlin, Professor Vesselovsky already pointed out that " there can be no doubt that the whole legend of Merlin is based upon the apocryphal history of Solomon ". " The legend of Merlin," he goes on to say, " is more archaic than the German poem of Solomon and Morolf, and more nearly approaches the Talmudic-Slavonic legend.[1]

Vortigern, King of Britain, having determined to erect an impregnable castle, sent for artificers, carpenters, and stonemasons, and collected all the materials requisite to building. When the materials collected repeatedly vanished during the night, Vortigern inquired of his wise men and astronomers the cause of this. The wise men thereupon advised the King to find a child born without a father, put him to death, and sprinkle with his blood the ground on which the castle was to be built. Vortigern's messengers, searching throughout Britain for a child born without a father, found Merlin, whom they decided to bring alive to the King. On their way they passed a market town, the streets of which were crowded with merchants. Merlin suddenly burst out into a violent fit of laughter. On being questioned about the cause of his mirth, Merlin pointed out a young man who was bargaining for a pair of shoes. "See you not that young man," he said, that has shoon bought, and strong leather to mend them?" The young man, Merlin swore, would be dead before he entered his gate. And so it really happened.

"In Vortigern and Merlin," writes Gaster, " we have the counterpart of that famous Talmudical legend of Solomon and Ashmedai." [2]

We find many tales and legends in Eastern and Western literature where a ruler, guilty of some transgression and particularly of arrogance and pride, is dethroned and his place occupied either by an angel, a demon, or a sorcerer. These tales and legends have been rightly called the *magnificat of pride*, and appear in numerous mediæval and modern versions dating from the thirteenth century to modern times.

[1] See Vesselovsky, *Iz istorii literaturnavo obshtshenia vostoka i zapada*, St. Petersburg, 1872; see also Dunlop, *History of Prose Fiction*, Vol. I, pp. 458-459.

[2] M. Gaster, *Jewish Sources of and Parallels to the Early English Metrical Romances of King Arthur and Merlin*, in Papers read at the Anglo-Jewish Historical Exhibition, London, 1888, p. 247.

Let us briefly enumerate the legends which in one way or another are known in mediæval and modern literature. The most popular and probably most ancient version is that contained in the *Gesta Romanorum*. It is told of the Roman Emperor Jovinianus.

One day, when the Emperor Jovinianus was reposing on his couch, his heart was filled with pride, and he spoke in his heart: " Is there another God besides me?" His blasphemy soon met with the punishment it so well deserved. On the following day he went out hunting, accompanied by his warriors. The day being very hot, he made up his mind to seek coolness in the waters of a river that was flowing past. Scarcely had the Emperor undressed and entered the water, when another man, closely resembling Jovinianus, appeared and dressed himself in the garments Jovinianus had left on the river bank. Thus arrayed, the usurper, accompanied by the Imperial suite, returned to the palace. Jovinianus, not finding his clothes, returned naked to the palace, knocked at the gate, and demanded admittance, but no one recognized him. When he informed the gatekeeper that he was the Emperor, the indignant servant insulted him, calling him a liar and a deceiver. He had himself seen with his own eyes the Emperor entering the palace. As the naked Emperor still insisted, the gate-keeper led him before him whom he believed to be the real Emperor. The usurper gave instructions to have the imposter beaten and thrown out of the palace. In his distress Jovinianus addressed himself to the Duke, his former trusted adviser, but the Duke, too, did not know him. Jovinianus was at last thrown into prison, where he was compelled for some time to live on bread and water; he was then chastised and ordered to leave the city.

Once more Jovinianus went to the palace and asked the gate-keeper to inform the Empress of his distress. He asked his wife to send him some clothes, for he was her true husband.

To prove his words, he reminded her of certain intimate occurrences which were known only to herself and her husband. On hearing these words, the Empress was greatly astonished, for how could the mad beggar know what had happened in her intimate conjugal life?

The pretender was once more brought into the presence of the new Emperor and the Empress. Scarcely, however, had Jovinianus entered the hall when a dog which had been very devoted to him caught him by the throat, whilst his favourite falcon hurriedly flew out of the room. The Empress and the entire court solemnly declared that they knew him not, had never set eyes on him, and that he was an impostor.

The new Emperor threatened Jovinianus with a shameful death should he ever dare again appear in his presence with his ridiculous claim. In his distress the dethroned ruler now remembered his confessor, a hermit who lived in the neighbourhood, and hoped that the latter would recognize him. When, however, he told the hermit that he was the real Emperor, the latter bade him go, accusing him of being the devil in person.

It was now that Jovinianus thought of his former arrogance, and, prostrating himself in humility, repented his sin and confessed all to the hermit. The hermit now recognized him as the real Emperor, gave him absolution, and provided him with garments. Once more Jovinianus returned to the Imperial palace, where the gate-keeper immediately saluted him as the Emperor. Brought into the palace, he was also recognized by the entire court and the Empress. The usurper now informed all present that the Emperor had been punished for his arrogance and presumption, and that he himself who, in Jovinianus' semblance, had assumed the crown was his tutelary angel who had come to teach the Emperor a lesson in humility.[1]

[1] *Gesta Romanorum*, ed. Oesterley, p. 722; ed. Graesse, p. 263; see also Graesse, *Literärgeschichte*, III, p. 964.

Numerous are the mediæval and modern productions based on this legend. Thus in 1549 Hans Sachs wrote a poem entitled *Der hochfertig Keiser*, and a comedy, *Julianus der Keyser*, in 1556. The trouvère Jehan de Condé, who lived in the fourteenth century, treated the subject in his *Dit du Magnificat*, and an unknown English poet, a contemporary of Jehan de Condé, wrote a poem on the subject, wherein King Robert of Sicily went to sleep after having declared the *magnificat* as stupid.[1] An English morality play, *Robert Cycyl*, was performed at Chester in 1529.[2] A French morality play, entitled *L'orgueil et présomption de l'empereur Jovinian*, appeared in 1581. During the first half of the thirteenth century a poet known as *der Stricker* wrote a poem entitled *Der König im Bade*, whilst another poet living during the second half of the same century, Herrand von Wildonie, dealt with the subject in a poem entitled *Von dem nackten Kaiser*.[3] All these European stories of the proud and arrogant King have forgotten the name of Solomon, substituting another personality for him, such as Jovinian, Robert, Gorneus, or Nimrod. Giovanni Sercambi, who lived in the second half of the fourteenth century and in the first half of the fifteenth, deals with the subject in one of his legends, where the name of the punished King is Anibretto of Navarre.[4]

Another similar story in Oriental lore is related in *Thousand and One Nights* (17th night), and also in the *Forty Viziers* of the Sheikh Shehabeddin. It runs as follows:

An Egyptian Sultan refused to believe that in the course of a few seconds the Prophet had been able to visit the seven heavens, the hells and Paradise, and to have exchanged with Allah ninety thousand words. He could not admit that all this had taken place in such a short span of time so that when

---

[1] Horstmann, *Sammlung Altenglischer Legenden*, 1878, p. 209; see also Ellis, *Specimens*, ed. Halliwell, p. 474.
[2] Collier, *The History of English Dramatic Poetry*, II, pp. 128, 415.
[3] Von der Hagen, *Gerammtabenteuer*, III, p. cxv.
[4] D'Ancona, *Novelle di Giovanni Sercambi*, Bologna, 1871, p. 235.

the Prophet returned to the bed he had so hastily left, he found it still warm and that the water had not entirely run out of a jug he had overturned in his hurry. In vain did the wise men at his court try to convince the Sultan of the truth of the assertions in the Koran.

Now one day there appeared in the palace the famous Sheikh Shehabeddin, who had heard of the Sultan's unbelief. After giving the Sultan some proof of his wonder-working powers, he gave instructions for a tub full of water to be brought in, and then invited the Prince to undress, enter the bath, and then submerge his head under the water. The Sultan, curious to see the results, obeyed. Scarcely, however, had he submerged his head under the water when he found himself at the seashore, at the foot of a barren and lonely mountain. A few woodcutters whom he met provided him with some clothes and directed him to the nearest town.

Here fortune favoured him, for he met and married a beautiful and wealthy woman, with whom he lived seven years and who bore him several children. When the wife's money was all exhausted, the Sultan was compelled to earn his living, and he became a carrier. One day he came to the seashore, and as he had to perform some ablutions, he undressed and entered the water and submerged his head. When he raised it up again, he was in his own palace, seated in the bath he had entered seven years ago.

When he beheld the Sheikh and his courtiers all standing round, he waxed wroth, but the Sheikh thus addressed him:

"Why art thou so angry, O Sultan? Thou hast submerged thy head only once and immediately raised it up again; if thou dost not believe my words, ask thy servants." The latter all said: "It is true," but the Sultan exclaimed:

"What do ye know? I tell ye that I have been away from throne and crown, wandering as a stranger over the world, for seven years!" Then the Sheikh said: "Why shouldst thou

be angry with me on this account, O Sultan? Look, I, too, will
enter the bath and submerge my head under the water."
Saying this, the Sheikh entered the bath. The Sultan then
beckoned to his executioner and commanded him to cut off
the Sheikh's head the moment he raised it again to the surface.
But when the Sheikh had submerged his head he at once
became invisible and found himself at Damascus. From that
city he sent a letter to the Sultan in which he wrote: " You
and I, O Sultan, are God's, the exalted One's, creatures;
He, who had created the whole world in one moment in which
He said, " Let it be," showed thee in one brief moment
seven years. He has also shown to His beloved Prophet 18,000
worlds in such a short span of time that when the latter returned to the earth he found his bed still warm. And because
thou didst refuse to believe this I performed the deed on
thee." [1]

In *Old Deccan Days*, or *Hindoo Fairy Legends*, collected
by M. Frere, a similar story is told under the title of *The
Wanderings of Vicram Maharajah*.

Vicram learned wisdom from the Hindu God of Wisdom,
Gunputti, but it happened that near the palace there lived the
son of a carpenter who was very cunning. When he heard that
the Rajah went to the temple to learn wisdom, he determined
to go and see if he could not learn it also. Each day, when
Gunputti gave Vicram Maharajah instructions, the carpenter's
son would hide close behind the temple and overhear all
their conversation; so that he also became very wise.

One day Gunputti said to the Rajah: " Vicram, what gift
dost thou choose?" And Vicram replied: " Most wise, give
me the power to leave my own body when I will, and translate
my soul, and sense, and thinking powers, into any other body
that I may choose, either of man, or bird, or beast—whether
for a day, or a year, or for twelve years, or as long as I like."

[1] Behrnauer, *Die Vierzig Viziere*, Leipzig, 1851, p. 16 ff; see also *Germania*, II, pp. 432–434.

His request was granted, and he was instructed by what means he should translate his soul into another body, and he also received something which, being placed within his own body when he left it, would preserve it from decay until his return. The carpenter's son, who had been listening outside the temple, heard and learnt the spell whereby Gunputti gave Vicram Maharajah power to enter into another body; but he could not see nor find out what was given to the Rajah to place within his own body when he left it, to preserve it; so that he was master only of half the secret.

Vicram transported himself into the body of a parrot and flew to the Pomegranate country, and brought the little Queen Anar Ranee whom he married. He thereupon decided once more to make use of the gift bestowed upon him, and to fly all over the world in the shape of a parrot. Scarcely, however, had he left his own body when the carpenter's son entered it, giving himself out to be the Rajah. The secret was discovered by the Rajah's vizier, Butti, and he so contrived it that the pretender's life was made rather miserable. He would gladly have returned to his own body, but alas! having no power to preserve it, his spirit had no sooner left it than it began to decay, and at the end of three days it was quite destroyed; so that the unhappy man had no alternative but to remain where he was. After many vicissitudes Vicram returned into his own body, the pretender having escaped it to enter that of a ram which Butti, however, soon killed.[1]

In the *Peregrinaggio de tre figliuoli del Re di Serendippo*, as well as in the French imitation *Les Soirées Bretonnes*, there is told the story of an eastern King who possessed the power of animating a dead body by flinging his own soul into it, but having incautiously shot himself into the carcass of a fawn, which he had killed while hunting, his favourite vizier, to whom he had confided the secret whereby the transmigration was

---

[1] Mary Frere, *Old Deccan Days*, pp. 103–106.

accomplished, occupied the royal corpse, which had been thus left vacant, and returned to the palace, where he personated the master. At last the King had an opportunity of passing into the remains of a parrot, in which shape he allowed himself to be taken captive and presented to the Queen. The vizier afterwards, in order to gratify Her Majesty by a display of his mysterious science, animated the carcass of a favourite bird which had died. Thereupon the King seized the opportunity of re-entering his own body, which the vizier had now abandoned, and instantly he twisted off the neck of his treacherous minister.[1]

The legend of the punishment meted out to the proud and arrogant King forms also the subject of Longfellow's famous poem, *King Robert of Sicily*, and of a Danish poem, *Den forvandlede Konge* (The changed King).[2]

Now the legends told respectively in the *Gesta Romanorum* and in the above-mentioned mediæval poems are based upon the tale of Solomon as told in the Talmudic and particularly upon the version given in the *Jerushalmi Talmud*. It has been pointed out that the Jews themselves have been influenced by the literature of India. " Legends told of Vikramaditya," wrote Benfey, " have been applied to Solomon. This legend, with insignificant alterations, was taken over by the Mohammedans, who brought it to Europe, where it gave rise to the legend told of Emperor Jovinianus, or of King Robert of Sicily. It is changed in a Christian sense, and the usurper is not a demon but an angel, the tutelary angel of the ruler."[3] This theory of Benfey has been adopted by Varnhagen.[4] According to this author, India was the cradle of all the imaginative tales, of myths and legends which delighted the mediæval ages and have been handed down to modern times. The legend of Solomon which has been applied to other

[1] See Dunlop, *loc. cit.*, Vol. II, p. 504; *The Spectator*, No. 578; L'Oiseleur Deslongchamps, *Essai sur les Fables Indiennes*, p. 175, note 5.
[2] Varnhagen, *Ein Indisches Märchen*, Berlin, 1882, p. 73; see also Vesselovsky, *loc. cit.*, p. 558.   [3] *Panschatantra*, I, pp. 129–130.   [4] *loc. cit.*

personalities is traced back to an Indian *Märchen*. It is told of King Vikramaditya.

This sovereign had ruled for a long time over his people, but with advanced age had grown feeble and impotent. The magician Samadra-Pala, who knew the art how to divest himself of his own body and to enter another, taught his Sovereign this art, and one day he thus spoke to him: " I will teach thee the art how to divest thyself of thy own body, and then thou canst choose another, more vigorous body of a young man as thy abode." The King listened to the advice of the magician, and when he had been instructed by the latter in the wonderful art, he divested himself of his own feeble body, and his soul entered that of a young man who had recently died. Immediately the soul of the magician entered the vacated body of the King, killed the deceived ruler, and ascended the throne.

According to another version, the magician did not put to death his royal master, and the latter, after many sufferings, regained his throne and crown. It is told of King Mukunda, who lived in the city of Lilavati, into whose vacated body the soul of a hunchback clown enters.[1]

According to these theories, the story of the King who had lost his throne originated in India, whence by way of Persia it travelled to the Jews, who turned it into a legend told of their wise King Solomon. The legend was then taken over by the Arabs, who combined it with another version. From the Arabs the legend migrated to Byzantium, whence it was brought to the West. The hero is alternatively Vikramaditya, Nanda, Mukunda, Solomon, Nebuchadnezzar, the Roman Emperors Jovinianus, Julianus or Gorneus, Anibretto, King of Navarre, or Robert, King of Sicily, whilst the usurper is either a magician, the demon Ashmedai, Sakhr among the Arabs, or an angel.[2]

[1] Benfey, *loc. cit.*, pp. 125–127.
[2] Cf. M. Landau, *Die Quellen des Dekameron*, 1884, p. 72; Von der Hagen, *loc. cit.*, cxv–cxx; Jellinek, *Beth-Hamidrash*, VI, p. xxvi; cf. Grünbaum, *ZDMG*, Vol. XXXI, pp. 214–224.

Now there is not the slightest doubt that Egyptian, Persian, Babylonian, and Indian civilizations have left their traces upon Judaism, and that Jewish myths and legends are subject to foreign influences. To maintain, however, with Benfey, that India is the sole cradle of all Jewish and mediæval legends appears to us to be an exaggeration. Such may be the case with many Midrashic and Haggadic tales and legends, but the legend of Solomon, dethroned and exiled, wandering as a tramp and a beggar all over the cities and villages of Palestine, is of purely Jewish origin. It must be borne in mind that the entire legend not only clusters round a Biblical personage, Israel's great King, but is based upon a passage in *Ecclesiastes*, i, 12: " I, Koheleth, the Son of David, *was* King of Israel in Jerusalem ". The Rabbis were struck by the verb used in the past tense. If Solomon said that he *was* King of Israel, then he evidently had lost the throne, and yet no mention of this fact is made in the *Book of Kings*. The Rabbis therefore imagined that Solomon had been dethroned and that someone who had taken his semblance was reigning in his stead. The incident of Solomon's sin, of his arrogance and presumption, and the subsequent punishment meted out to him as a lesson in humility and as explained in the Haggada, is also based upon the Biblical text. This legend of Solomon's exile and sufferings also explains his fear and terror during the later part of his life.

Paulus Cassel, in his essay entitled *Schamir*, derives the story in the *Gesta Romanorum* from Jewish sources. " Holy Scripture," writes Cassel, " relates of the errors into which Solomon had fallen, and Jewish legendary lore explains the discrepancies and contradictions by the story of Ashmedai who had deprived Solomon of his signet-ring and taken his semblance. This legend has roots in the old Iranian tale of Jemshid who, like Solomon, after reigning wisely for a long time, had grown arrogant and deviated from the right path.   It has analogies with the legend told about Emperor Jovinianus." [1]

It must also be pointed out that there is a difference between the Jewish and the subsequent Christian legends and the Indian tale.   Both Solomon and the Christian arrogant King remain in their own bodies, whilst Ashmedai, or the angel, assume their semblance and take their places.   In the Indian tale the King's soul wanders into another body, whilst his own vacated body is occupied by the soul of his rival.[2]

In the majority of Haggadic legends imagination certainly plays a part, but this imagination is based upon a Biblical text, inspired by some etymological derivation, and usually follows some Biblical narrative.   Now a Biblical narrative resembling to some extent the legend of Solomon's exile is found in the story of Nebuchadnezzar [3] who, on account of his arrogance, was deprived of his throne.   There is no reason whatever, in our opinion, to maintain that the entire legend was borrowed from India.[4]

On the other hand, it seems to us that although the Arabs borrowed the legend of Solomon's exile from the Jews and transmitted it to the Byzantines, it is not the latter but the Jews themselves who brought it to the West.   Peter Comestor's work *Historia Scholastica* is full of passages borrowed from Midrash and Talmud; Petrus Alphonsus, author of *Disciplina Clericalis*, and John of Capua, two converted Jews, acquainted mediæval Europe with the legendary lore of the East, and Eisenmenger and Raymondus Martinus have collected a great number of texts from Jewish legendary lore.   There is therefore but little doubt that many other works compiled either by such converted Jews or by priests who had a close acquain-

---

[1] P. Cassel, *Schamir*, p. 53.
[2] Koehler, in *Archiv für Litteraturgeschichte*, Vol. XI, p. 582; A. D'Ancona, *loc. cit.*, p. 293 and *Sacre Rappresentazioni*, Firenze, 1872, III, 175; see also *Lemke's Jahrbuch*, XII, 407.   [3] *Daniel*, vi, 22–36.
[4] See also Israel Lévi in *Revue des Études Juives*, Vol. XVII, pp. 58–65.

tance with learned Jews must have existed during the early
Middle Ages.[1]

Indeed the legends related in the *Gesta Romanorum* and in
the other European works mentioned above closely resemble
not the Arab version of the story but that given in the Talmud
of Jerusalem, where it is not a demon but an angel who takes
the place of Solomon, an angel sent from heaven to punish
the King for his pride and arrogance and to teach him a lesson
in humility.

The version of the Jerusalem Talmud runs as follows:
Solomon boasted of having trodden under foot the three
commandments given to the King.

Thereupon the Lord said unto him: " What is the crown
which thou art wearing doing upon thy head? Get thee down
from my throne." Then an *angel* came down from heaven and
casting Solomon from his throne seated himself upon it. As
for the King, he wandered from town to town, and at the
doors of the synagogues and schools called aloud: " I,
Koheleth, was King over Israel in Jerusalem." Then the people
mocked him and said: " The King is seated upon his throne,
and thou sayest that thou art Koheleth, the son of David."
And they beat him and gave him a dish of ground beans to eat.[2]

Rightly writes Professor Vesselovsky: " I do not see why
Benfey thought it necessary to assume that the Arabic version
must have served as the intermediary between the original
Talmudical legend and its European imitations. There is no
need for such an assumption, and in the case of the Slavonic
version it is right down impossible." [3] The European legends
of the proud King have forgotten the name of Solomon, substituting for it those of Jovinian, Robert, Gorneus, Nimrod,
or Anibretto, the punishment of the Emperor is everywhere

---

[1] See also Israel Lévi in *Revue des Études Juives*, Vol. XVII, p. 65.
[2] *Leviticus Rabba*, XIX; *Shir ha-Shirim Rabba*, V, 9; *Eccles Rabba*, II, 2; *Pesikta de
Rab Kahana*, pp. 168b–169a; *Midrash Tanchuma*, ed. Buber, III, p. 28.
[3] *Archiv für Slavische Philologie*, Vol. VI, p. 556.

considered as a trial, *but* the demon is changed into an angel.
Now this coincides with the version given in the Talmud of
Jerusalem, where it is an angel and not a demon who takes the
place of the King.[1]

ROBERD OF CISYLE

Princes proude þat beþ in pres,
I wil ȝou telle þing nobles.
In Cisyle was a noble kyng,
Fair and strong and sumdel ȝyng.
He hadde a broþer in grete Rome,   5
Pope of all Cristendome;
Anoþer broþer in Almayne,
Emperour, þat Sarzins wrouȝte payne,
Þe kyng was hote Kyng Roberd;
Neuer man wiste him ferd;   10
He was kyng of gret honour,
For þat he was Conquerour;
In all þe worlde nas his per,
Kyng ne prince, fer no ner.
And for he was of chiualrye flour,   15
His broþer was mad Emperour,
His oþer broþer Godes vikere,
Pope of Rome, as I seide ere.
Þe pope was hote Pope Vrban:
He was good to God and man;   20
Þe emperour was hote Valemounde:
A strengur werreour was non founde
After his broþer of Cisyle,
Of whom þat I schal telle a while.
Þe kyng þouȝte he hadde no per   25
In all þe worlde, fer no ner;
And in his þouȝt he hadde pride,
For he was nounper in ech a side.

[1] See also Vogt, *Die deutschen Dichtungen von Salomon und Markolf*, Halle, 1880, p. 213;
Revue des Études Juives, Vol. VIII, p. 204.

At midsomer, a seynt Jones niȝt
Þe kyng to cherche com ful riȝt,   30
Forto heren his euensong.
Him þouȝte he dwelled þer ful long:
He þouȝte more in worldes honour
Þan on Crist, oure saueour.
In Magnificat he herde a vers: 35
He made a clerk hit him rehers
In langage of his owne tonge—
In latyn he niste what þei songe.
Þe vers was þis, I tele þe:
Deposuit potentes de sede   40
Et exaltauit humiles—
Þis was þe vers, wiþouten les.
Þe clerk seide anon riȝt:
" Sire, such is Godes miȝt
Þat he may make heyȝe lowe,   45
And lowe heyȝe, in litel þrowe.
God may do, wiþoute lyȝe,
His wille in twynkling of an eiȝe.'
Þe kyng seide wiþ herte vnstable:
" Al ȝoure song is fals and fable.   50
What man haþ such pouwer
Me to bringe lowe in daunger?
I am flour of chiualrye,
Min enemys I may distrye,
Noman liueþ in no londe   55
Þat me may wiþstonde:
Þan is þis a song of nouȝt."
Þis errour he hadde in þouȝt.
And in his þouȝt a slep him tok
In his pulpit, as seiþ þe bok   60
Whan þat euensong was al don,
A kyng ylich him out gan gon,
And alle men wiþ him gan wende—
Kyng Roberd lefte out of mynde.
Þe newe kyng was, I ȝou telle,   65
Godes angel, his pride to felle.

Þe angel in halle joye made,
And alle men of him were glade.
Þe kyng waked, þat lay in cherche:
His men he þouȝte wo to werche 70
For he was left þer alon
And derk niȝt him fel vppon.

    .   .   .   .   .   .

Þe angel seide to kyng Roberd: 141
" Þou art a fol, þat art nouȝt ferd
Mi men to do such vileynye;
Þi gult þou most nede abye.
What art þou?" seide þe angel. 145
Quaþ Roberd: " Þou schalt wite wel:
I am kyng, and kyng wil be;
Wiþ wronge þou hast mi dignite.
Þe pope of Rome is mi broþer,
And þe emperour min oþer; 150
Þei wil me wreke, for soþ to telle,
I wot þei nille nouȝt longe dwelle."
" Þou art mi fol," seide þe angel,
" Þou schalt be schore euerichdel
Lich a fol, a fol to be— 155
Wher is now þi dignite?
Þi counseyler schal ben an ape,
And o cloþyng ȝou worþ yschape:
I schal him cloþen as þi broþer
Of o cloþyng—hit nis non oþer; 160
He schal be þin owne fere—
Sum wit of him þou miȝt lere.
Houndes, how so hit falle,
Schulen ete wiþ þe in halle;
Þou schalt eten on þe ground, 165
Þin assayour schal ben an hound
To assaye þi mete bifore þe.
Wher is now þi dignite?"

    .   .   .   .   .   .

" I am an angel of renoun, 405
Sent to kepe þi regioun.

More joye me schal falle
In heuene among mi feren alle
In an oure of a day,
Þan in erþe, I þe say,   410
In an hundred þousend ȝer,
Þeiȝ al þe world fer and ner
Were min at mi likyng.
I am an angel, þou art kyng."
He went in twynklyng of an eȝe.
No more of him þer nas seȝe.

     C. HORSTMANN, *Sammlung Altenglischer Legenden*,
        1878, pp. 209–219 (*Roberd of Cisyle*).

THE SICILIAN'S TALE

KING ROBERT OF SICILY

Robert of Sicily, brother of Pope Urbane
And Valmond, Emperor of Allemaine,
Apparelled in magnificent attire,
With retinue of many a knight and squire,
On St. John's even, at vespers, proudly sat
And heard the priests chant the Magnificat
And as he listened, o'er and o'er again
Repeated, like a burden or refrain,
He caught the words, " Deposuit potentes
De sede, et exaltavit humiles;"
And slowly lifting up his kingly head
He to a learned clerk beside him said,
" What mean these words?" The clerk made answer meet,
" He has put down the mighty from their seat
And has exalted them of low degree."
Thereat King Robert muttered scornfully,
" 'T is well that such seditious words are sung
Only by priests and in the Latin tongue;
For unto priests and people be it known,
There is no power can push me from my throne!"
And leaning back, he yawned and fell asleep,
Lulled by the chant monotonous and deep.

When he awoke, it was already night;
The church was empty, and there was no light,
Save where the lamps, that glimmered few and faint,
Lighted a little space before some saint.
He started from his seat and gazed around,
But saw no living thing and heard no sound.
He groped towards the door, but it was locked;
He cried aloud, and listened, and then knocked;
And uttered awful threatenings and complaints,
And imprecations upon men and saints.
The sounds reëchoed from the roof and walls
As if dead priests were laughing in their stalls.
At length the sexton, hearing from without
The tumult of the knocking and the shout,
And thinking thieves were in the house of prayer,
Came with his lantern, asking " Who is there?"
Half choked with rage, King Robert fiercely said,
" Open: 't is I, the King!   Art thou afraid?"
The frightened sexton, muttering, with a curse,
" This is some drunken vagabond, or worse!"
Turned the great key and flung the portal wide;
A man rushed by him at a single stride,
Haggard, half naked, without hat or cloak,
Who neither turned, nor looked at him, nor spoke,
But leaped into the blackness of the night,
And vanished like a spectre from his sight.
Robert of Sicily, brother of Pope Urbane
And Valmond, Emperor of Allemaine,
Despoiled of his magnificent attire,
Bareheaded, breathless, and besprent with mire,
With sense of wrong and outrage desperate,
Strode on and thundered at the palace gate;
Rushed through the courtyard, thrusting in his rage
To right and left each seneschal and page,
And hurried up the broad and sounding stair,
His white face ghastly in the torches' glare.
From hall to hall he passed with breathless speed;
Voices and cries he heard, but did not heed,

Until at last he reached the banquet-room,
Blazing with light, and breathing with perfume.

There on the dais sat another king,
Wearing his robes, his crown, his signet-ring,
King Robert's self in features, form, and height,
But all transfigured with angelic light!
It was an Angel; and his presence there
With a divine effulgence filled the air,
An exaltation, piercing the disguise,
Though none the hidden Angel recognize.

A moment speechless, motionless, amazed,
The throneless monarch on the Angel gazed,
Who met his look of anger and surprise
With the divine compassion of his eyes;
Then said, " Who art thou? and why com'st thou here?"
To which King Robert answered with a sneer,
" I am the King, and come to claim my own
From an impostor, who usurps my throne!"
And suddenly, at these audacious words,
Up sprang the angry guests, and drew their swords;
The Angel answered, with unruffled brow,
" Nay, not the King, but the King's Jester, thou
Henceforth shalt wear the bells and scalloped cape,
And for thy counsellor shalt lead an ape;
Thou shalt obey my servants when they call,
And wait upon my henchmen in the hall!"

Deaf to King Robert's threats and cries and prayers,
They thrust him from the hall and down the stairs;
A group of tittering pages ran before,
And as they opened wide the folding-door,
His heart failed, for he heard, with strange alarms,
The boisterous laughter of the men-at-arms,
And all the vaulted chamber roar and ring
With the mock plaudits of " Long live the King!"

Next morning, waking with the day's first beam,
He said within himself, " It was a dream!"
But the straw rustled as he turned his head,
There were the cap and bells beside his bed,
Around him rose the bare, discoloured walls,
Close by, the steeds were champing in their stalls,
And in the corner, a revolting shape,
Shivering and chattering sat the wretched ape.
It was no dream, the world he loved so much
Had turned to dust and ashes at his touch!

Days came and went; and now returned again
To Sicily the old Saturnian reign;
Under the Angel's governance benign
The happy island danced with corn and wine,
And deep within the mountain's burning breast
Enceladus, the giant, was at rest.

Meanwhile King Robert yielded to his fate,
Sullen and silent and disconsolate.
Dressed in the motley garb that Jesters wear,
With look bewildered and a vacant stare,
Close shaven above the ears, as monks are shorn,
By courtiers mocked, by pages laughed to scorn,
His only friend the ape, his only food
What others left,—he still was unsubdued.
And when the Angel met him on his way,
And half in earnest, half in jest, would say,
Sternly, though tenderly, that he might feel
The velvet scabbard held a sword of steel,
" Art thou the King?" the passion of his woe
Burst from him in resistless overflow,
And lifting high his forehead, he would fling
The haughty answer back " I am, I am the King!"

Almost three years were ended; when there came
Ambassadors of great repute and name
From Valmond, Emperor of Allemaine,

Unto King Robert, saying that Pope Urbane
By letter summoned them forthwith to come
On Holy Thursday to his city of Rome.
The Angel with great joy received his guests,
And gave them presents of embroidered vests,
And velvet mantles with rich ermine lined,
And rings and jewels of the rarest kind.
Then he departed with them o'er the sea
Into the lovely land of Italy,
Whose loveliness was more resplendent made
By the mere passing of that cavalcade,
With plumes, and cloaks, and housings, and the stir
Of jewelled bridle and of golden spur.
And lo! among the menials, in mock state,
Upon a piebald steed, with shambling gait,
His cloak of fox-tails flapping in the wind,
The solemn ape demurely perched behind,
King Robert rode, making huge merriment
In all the country towns through which they went.

The Pope received them with great pomp and blare
Of bannered trumpets, on Saint Peter's square,
Giving his benediction and embrace,
Fervent, and full of apostolic grace.
While with congratulations and with prayers
He entertained the Angel unawares,
Robert, the Jester, bursting through the crowd,
Into the presence rushed, and cried aloud,
" I am the King! Look, and behold in me
Robert, your brother, King of Sicily!
This man who wears my semblance to your eyes,
Is an impostor in a king's disguise.
Do you not know me? does no voice within
Answer my cry, and say we are akin?"
The Pope in silence, but with troubled mien,
Gazed at the Angel's countenance serene;
The Emperor, laughing, said, " It is strange sport
To keep a madman for thy Fool at court!"

And the poor, baffled Jester in disgrace
Was hustled back among the populace.

In solemn state the Holy Week went by,
And Easter Sunday gleamed upon the sky;
The presence of the Angel, with its light,
Before the sun rose, made the city bright,
And with new fervor filled the hearts of men,
Who felt that Christ indeed had risen again.
Even the Jester, on his bed of straw,
With haggard eyes the unwonted splendor saw,
He felt within a power unfelt before,
And, kneeling humbly on his chamber floor,
He heard the rushing garments of the Lord
Sweep through the silent air, ascending heavenward.

And now the visit ending, and once more
Valmond returning to the Danube's shore,
Homeward the Angel journeyed, and again
The land was made resplendent with his train,
Flashing along the towns of Italy
Unto Salerno, and from thence by sea.
And when once more within Palermo's wall,
And, seated on the throne in his great hall,
He heard the Angelus from convent towers,
As if the better world conversed with ours,
He beckoned to King Robert to draw nigher,
And with a gesture bade the rest retire;
And when they were alone, the Angel said,
" Art thou the King?" Then, bowing down his head,
King Robert crossed both hands upon his breast,
And meekly answered him: " Thou knowest best!
My sins as scarlet are; let me go hence,
And in some cloister's school of penitence,
Across those stones, that pave the way to heaven
Walk barefoot, till my guilty soul be shriven!"
The Angel smiled, and from his radiant face
A holy light illumined all the place,

And through the open window, loud and clear,
They heard the monks chant in the chapel near,
Above the stir and tumult of the street:
" He has put down the mighty from their seat,
And has exalted them of low degree!"
And through the chant a second melody
Rose like the throbbing of a single string:
" I am an Angel, and thou art the King!"

King Robert, who was standing near the throne,
Lifted his eyes, and lo! he was alone!
But all apparelled as in days of old,
With ermined mantle and with cloth of gold;
And when his courtiers came, they found him there
Kneeling upon the floor, absorbed in silent prayer.

LONGFELLOW, *King Robert of Sicily*.[1]

---

[1] There is no need to assume that Longfellow borrowed the contents of his poem from Leigh Hunt's story told in " A Jar of Honey from Mount Hybla " (*Ainsworth's Magazine*, 1844). If he was unacquainted with the Hebrew and Oriental sources, then he must have probably availed himself of the Anglo-Saxon poem.

CHAPTER XIV

Solomon and Marcolf, or
Salman and Morolf

The dialogues of Solomon and Marcolf—Solomon and Saturn—Christian wisdom and heathen wisdom of the East—Solomon and Marcolf in Western literature—The wit combat between Solomon and Marcolf—Marcolf's riddles—Fresh milk and curds—Marcolf before the King—He is snoring and thinking—The black and white feathers of the magpie—The vertebræ of a hare—Milk and daylight—Marcolf, or Morolf, proves his assertion—His sister Fudasa—The cat and the mouse—Nature is stronger than education—The two harlots—The revolt of the women—Solomon's diatribe against women—Marcolf's triumph—A tree to his liking—Solomon and his wife—The heathen prince—The magic herb—Morolf finds the Queen—Solomon defeats the heathen king—The Queen is put to death—Solomon Emperor of Christendom—Salomé, the beautiful daughter of King Cyprian—Faro, the son of Memerolt—Salomé's apparent death—She is carried off by Faro—Morolf's search for Salomé—Solomon disguised as a pilgrim—Faro's beautiful sister falls in love with Solomon—Salomé is carried off by Prince Princian of Ackers—The Morolf legend in Little Russian literature—The *bylini*—Emperor Vassilj and Ivashka—Solomon and Kitovras—The golden cup and the ring—The three armies and the three nooses.

It does not enter within the scope of this work to relate all the legends clustering round Solomon found in European lore, but it will be interesting to deal here with the famous dialogues of Solomon and Marcolf.

"There are two dialogues," writes Stopford A. Brooke, " between Solomon and Saturn with which we may close the poetry of the ninth century. The oldest is the second in the MS. Saturn had wandered through all the East, and Solomon asks him about ' the land where none may walk '. Saturn answers. Then Solomon answers and Saturn begins his questions. Their wits are set over one against the other. Solomon stands as the representative of Christian wisdom, Saturn of the heathen wisdom of the East. The other poem, although it begins the MS., is the later of the two. Saturn asks Solomon to explain to him the power of the Paternoster. The answer takes up the whole poem, and in the course of it many interesting examples of folk-lore and superstitions occur.[1] Now these Solomon dialogues have become common in Western literature under the title of Dialogues of Solomon and Marcolf. Marcolf does not play the grave part of Saturn, the Eastern sage, but that of the peasant or mechanic full of uneducated mother-wit and rough humour. It suited the mediæval temper, a little in rebellion against the predominance of Church, noble and King."[2] The contents of the Dialogues of Solomon and Marcolf are briefly as follows:

SOLOMON AND MOROLF

Sitting in all his glory upon the throne of his father David, Solomon one day saw a misshapen, coarse, and clownish man come into his presence, accompanied by a foul sluttish woman, his wife, in every way answering to himself. This was Morolf. When he mentioned his name, he was immediately recognized by the King as a person quite famous for his shrewdness and wit. Solomon now challenged him to a trial of wisdom, promising him great rewards, should he prove victorious. Solomon begins the contest, uttering at first some moral common-places or reciting some of his own Biblical proverbs. These are immediately paralleled or contradicted by Morolf, who ridicules the King's sayings in the very coarsest terms. Moreover, Morolf always draws his illustrations from the most common events of homely life, expressing himself in popular

---

[1] Stopford A. Brooke, *English Literature from the Beginning to the Norman Conquest*, 1898, pp. 210–211.   [2] *Ibid.*, p. 210, note 1.

proverbs. Solomon is at last exhausted and wishes to discontinue the contest, but Morolf is ready to go on. He calls on the King to declare himself beaten and give him the promised rewards. Solomon, refusing to listen to his councillors who urge him to drive Morolf out of court, keeps his promises and dismisses Morolf with many gifts. Morolf leaves the court, uttering the words: " Where there is no law, there is no King."

One day, whilst out hunting, Solomon suddenly comes upon Morolf's hut. He calls upon him and receives a number of enigmatic answers which foil him completely. The King, unable to find the solution of the riddles, is compelled to have recourse to Morolf. He leaves his hut, but desires him to come to court the next day and to bring with him a pail of fresh milk and curds from the cow. Morolf does this on the next day, but on the road he grows hungry, eats the curds, and covers up the milk with cow-dung. When he appears before Solomon, the latter, not seeing the curds, asks him what he had done with them. Morolf answers that he had eaten them, but that the dung he had used to cover up the milk was also curd from the cow. Now Solomon condemns Morolf to sit up all night in his company, and should he fall asleep he would be put to death in the morning. Morolf submits, sits down, and begins to snore aloud. Solomon asks him whether he is asleep, to which Morolf replies that he is *thinking*.

" And what art thou thinking about?" asks Solomon.

" I am thinking," replied Morolf, " that there are as many vertebræ in a hare's tail as there are in his backbone."

The King imagines that Morolf will not be able to prove his assertion, and quickly says:

" If thou canst not prove this thou shalt die in the morning."

Morolf now again begins to snore and is frequently awakened by Solomon. He informs the King every time that he is thinking. He asserts that there are as many white as black feathers in a magpie, that milk is not whiter than daylight, that nothing can be entrusted to a woman, and that nature is stronger than education. All these assertions he is to prove in the morning, otherwise he is to die.

Solomon now becomes sleepy and Morolf leaves him. He runs to his sister Fudasa, and under the seal of secrecy informs her that he had been so badly treated by the King that he had made up his mind to kill him. Taking up a knife, he hides it ostentatiously in his bosom. Fudasa swears to her brother to respect his secret, and Morolf returns to the King and is present at the latter's waking. Then a magpie and a hare are brought, and Morolf proves that he was right. In the meantime he placed a pan of milk in a dark closet and suddenly called the King to him. Solomon, on entering the closet, stepped into the milk, splashed his clothes, and nearly fell on his face. He turns to Morolf in a rage and asks him what he meant by it.

" Merely to show to your Majesty," calmly replies Morolf, " that milk is not whiter than daylight."

Now Solomon sits down on his throne and Morolf cites his sister Fudasa before him, accusing her of various crimes. The astonished woman immediately reveals the secret her brother had entrusted to her, that he intended to murder the King. Morolf thus proves to the much amused King that a woman could not keep a secret.

The King now commands Morolf to prove his last assertion, that nature is stronger than education, and the latter promises to do this at supper-time.

Now it happened that Solomon had a cat which had been trained to sit upon the table and to hold up in its paws a lighted candle whilst the King was having his supper. When all were seated at supper and the cat had taken up her post, Morolf suddenly threw a mouse at her feet. The cat did not budge,

THE CAT AND THE CANDLE

but when a second mouse was thrown the candle began to tremble in the cat's paws, and when at last a third mouse was let loose the cat could no longer resist, threw down the lighted candle, and gave chase to the mouse.[1]

Instead of rewarding Morolf, the King, however, commands him to be thrown out of the palace and that the dogs be set on him should he ever dare to return. The next day Morolf provided himself with a live hare, threw it to the dogs, and appeared in the presence of the King. Solomon does not punish him, but merely warns him not to commit any impropriety in the hall of audience and not to spit, except on some bare spot. Unfortunately the only bare spot in the audience hall is the bald head of one of the nobles. In the meantime the two women arrive and the famous judgment is given. Morolf is all the while sneering, and he frequently abuses womankind in general. An altercation between the King and Morolf follows, and the latter remarks to the King: " You praise women now, but I assure you that I shall live to hear you abuse them with all your heart."

The King now orders him out of the palace, and Morolf immediately sets out to find the two harlots, whom he informs that the King had decreed that every man shall have seven wives. Such an arrangement, Morolf endeavoured to prove to the women, would only result in great mischief. The news spread all over the city, and soon the women of Jerusalem congregated under the windows of the palace, vociferated against the royal decree, and abused the King in no measured terms. The King, who was quite unaware of the cause of this feminine outburst, tried to pacify the assailing women, but was received with a tempest of abuse. He now lost patience and burst out into a most furious diatribe against women. Morolf, who was standing by, was delighted and sneeringly approached

---

[1] Cf. for a similar incident in a story by Marie de France; C. A. Robert, *Fables Inédites*, I, 155; cf. also R. Koehler, *Kleinere Schriften*, II, p. 640, where other passages are quoted.

to thank the King, who had taken such trouble to prove the truth of his assertions. Solomon now becomes aware of the trick played upon him, pacifies the infuriated ladies, and orders Morolf to be turned out. " Never," added the King, " let me see thy ugly face again."

Some time afterwards, on a snowy night, Morolf made an extraordinary track, and in the morning managed to allure the King and his courtiers to follow him into the forest. The King is thus led to a hollow tree wherein Morolf had so placed himself that the King is unable to look him in the face. Solomon now gives orders to have Morolf hanged, but the latter implores the King to allow him at least to choose his own tree. The request is granted, and Morolf, accompanied by his guards, sets out to find a tree to his own liking. He is naturally in no hurry, and leads the guards backwards and forwards all over Palestine. In the end the guards are so wearied out that they let him go, dismissing him with his life, upon his promising never to show his face at the court.[1]

This wit combat or Dialogue of Solomon and Morolf is preceded by another poem wherein the story of Solomon and his wife Salomé is related.

Solomon's wife has bestowed her love on a heathen with whom she corresponds. She is anxious to be united to him, and for that purpose feigns to be sick. The heathen King, whom she has managed to inform of her design, sends two minstrels to her who are also well versed in the art of magic. They pretend to be hailing from Greece and to be able to cure sick folk with their songs and music. They are admitted to the presence of the Queen. They place an herb under her tongue which has the power to throw her into a death-like sleep, although her colour never changes.

[1] Kemble, *The Dialogues of Solomon and Saturn*, pp. 25–30; Von der Hagen, *Deutsche Gedichte des Mittelalters*, Berlin, 1808, Vol. I (Salman and Morolf), pp. 44–64; see also Dr. P. Piper, *Die Spielmannsdichtung* (in J. Kürschner's *Deutsche Nationallitteratur*, II, 1, pp. 206–209).

When the news of the Queen's death becomes known, no one will believe that she is really dead since her mouth is still so red. Morolf or Marcolf should advise in the matter, but he is nowhere to be found, since he is in hiding. He is at last brought to court by a ruse. When he hears what has happened, he immediately suspects foul play and is quite convinced that the Queen is not really dead. He tries to make the Queen show some sign of life by pouring molten lead into the palm of her hand. All in vain, the beautiful Salomé remains to all appearance dead, and all are convinced of her death except Morolf. In the third night the minstrels manage to carry off the dead Queen to their master, the heathen King.

The King now entreats Morolf in strict confidence to advise him, and Morolf declares himself ready to set forth to find the Queen. He traverses many lands until he at last learns the whereabouts of the Queen. He immediately returns and informs Solomon of the place where his wife is living. Accompanied by an armed force, Solomon and Morolf go to the castle where the Queen is dwelling. Whilst Morolf and the armed force remain hidden in the adjoining wood, Solomon, disguised as a pilgrim, goes alone to the castle, where he begs for food. His companions, it is arranged, are only to come to his rescue when they hear him blow his horn. Now when the faithless wife sees Solomon she immediately recognizes him, in spite of his disguise, and informs the heathen of his presence. The heathen is overjoyed when he hears the news that Solomon is now in his tower. " Now," said the heathen, " what should be my death, were I in thy hands?"

Solomon sighs and replies: " I wish to God it were so, for I would take thee to the nearest wood and there let thee choose a tree and hang thee on it."

" Then such shall also be thy death," replies the heathen.

Accompanied by his entire suite, he took Solomon to the nearest wood and bade him choose his tree. Solomon, remind-

ing the heathen that he is of kingly strain, asks as a special
boon to be allowed to blow his horn three times before he dies.
In spite of the objections of the Queen, who fears some ruse
on the part of Morolf, the heathen grants Solomon's request.
The latter blows his horn, and immediately Morolf arrives
with Solomon's men. The heathen King is strung up, his
men are all slain, and the Queen is taken back to the land of
the Jews, where, at Morolf's advice, she is put to death by
opening her veins in a bath.[1]

A longer version of this legend, where Morolf is Solomon's
brother, runs as follows:

Solomon, King of Jerusalem and Emperor of all Christendom, has abducted Salomé, the beautiful daughter of Cyprian,
King of India, and compelled her to embrace Christianity.
Beyond the seas, on the shores of the Mediterranean, there
ruled a mighty heathen King named Fore, or Faro, the son of
Memerolt. One day, when he asked his heroes to find him a
wife, the latter called his attention to the beautiful Salomé,
wife of Solomon, of whose beauty they had heard. Faro decides to do battle for her and to take her by force from her
husband. Faro lands with 40 ships and an army of 15,000
heroes before Jerusalem, and a fierce battle is waged. Faro
and his whole host are defeated, and the King is made prisoner.
Morolf advises Solomon to put the heathen King to death,
but the King of Jerusalem spares his enemy's life and com-
mits him to the keeping of the Empress. In vain does Morolf
warn Solomon, pointing out to him that it is dangerous to
put temptation in the Empress's way and to give her an opportunity of thus becoming familiar with the heathen King.
Solomon ignores the arguments of Morolf, having implicit
faith in Salomé. Soon, however, he has cause to regret his
rash conduct.

[1] Von der Hagen, loc. cit., pp. 62–64, verses 1605–1875; Vogt, Salman und Morolf, pp.
lxi–lxii; Piper, loc. cit., pp. 209–210; F. J. Child, The English and Scottish Ballads, Vol. IX,
pp. 3–5.

Thereupon Faro received a magical ring from his nephew, the sorcerer Elias, and of which he made a present to the Empress. Scarcely had the latter put the ring on her finger than she fell violently in love with the heathen King. The lady helped the prisoner to escape, and even promised him to leave her husband and rejoin him. When half a year had elapsed, Faro sent Salomé, through a heathen minstrel, a magical root which she placed under her tongue. Immediately she fell down dead, although her beautiful colour remained unchanged. Morolf pretended that the Queen was still alive, and endeavoured to bring her back to life by pouring molten gold into her hands. To all appearance, however, the Empress remained dead, and Morolf was only rebuked by his brother Solomon.

The Empress was laid in a golden coffin and buried, but within a few hours the minstrel carried her off to his master Faro. Morolf now decides to seek the Empress. He kills an old Jew named Berman, takes off his skin, which he puts on, and thus disguised begs money from the King, to whom he afterwards reveals his true identity. Solomon now consents to his going out in search of Salomé, and Morolf, after seven years' wandering, discovers the whereabouts of the faithless Empress and enters her palace. He is immediately recognized by Salomé and condemned to death. After having intoxicated the guards and clipped their hair, he manages to escape to Jerusalem under water by means of a long leather tube which made it possible for him to breathe from the surface.

Solomon now arms a large host and, accompanied by Morolf, sets out to recover his wife. Whilst Morolf and Solomon's men are hiding in a wood near by, Solomon, disguised as a pilgrim, enters Fore's city. He is brought before the Empress, who immediately recognizes him. In vain does Solomon now try to recall his wife to her duty. She informs him, however, that she loved Fore and would stick to him.

Solomon is put in a side room where he can hear how tenderly Fore, who had in the meantime returned, is embraced by Salomé.

When the two sit down to their meal, Salomé informs Fore of the arrival of the handsome pilgrim, and that Solomon, King of Jerusalem, was now in his power. Solomon, led into the presence of Fore, is asked by the latter what he would do with *him* were he in Jerusalem, to which he replied that he would keep him a prisoner till the morning and then hang him. Fore declares that such shall be Solomon's own doom.

Solomon, however, has found a friend in Fore's beautiful sister, who had been smitten with a violent love for the pilgrim. She now intercedes on Solomon's behalf, and ultimately persuades Fore to commit the prisoner to her custody till the morning. She takes him into a sumptuous room, relieves him of his chains, and sets food and drink before him. Solomon listens to the lays of a famous minstrel, and himself, forgetting all care and the doom awaiting him, plays the harp, to the delight of the beautiful heathen maid. The latter urges him to escape, but he loyally refuses to do so, assuring her that his angels in the wood would save him in the morning. In the morning Solomon is led to the place of execution, and under the gallows he asks as a last favour to be allowed to blow his horn thrice. He alleges that he wishes to do this so as to give notice to St. Michael and the angels to come and take his soul in charge. Salomé objects, but Fore gives his permission to Solomon's request. Morolf had in the meantime divided his army into three divisions, a black, a white, and a pale. When Solomon sounds his horn, Morolf and his army burst from their ambush and slay the heathen host. Faro is hanged upon the gallows which had been erected for Solomon. The latter, accompanied by Salomé and the beautiful sister of Faro, now returns to Jerusalem, where Morolf persuades the heathen maid to become a Christian, promising her that should Salomé die, Solomon would take her to wife.

Seven years again elapse, and once more the Empress runs away. This time it is Prince Princian of Ackers, another heathen King who had heard of Salomé's beauty, who makes up his mind to capture her. He sends the Empress a magical ring, and the lady falls in love with him and once more elopes with the heathen Prince. Once more Morolf is asked to go out in search of the Empress. He promises to do so, but not until Solomon has given him his promise that should he recover the flighty Empress he could deal with her at his pleasure. Morolf discovers the whereabouts of the Empress, but when he returns Solomon is not anxious to expose his own life. Morolf, therefore, accompanied by a great host, sets out himself and invades King Princian's land. With the help of a mermaid and dwarfs, he slays the King and carries the Empress back to Jerusalem, where, however, he puts her to death in a bath. Solomon then marries the beautiful heathen maid, the sister of Fore, who had been baptized and who reigned as Empress in Jerusalem for thirty years.[1]

An imitation of the Morolf legend is told in Little Russian literature.

The tsar Solomon took to wife the daughter of a heathen tsar; she hated him, and refused to go to Church. At last she concerted an elopement with a heathen tsarevitch, and pretended to be dead. Solomon burned her hands through and through with a red-hot iron. The lady, however, uttered no sound, and was consequently buried in the evening. She was immediately disinterred and carried off by her lover. Now Solomon went to the house of the tsarevitch attended by three armies, a black, a white, and a red, but which were lying in ambush in a neighbouring wood. The tsarevitch recognizes

[1] Vogt., *loc. cit.*, pp. xxi–xxxiii; Vincenti, *Die altenglischen Dialoge von Salomon und Marcolf*, pp. 18–19; Kemble, *loc. cit.*, pp. 17–20; Child, *loc. cit.*, p. 4; (cf. *The Scottish Ballad John Thomson and the Turk, ibid.*, Vol. IX, p. 9).

Solomon and has a gallows set up, but Solomon craves the
permission to play on his three pipes before dying. The request is granted, and the sound of the first pipe brings out the
red army, that of the second the white, and that of the third
the black. The tsarevitch is hanged, whilst the tsaritsa is
dragged at a horse's tail.[1]

From the East the legend of Solomon wandered to the West.
According to Vogt, the oldest version is the Greeko-Byzantine,
which developed directly from the Oriental sources and gave
rise to the Russian versions.[2]

The tale of the capture of Solomon's wife and the revenge
taken by him is related as follows in the *bylini*, or ballads:

A certain Emperor Vassilj Okulyeviez is feasting with his
nobles. When he is of good cheer, he asks his heroes to find
him a wife who shall be a match to him in stature, beauty, and
wit. One of the company, a certain Ivashka, undertakes to
get for his master the wife of Solomon, the beautiful Salamaniya. He manages it by making use of a ruse. In a fine ship
full of beautiful things Ivashka and his company set out and
sail to Jerusalem. Solomon is just away from his capital, and
the wily Ivashka, after having presented the Empress with
costly gifts, manages to entice her on board the ship, where
she is promised even finer things. Here she is made drunk
and falls asleep. The ship immediately sails away, carrying
the lady off to the Emperor Vassilj, with whom she lives for
three years. Solomon, attended by a large army of winged
horsemen, sets out to retrieve his wife, hides his men in a
grove, whilst he presents himself, disguised as a pilgrim, at the
palace of the Emperor. He is recognized by his wife, who
shuts him up in an iron cage.

When the Emperor returns to the palace from hunting, the

---

[1] Dragomanov, *Popular Traditions and Tales*, 1876, p. 103; *Revue des Traditions Populaires*, Vol. II, pp. 518–520.
[2] Vogt, *loc. cit.*; Vincenti, *loc. cit.*, p. 13; see also Vesselovsky in *Archiv für Slavische
Philologie*, Vol. VI, pp. 405–410, and 554 ff; Dunlop, *loc. cit.*, p. 637; Varnhagen, *loc. cit.*,
p. 48; Gaster, *Literatura populara Romana*, 1883, p. 332.

lady informs him of what had occurred and advises him to put Solomon to death. The execution is decided upon, and, at his own request, Solomon is to be hanged instead of beheaded. Under the gallows he begs permission to be allowed to blow his horn. In spite of the objection of the Empress, his request is granted. At the first sound of Solomon's horn all the animals and birds gather round him, and Solomon explains that they have come to be present at his execution. At the second sound of his horn all the trees in the forest tremble, and the roar of all the seas is heard. At the third sound Solomon's winged horsemen appear. Ivashka, who had carried off the wife of Solomon, the Emperor Vassilj, and Salamaniya are all hanged in the three nooses which, at Solomon's request, had been provided.[1]

In addition to the popular ballads or *bylini*, there are also Russian prose versions of the same legend. Here the wife of Solomon is stolen from him not by the Emperor Vassilj but by Solomon's own brother Kitovras, who, during the day, ruled over men, and during the night, changed into an animal, ruled over the animal world. Kitovras sends to his brother a magician disguised as a merchant, who offers for sale to the King a magnificent purple robe. Solomon buys the robe and invites the merchant magician to his table. After enveloping the King and his people in darkness, the magician brings a heavy sleep upon the Queen, and thus carries her off to his master Kitovras.

When Solomon learns that his wife is in the possession of his brother King Kitovras, he sets out with an army in order to retrieve his wife. He instructs his men to come forward when they hear him sound his horn thrice. As an old beggar, he proceeds to his brother's castle and enters the garden. Here he meets a girl who is going to draw water with a golden cup, and asks her to allow him to drink from this cup. The girl at

[1] Vogt, *loc. cit.*, pp. xlii–xliii; Vincenti, *loc. cit.*, p. 14; Child, *loc. cit.*, p. 2.

first refuses, but in the end grants his request, induced by the gift of a golden ring. When the Queen notices the ring on the girl's finger, she asks who gave it to her.

" An old pilgrim, or beggar," replies the girl.

" No," retorts the Queen, " it is not an old pilgrim, but my husband Solomon."

She now gives instructions to have Solomon brought into her presence, and asks him what he had come for.

" I have come to put you to death," says Solomon, to which the Queen rejoins: " It is you who will die, you will be hanged." She sends for Kitovras, who pronounces Solomon's doom.

" You will neither see your wife back in your house nor go away alive from here," says Kitovras. Solomon now begs his brother to allow him at least to die in regal style. Kitovras, the Queen, and the whole court, with all the people in the city, should attend the execution, ample food and drink should be provided, and under the gallows there should be a feast. His request is granted. He furthermore begged that three nooses should be provided, one of bast, another of red silk, and a third of yellow. This request was also granted.

Under the gallows Solomon once more reminds Kitovras of their brotherhood, and implores him to grant him, as his brother, the permission to blow his horn. The whim is complied with, and upon the third blast Solomon's army appears. Kitovras, the Queen, and the magician are all hanged, the first two in the red and yellow silken nooses and the magician in the bast.[1]

[1] Vogt, *loc. cit.*, pp. xliii–xliv; Jagic, *Archiv für Slavische Philologie*, Vol. I, p. 110 ff; Vesselovsky, *ibid.*; Vincenti, *loc. cit.*, pp. 14–15; Child, *loc. cit.*, pp. 2–3.

CHAPTER XV

David in Mohammedan Tradition

David's melodious voice—The chapel in the mountain—The birds and beasts come to listen to the King's voice—The merits of David and Abraham—David's request—God grants his prayer—The beautiful bird—David is fascinated—The secluded lake—The beautiful woman—Saya, daughter of Josu—David falls in love—The angels in disguise—David's punishment—His tears and repentance—The reed of iron and the little bell—The pearl in the stick—The silent bell—The reed and bell are taken away from David—David's companion in Paradise—The King wanders over Palestine—The old man carrying a bundle of faggots—The cave in the mountains—The hermit reciting his prayers—Mata, the God-fearing stranger—The wet patch on the summit of the mountain peak—David's surprise—The mysterious stranger—Mata's prayer—David and the angel of death—The death of David and the angel Gabriel.

David was not only a great warrior and a wise ruler, but also a great Prophet. God revealed unto him seventy psalms, and endowed him with a voice such as had never been vouchsafed to any mortal man. No other human voice had ever equalled his in power and sweetness. His voice was as loud as the deafening peal of thunder or the roaring of the lion, and as sweet as the warble of the nightingale. There was no musician or singer in Israel like David. Every third day he sang in a chapel hewn in a mountain, and when he sang not only men gathered to hear him, but also birds and beasts came from a distance to listen to his wonderful song.

He divided his time into three parts, devoting one part of it to affairs of State, one to the service of God, and the third to his wives, of whom he had ninety-nine, besides his concubines. One day, as David was returning home from prayer, he heard two of his subjects discussing his merits and comparing him with Abraham.

"Was Abraham or David the greater Prophet?" the men were asking.

"Was not Abraham," said the first man, "saved from the fiery furnace?"

"Didst not David," asked the other, "slay the giant Goliath?"

"But what has David done," retorted the first speaker, "that can be compared with the obedience of Abraham when he was ready to offer his only son as a sacrifice?"

When David reached home he fell on his face before God, and thus he prayed: "Lord, Thou who didst put to the test in the pyre the faithfulness and obedience of Abraham, grant me, too, an opportunity wherein I may be able to prove to my people that my love for Thee can resist temptation."

God granted David's prayer. When on the third day David was singing psalms before the congregation, he suddenly beheld a bird that was so beautiful that it attracted all his attention. David was greatly perturbed, and the sight of the beautiful bird fascinated him in a strange manner. He followed its movements and sang less psalms on that day than usual. He could scarcely sing when the bird disappeared from his view, and his voice became very soft and melodious whenever the beautiful bird once more came in sight.

To the great surprise of the congregation the King concluded the recitation of his psalms earlier than usual, and immediately went out alone in pursuit of the beautiful bird. From bush to bush and from tree to tree did the beautiful bird fly, leading the King onwards until towards sunset it brought him to the bank of a secluded lake. Here the bird vanished in the water, and David soon forgot it, for in its place there emerged out of the water a beautiful woman who dazzled the King like the midday sun. Anxious not to startle the bathing woman, David hid behind the bushes and waited until she was dressed, then he approached and asked her name.

" My name," replied the woman, " is Saya, the daughter of Josu, and I am the wife of Uriah Ibn Hanan, who is with the army." David went home, but his passion was so violently inflamed that he immediately sent instructions to the captain of his hosts to set Uriah in the most dangerous place in battle. The King's command was obeyed, and soon Uriah was killed in battle. Thereupon the King married the widow.

On the day after his marriage the angels Michael and Gabriel appeared in human form before David at his court, and Gabriel thus said to the King: " The man thou seest here possesses ninety-nine sheep, whilst I have only one, and yet he is pursuing me constantly and claiming my ewe lamb."

" This is unfair, and shows an evil and unbelieving heart and a bad nature," replied David.

" There are plenty of noble and learned believers," Gabriel interrupted the King, " who permit themselves worse things."

David now understood that the man was alluding to his own conduct with regard to Uriah, and his wrath was kindled. Seizing his sword, he wanted to pierce Gabriel, when Michael suddenly burst out into loud laughter. Both angels, now rising up on their wings, exclaimed:

" Thou hast given judgment against thyself, and hast declared thine own action to be that of a wicked unbeliever. Therefore God has decided that the power He had intended to give thee will only be granted to one of thy sons. Thy sin is the more heinous because thou thyself didst ask God to put thy piety to the test and to give thee a trial, but when the opportunity was afforded thee thou wast too weak to resist temptation." Thus spoke the angels and vanished, and David felt now the greatness of his sin. He tore his golden crown from his head and his royal purple robe from his body, and clad in rough woollen clothes went out into the desert, where he shed tears and repented of his sin. Thus he wandered about in the desert for three years, and the angels in heaven had pity on the repentant King and prayed to God to forgive him. After three years David heard a heavenly voice which informed him that the all-merciful God had opened unto him the Gates of Grace.

David was now consoled and returned home, where he soon regained his physical strength.[1]

According to other sources, David only wept and repented for forty days and forty nights, praying to the Lord for forgiveness. He shed more tears during these forty days and nights than all the men in the world have ever shed. He had written the history of his sin upon the palm of his hand, and whenever he looked at it his hand trembled. For shame David never dared lift his eyes to heaven, until, after the expiration of forty days, God bade him lift up his head, for his sin had been forgiven.

Thereupon David said: "O Lord, Thou art a just judge; when on the day of Resurrection Uriah, blood soiled, will appear before Thy Throne and say: 'Lord, ask this man why he did slay me,' what wilt Thou reply?"

And God answered: "I will ask him to forgive thee, and as his reward I will give a great inheritance in Paradise." Thereupon David said: "Now I know that I am pardoned." [2]

Although David was now again being loved and honoured by his people, he never dared, remembering the incident with the two angels, to give sentence in cases brought before him. He had already appointed a judge to give sentence in his place, when one day the angel Gabriel brought him a reed of iron and a little bell, and thus said unto him: "God has seen thy humility and is pleased with it, and He therefore sends thee this reed of iron and this little bell, which will enable thee to give judgment and to uphold right and justice in Israel. Place this reed in thy judgment hall and hang up the bell in

---

[1] Weil, *Biblische Legenden der Muselmänner*, pp. 208-212.
[2] Grünbaum, *Neue Breitäge zur semitischen Sagenkunde*, p. 197.

the middle. When a case is brought before thee, place the accuser on one side and the accused on the other, and always give sentence in favour of him who will cause the bell to tinkle when he touches the reed."

Thus spoke Gabriel, and David was greatly pleased with the gift which enabled him to give righteous judgment. Henceforth men feared to commit evil or do wrong, because they were certain to be discovered by the tinkling of the bell.

Now one day two men came before David, and one accused the other that he had left in the charge of his friend a costly pearl, but when he claimed it back the accused denied it to him. The latter swore that he had indeed returned the pearl. David, as usual, bade the men each to lay his hand on the reed, but the bell remained silent in both cases, so that David knew not which of the two had spoken the truth, and he began to doubt the power of the reed. He bade the men try again, but the result was the same. When he had made them try several times, he noticed that whenever the defendant went up to the reed to lay his hand on it he gave his stick to the plaintiff to hold. David's suspicion was aroused, and he made the men try again, but when the defendant went up to the reed to lay his hand on it David took the stick himself, and lo! when the accuser touched the reed the bell began to tinkle. David now examined the stick and found that it was hollow and the pearl was concealed in it, so that the accused had really spoken the truth when, after giving his stick to the plaintiff to hold, he maintained that he had returned the pearl to him. But because David had doubted the power of the heavenly gift, God was displeased with him, and the reed and bell were taken from him and returned to heaven whence they had come. After that David often erred in his judgment until his son Solomon, whom Saya had borne unto him, gave him the benefit of his wise counsel.[1]

[1] Weil, *loc. cit.*, pp. 213–215.

DAVID AND MATA

When the time of his death was approaching, David prayed to the Lord to let him see the man who was destined to be his companion in Paradise. His prayer was granted, and a voice fell from heaven and bade him give up his royal power and go forth as a poor pilgrim and wander about until he found the man who was to be his friend and comrade in the abode of the Blessed.

David immediately appointed Solomon as Regent to rule in his absence, whilst he himself, arrayed in pilgrim's garb and staff in hand, went forth in search of the man who was to be his companion in Paradise. From city to city and from village to village did the King of Israel wander, and everywhere he inquired after the pious and God-fearing men and made their acquaintance. For weeks, however, he had already wandered all over Palestine without finding a man whom he could deem worthy of being his companion in Paradise.

One day he reached a village on the shores of the Mediterranean Sea and met a man who was walking alongside of him. Poorly dressed, the old man was carrying on his head a very heavy load consisting of a bundle of faggots. The man was very old, and looked so reverend that David was interested and followed him to see where he lived. The old man walked on, but never entered any house in the village. He sold his bundle of faggots, and then gave away half the amount of the money he had received to a poor person who begged him for alms. Thereupon he bought bread for his money and retired from the town, wending his way to the mountains whence he had come. David followed him. He saw the old man break his bread in half and give a big portion to a blind woman whom he met on the way. " This man," thought David, " is worthy to be my companion and comrade in Paradise, for he is old and reverend and his actions prove him to be very pious and charitable. I must try and become more closely acquainted with him."

At some distance, therefore, David followed the old man, who was walking for several hours until he reached a cave among the rocky mountains which was lighted by a rent above. David remained at the entrance of the cave and heard the old man recite his prayers, then read the Thora and the Psalms till the sun had set. He then lighted a lamp and recited his evening prayers, and then only he drew forth his piece of bread and ate about half of it. David, who had not ventured to interrupt the old man in his devotions, now approached, entered the cave, and saluted the hermit.

" Who art thou?" asked the pious hermit, after returning the salute of David. " I have seen no human being in these mountains except the God-fearing Mata Ibn Juhana, who is destined to be King David's companion in Paradise."

David now revealed his identity to the hermit, and asked him to give him information where he could find this Mata. But the hermit replied: " I am not permitted to tell thee where he dwells, but if thou wilt go over these mountains, search very carefully and observe everything well, thou canst not miss the place where thou wilt meet Mata."

David continued his search, and wandered about for a long time without, however, noticing any trace of a human foot. He was just abandoning hope, and had made up his mind to return to the hermit and ask him for more precise information, when suddenly on the summit of a rugged mountain peak he noticed a spot that was wet and soft. David was surprised.

" It is rather strange," thought he, " that just on the summit of this rugged mountain peak the ground should be so soft and sloppy; it is impossible that there should be a spring here."

And whilst he was thus musing and wondering at this

strange patch of soft ground, an old man came up from the other side of the mountain. He resembled an angel rather than a mortal man, and his eyes were depressed to the earth, so that he did not notice the presence of David. He stood still on the wet patch and began to pray with such fervour that the tears flowed from his eyes like two rivulets. David now understood why the ground on the topmost peak of the rocky mountain was so wet and sloppy, and he thought in his heart: " A man who can pray to the Lord with such fervour, shedding tears in such abundance, well deserves to be my companion and comrade in Paradise."

He did not venture, however, to interrupt the pious and God-fearing Mata until he heard him pray as follows: " O my God! Forgive King David his sins and let him not be led into temptation and save him from further trespass; be merciful to him for my sake, since Thou hast destined me to be his comrade in the life to come!"

David now ran towards the old man, but when he reached him Mata was dead. David dug into the soft ground with his staff, washed the body, and laid it in the grave, reciting the funeral prayer. He then covered the grave and returned to his capital. In his harem he found the angel of Death awaiting for him. The latter greeted the King with the following words:

" The Lord has granted thy request, but now thy life has reached its end."

" The Lord's will be done," said David, fell to the ground, and expired.

Thereupon the angel Gabriel came down to console Solomon, and brought him a heavenly shroud wherein to wrap his father. All Israel followed the bier of David to the entrance of the cave of Machpelah, where lies buried the Patriarch Abraham.[1]

---

[1] *Ibid.*, pp. 220–224.

CHAPTER XVI

Solomon in Mohammedan Legend

Solomon's signet-ring—The angels who rule over the light winds—
The wonderful jewel—The angels who rule over all the living creatures—
The power of the precious stone—The living creatures assemble before
Solomon—Solomon's conversation with the beasts, birds, and fishes—The
language of the birds—Their wise sayings—The song of the nightingale,
the call of the turtle-dove, and the piping of the peewit—The swallow, the
pelican, the dove, and the eagle—Solomon strokes the dove—Solomon
is given dominion over the spirits—The Jinns in their natural and original
shape—Loathsome beings as a result of a sinful life—The building of the
Temple—The power of Solomon's signet-ring—The male and the female
Jinns—Their various tasks—The terrible noise—The demon Sakhr—The
capture of the demon—Water and wine—The eggs out of a raven's nest
—The stone Samur—Solomon and the ants—Solomon's conversation with
the Queen of the ants—My power is greater than thine—The piteous cry
of the aged man—The reason of his old age—The angel of death—The tree
Sidrat-Almuntaha—The magic carpet—Solomon visits the cities of Mecca
and Medina—The absence of the peewit—The Queen of Sheba—The
riddles of Balkis—The boys disguised as maidens—The contents of the
box—The diamond cut in zigzags—The water that comes neither from
heaven nor from earth—Solomon solves the riddles of Balkis—The throne
of Balkis—Solomon falls in love with Balkis—The jealousy of the ladies of
the harem—The palace with a crystal floor—The hairy legs of the Queen—
The wonderful throne of gold—The coffin of Queen Balkis—Princess
Djarada—The statue of King Nubara—Asaph rebukes the King—Solomon's penance—The lost ring—Amina and the demon Sakhr—The exiled
King—The enamoured Princess—The ring found in the fish—Solomon
returns to Jerusalem—The punishment of Sakhr—The death of Solomon
—The attitude of prayer—The trees in Solomon's garden—The white ant
which gnawed the King's staff—The Jinns discover that Solomon is dead.

SOLOMON'S SIGNET-RING

When he had shown to his father David the last offices,
Solomon, having sat down to rest in a valley between Hebron
and Jerusalem, fell asleep. Awaking from his sleep, he suddenly
beheld eight angels standing before him. Each had countless

wings of various shapes and colours and bowed three times before the King.

" Who are ye?" queried Solomon, his eyes still half closed.

" We are the angels appointed to rule over the light winds, and the Lord, our and thy creator, has sent us to pay homage unto thee and to give thee the dominion and power over us and over the winds which are subject to our command. Henceforth, at thy command, the winds will be either stormy or mild, blowing from the side to which thou wilt turn thy back. At thy command, too, the winds will rise up and bear thee above the highest mountains."

Thus spoke the angels, and the greatest of them gave Solomon a jewel inscribed with the words, " To God belong power and greatness ". " Whenever thou hast a command for us," said the angel, " then raise this stone towards heaven, and at once we shall appear before thee as thy servants." Thus spoke the greatest angel, and they all departed.

Thereupon four other angels appeared, each greatly differing from the others. One had the shape of an immense whale, the second that of an eagle, the third was like a lion, and the fourth like a serpent. They bowed before Solomon and said: " We rule over all the living creatures that move on the earth and in the water, and have come at the command of God to pay homage unto thee and to give thee dominion over us. Command us according to thy wish, and we will grant unto thee and thy friends all the good which the Lord has placed in our power, and will use all the evil against thine enemies."

Thereupon the angel who ruled over the winged fowls handed to Solomon a precious stone inscribed with the words, " All creatures praise the Lord ". " Raise this stone," they said, "above thy head, and by virtue of it thou canst call us at any moment to thy assistance and give us thy commands."

Solomon immediately decided to test the power of the stone and ordered the angels to bring him a pair of every living creature that moved and lived in the water, upon earth, or in the air. The angels vanished, and in an instant there were assembled before Solomon all sorts of creatures, from the elephant to the smallest worm, and also all sorts of fishes and birds. Solomon conversed with them and was instructed in all their different habits. He also listened to their complaints and rectified many abuses and evil customs amongst the beasts, birds, and fishes. It was, however, with the birds that he entertained himself longest, both on account of their beautiful and melodious speech, which he understood as well as the language of man, and the sentences full of wisdom which they uttered.

Translated into the speech of man, the cry of the peacock signified: " As thou judgest others, so shalt thou thyself be judged." The song of the nightingale, expressed in human speech, signified: " Contentment is the greatest happiness." The call of the turtle-dove meant: " It were better for some created things that they had never been created." The piping of the peewit signified: " He who hath no mercy will never find mercy himself," whilst the bird *syrdar* called: " Return to the Lord, ye sinners." The swallow said: " Do good, and one day ye shall receive your reward." The pelican said: " Praised be the Lord in heaven and upon earth." The dove said: " Everything in the world passeth away, God alone remaineth eternal," whilst the *kata* uttered: " He who is silent will certainly pass through." The eagle's cry signified: " May our life be ever so long, it inevitably ends in death." The raven croaked: " The farther I am from man, the better I feel." The cock crowed: " Remember the Creator, ye thoughtless men."

Solomon then chose the cock and peewit to be his constant companions, the first on account of the wise sentence it uttered, the second because it is able to see through earth as through a crystal, and therefore could indicate to him on his travels the place where a fountain of water was to be found, so that he would never lack water either to drink or for his ritual ablutions. He thereupon stroked the dove and bade it dwell in the Temple which he was about to build. In a few years this pair of doves, on account of the touch of Solomon, multiplied to such an extent that all those who came to visit the Temple moved from the farthest part of the town under the shadow of the wings of the doves.

When Solomon was again alone, there appeared an angel whose upper half was like earth, whilst his lower half was like water. Bowing very low before Solomon, he said: " I was created by God to do His will both on dry land and in the water. He has now sent me to do thy bidding, and through me thou canst rule over earth and water. The highest mountains will disappear at thy command, and others will rise up on level land. At thy command, rivers and seas will dry up, whilst fertile dry land will be changed into sea and ocean." Thereupon the angel gave unto Solomon a precious stone inscribed with the following words: " Heaven and earth serve God ".

Finally another angel brought the King a fourth precious stone inscribed with the words: " There is no God save the one God, and Mohammed is His messenger ". " By virtue of this stone," said the angel, " thou shalt have dominion and rule over the whole world of spirits, which is much greater and vaster than the world of men and beasts, for it occupies the entire space between earth and heaven. A portion of these spirits," continued the angel, " is faithful, worshipping the one and only God, whilst another portion is unfaithful. Some of the last adore fire, others worship the sun, the stars, the planets, or water. The first, who are the good spirits, always hover round the true believers, protecting them from evil and also from sin, whilst the evil spirits are always trying to injure and plague men, or to lead them into temptation.

Being invisible, and able to assume any shape they like, they often succeed in their endeavour."

Solomon now asked to be allowed to see the Jinns in their original and natural shape, and his request was granted. Like a column of flame the angel immediately shot up into heaven, and an instant later he returned accompanied by a host of Satans and Jinns. In spite of the power and dominion he had over them, Solomon shuddered when he beheld their horrible appearance. Never had he imagined that such loathsome beings existed in the world. He saw human heads attached to the necks of horses whose feet were those of an ass; he saw the wings of eagles attached to the humps of dromedaries, and the horns of gazelles upon the heads of peacocks. He asked the angel to explain the cause of such a strange mixture, to which the latter replied that it was the result of a sinful and shameless life.[1]

The Building of the Temple

When Solomon returned home, he gave instructions to have the four stones the angels had made him a gift of set in a signet-ring, so that he might at any moment make use of his power and dominion over the beasts and spirits, the earth and the wind. His first care was to subject the Jinns. He summoned them all in his presence, with the exception of the mighty Sakhr, who had concealed himself upon an unknown island in the ocean, and of Eblis, the master of all the evil spirits, to whom God had given complete independence and liberty until the day of the last Judgment. When all the Jinns had assembled before him, Solomon at once pressed his seal upon their necks, thus marking them as his slaves. Thereupon he commanded the male Jinns to construct many buildings, and especially the great temple similar to that of Mecca, but much greater. The female Jinns Solomon bade cook, bake, wash,

[1] Weil, *Biblische Legenden der Muselmänner*, pp. 225–231.

weave, carry water, and do all sorts of work. All that they produced he distributed among the poor. All the food they cooked was placed on tables which covered an area of one square mile. Thirty thousand oxen, and so many sheep, besides many birds and fishes, were devoured daily. The Jinns and Satans sat at iron tables, the poor at tables of wood, the heads of the people and the commanders of the army at silver tables, whilst the learned, the wise, and the pious sat at tables of gold. Solomon himself in person served the latter.[1]

When Solomon returned to Jerusalem, he heard a mighty noise of the hammers and other instruments of the Jinns who were constructing the Temple. The noise they made was so great that the inhabitants of Jerusalem could not hear one another speak. Solomon therefore commanded the Jinns to cease their work, and asked them whether any one of them knew of a means whereby the various metals could be cut without making such a tremendous noise. Thereupon one of the Jinns stepped forth and said that the means was known only to the mighty Sakhr, who had hitherto escaped the King's authority.

" And could not this Sakhr be captured?" asked Solomon.

" Sakhr," replied the Jinn, " is mightier and stronger than all the Jinns together, and he is superior to all of us both in strength and in speed. I know, however, that once a month he goes to the land of Hidjir, there to slake his thirst at a fountain. Thou mayest thus, O wise King, subdue him and bring him under thy sceptre."

Solomon immediately commanded a number of swift Jinns to fly to the land of Hidjir, to empty the fountain, and to fill it with strong wine. Some of the Jinns he bade remain in ambush by the side of the fountain and see what would happen. The Jinns accordingly emptied the source of water, filled it with wine, and hid themselves nearby behind trees. Soon

[1] Weil, *loc. cit.*, pp. 231–232.

Sakhr appeared, and smelling the wine, exclaimed: " O wine, thou art delicious, but thou dost deprive one of intelligence, makest stupid the wise, and causest regret." He left the source without having drunk out of it. On the third day, being tormented by thirst, he returned. " I cannot escape," he exclaimed, " the fate which God has decided to bring upon me." Thereupon he drank his fill, made a few steps, but fell down. From all sides the Jinns and Ifrits now appeared, hurried to the spot where Sakhr lay intoxicated, and put him in chains, whilst flames were issuing forth from his mouth and nostrils.[1] One day, when Solomon was standing on the terrace of his palace, he saw a Jinn flying swifter than the wind from the direction of Hidjir. " Great King," he said, " Sakhr lies drunk by the side of the fountain, securely bound with chains as thick as the pillars of the Temple, but when he will have slept off the wine he will snap them as if they were the hair of a maiden."

Solomon at once mounted the winged Jinn and in less than an hour was transported to the land of Hidjir. He was just in time, for Sakhr was already opening his eyes and awakening from his drunken sleep. Solomon had just time to press the signet-ring upon the demon's neck. Sakhr uttered such a cry that the whole earth rocked and trembled.

" Be without fear, mighty Jinn," said Solomon; " I will restore unto thee thy liberty as soon as thou wilt tell me how I can cut the hardest metals without making a noise."

" I know no means," replied Sakhr, " but the raven can certainly advise thee. Take thou now the eggs out of the raven's nest, cover them with a crystal globe, and then thou shalt see how the raven will break the glass."

Solomon did as Sakhr had advised him. When the raven came, he fluttered round the crystal globe but could not reach the eggs. He vanished, and soon returned carrying in his beak

---

[1] Grünbaum, *Neue Beiträge zur semitischen Sagenkunde*, pp. 227-228.

a stone called Samur, and with this stone he cut the crystal globe.

" Whence hast thou taken this stone?" asked Solomon.

" From the mountain in the Far West," replied the raven.

Solomon now commanded some of the Jinns to fly to that mountain and fetch more of these stones. Sakhr, however, he released, as he had promised. When the chains were taken off the demon, he uttered a loud cry of joy, but which sounded in Solomon's ears like mocking laughter.

The Jinns had in the meantime returned with the Samur stones, and Solomon was borne back to Jerusalem. Here he distributed the stones among the working Jinns, who were now able to continue their work without making the slightest noise.[1]

Solomon also built a great and splendid palace unto himself with vast riches in gold, silver, and precious stones as no other King before him had ever possessed. Some of the halls in the Temple had crystal floors and ceilings. He also built a throne for himself of sandalwood, set in with gold and precious stones.[2]

SOLOMON AND THE ANTS

Whilst the Jinns were building the Temple, Solomon undertook a journey to Damascus. He was borne on the back of a Jinn or, according to others, transported on his magic carpet. He was carried over a precipitous valley surrounded on all sides by craggy mountains with sharp peaks, so that no man had ever ventured to visit the spot. It was the valley of ants. When Solomon looked down he beheld a host of ants as large as wolves. They had grey eyes and grey feet, and from a distance looked like a cloud. When the Queen of the ants, who had never beheld a mortal man before, saw Solomon, she was filled with amazement and fear. She immediately com-

[1] Weil, *loc. cit.*, pp. 234–237; Grünbaum, *loc. cit.*, p. 229; Salzberger, *Tempelbau*. p. 47.
[2] Weil, *loc. cit.*, p. 237.

manded her army to fly and conceal themselves in their hiding-places. God, however, commanded the Queen of the ants not to fear but to summon all her subjects and do homage unto Solomon as King of all the insects.

From a distance of many miles Solomon heard the command of God and the answer of the Queen of the ants borne to him upon the wind. Gently he descended into the valley, and taking the Queen of the ants upon his hand, he began to converse with her.

"Why didst thou fear me?" he asked. "Art thou not surrounded by such a mighty host?"

"I did not fear thee," replied the ant, "for I fear God alone. Should any danger threaten my subjects then, at a sign from me, seven times as many would appear in an instant."

"Then why didst thou command thy subjects to run to their hiding-places?"

"Because I feared that they would look on thee with wonder and amazement, and thus forget for a moment to praise their Creator."

"Is my power greater than thine?" asked the King.

"No," replied the ant, "I am greater than thou, for thy throne is only a metal one, whilst I am now reposing in the palm of the hand of a mighty King."

"And hast thou any request to make unto me before I release thee?" asked Solomon.

"No," replied the ant, "I ask nothing of thee, but I will give thee some advice. Beware of acting on any occasion so as to have to be ashamed of thy name which signifies The Blameless. Moreover, never give the ring from thy finger before saying first, 'In the name of God the all merciful'."

"Lord," exclaimed Solomon, "Thy Kingdom is greater and by far exceeds mine." Thereupon he bade farewell to the Queen of the ants and departed.

On his return journey Solomon commanded the Jinn to

take another direction, as he did not wish to disturb the ants in their devotions. When he reached the borders of Palestine, he heard the piteous cry of someone exclaiming: " O God, Thou who didst choose Abraham as Thy friend, release me from this miserable life."

Solomon followed in the direction of the voice and descended. He beheld a very old man bent with age and trembling in all his limbs.

" Who art thou?" asked Solomon.

" I am an Israelite from the tribe of Judah."

" And how old art thou?"

" This God alone knows. I reckoned my years until they numbered three hundred, but then I ceased, and another fifty or sixty may have passed over me."

" And how came it," asked Solomon, " that thou hast attained an age that has not fallen to the lot of man since Abraham?"

" Because," replied the old Israelite, " I once prayed to God to be allowed to behold the greatest of all the Prophets before I died."

" Thy wish is now fulfilled," said Solomon, " for I am that Prophet. I am Solomon, King and Prophet, unto whom God has given power and dominion such as was never given to any man before. Thou hast now reached thy goal, and now prepare to die."

Hardly had Solomon uttered these words, when the angel of Death appeared in human shape and took the soul of the old man.

" Thou must have been very near," exclaimed Solomon, " to have been able to appear with such speed."

" Thou dost greatly err," replied the angel of Death. " Know that I rest upon the shoulders of an angel whose head reaches ten thousand years' journey above the seventh heaven, whilst his feet are five hundred years' journey beneath the earth. He is so strong that if God only gave him permission he would have destroyed the earth and all that it contains. It is he who tells me when I must fetch a soul. His eyes are always fixed on the tree Sidrat-Almuntaha, which has as many leaves as there are men in the world. Every time that a child is born a new leaf shoots forth on which its name is inscribed; and every time that a man is about to die the leaf withers and falls off. Then I come and fetch the soul."

" And what dost thou to the souls and whither dost thou lead them?"

" When a believer dies, Gabriel accompanies me. He wraps the soul in green silk, and a green bird carries it to Paradise, where it remains till the end of time. As for the souls of the sinners, I carry them myself in a tarred cloth to the gates of hell, where they wander about in misery until the day of Judgment.

Solomon thanked the angel for the information, and asked him, when his time came, to keep his death secret. Thereupon he washed the body of the old man, buried it, and prayed for his soul that it might be eased of the pains it would have to undergo during its purgation by the angels Ankir and Munkir.[1]

This journey on the backs of the Jinns had exhausted Solomon, and on his return to Jerusalem he ordered his serving Jinns and demons to weave a carpet of stout silk which could transport him and his entire household from one place to another. When he made up his mind to go on a journey he ordered the winds to blow, and they immediately wafted him whither he wanted to travel. One night the Patriarch Abraham appeared to him in a dream and commanded him to visit the city of Jathrib or Medina, where the greatest of Prophets will one day find shelter, and also the city of Mecca, where he will be born. The King was accompanied on his journey by such

---

[1] Weil, *ibid.*; pp. 237–242; Tabari, *Chronique*, Vol. I, pp. 457–459; Mirkhond, *Rauzat-us-Safa*, ed. Rehatsek, Part I, Vol. II, p. 82; Migne, *Dictionnaire des Apocryphes*, Vol. II, col. 856.

a great number of pilgrims that he ordered the Jinns to weave a new carpet of vast dimensions on which the whole caravan, the camels and the oxen, could be accommodated. When all was ready, Solomon ordered the winds to blow and to waft the carpets to Medina. In the vicinity of the city, at a sign from Solomon, the winds abated, and slowly the carpets sank to earth. He visited the spot where Mohammed was once to build a mosque and then returned to the carpet. Through the air the King and his suite then sailed to Mecca, where Solomon offered sacrifices and preached a sermon in the Kaaba, prophesying the birth of Mohammed. Three days Solomon, his suite, and all the pilgrims remained at Mecca and then returned to Jerusalem.

When Solomon remounted his throne on the carpet and the birds accompanying him spread out their wings, he noticed a ray of the sun piercing the ranks of the birds, and he knew that one bird had deserted its place. He immediately bade the eagle to ascertain which was the missing bird. When the eagle informed Solomon that it was the peewit who had deserted its place, the King commanded him to find and bring the runaway. The peewit, trembling in every limb, was brought before Solomon, and excused his absence by the news he had obtained of a land and a Queen whose names the King had never heard. It was the land of Sheba, and the name of the Queen was Balkis. A lapwing of that country had told the peewit that the name of King Solomon was absolutely unknown in his native land.[1]

THE QUEEN OF SHEBA

The peewit now related unto Solomon what he had learned of the land of Sheba and its Queen. Sheba was the name of the King who had founded the kingdom, and Sheba was also

---

[1] Weil, *loc. cit.*, pp. 242–247; Tabari, *loc. cit.*, pp. 436–438; Grünbaum, *loc. cit.*, pp. 211–217.

the name of the capital. King Sheba was succeeded by a number of rulers the last of whom was Scharabel, a tyrant of dissolute habits. He had a vizier of such extraordinary beauty that all the daughters of the Jinns fell in love with him, and even transformed themselves into gazelles so that they might walk alongside of him and admire his exquisite beauty. One of these damsels once appeared to the vizier and offered him her hand. Dazzled by the marvellous beauty of Umeira—such was the name of the daughter of the Jinns—the vizier was only too happy to marry her. She gave birth to a daughter whom they called Balkis. Now the vizier had promised his wife never to inquire after her origin, but one day he forgot himself and asked her to what race she belonged. Immediately the lady-Jinn uttered a wail of sorrow and vanished.

The vizier now lived in seclusion with his daughter Balkis, who grew up to be a maiden of extraordinary beauty. One day King Scharabel saw her, and the licentious ruler fell violently in love with her. Balkis consented to give him her hand, and the marriage was celebrated with great pomp. On the bridal night, however, the bride-elect plied the King with drink and then stabbed him to the heart with a dagger. As the people of Sheba were already furious against the licentious monster, they received the news of the tyrant's death with a shout of joy, and unanimously elected Balkis as their Queen and sole ruler. " Thus," concluded the peewit, " Balkis rules over Sheba, and the country is prosperous, but, like her predecessors, the queen is a worshipper of the sun." [1]

" We shall soon see," said Solomon, " whether thou hast spoken the truth or not."

He wrote a letter, sealed it with his ring, and bade the peewit carry the missive immediately to Queen Balkis. Like an arrow the bird flew away and arrived at Sheba on the following morning.

---

[1] Weil, *loc. cit.*, pp. 247–258; Grünbaum, *loc. cit.*, pp. 217–219.

And this is what Solomon wrote to Queen Balkis: "Solomon, the son of David, and servant of God, the most Merciful, sendeth greeting to Balkis, Queen of Sheba. In the name of the most merciful God, peace be to those who walk in His ways. Do what I bid thee and submit immediately to my power."

The Queen read this letter to her counsellors, and they told her to do as seemed best to her, but assured her of their fidelity. The Queen decided to propitiate Solomon with gifts. " If he accepts these gifts," said the Queen, " he is not above or greater than other kings, but if he refuseth them, then he is indeed a Prophet, and we must yield to his sway and do what he commandeth us." Thereupon she had five hundred boys dressed as girls and five hundred maidens dressed in men's clothes. She also sent Solomon as presents a thousand carpets of gold and silver tissue, a crown set with pearls and precious stones, and a box containing a pearl, a diamond cut in zigzags, and a crystal goblet. Then she sent a letter to Solomon, and this is what she wrote: " If thou art a Prophet, thou wilt be able to distinguish the boys from the girls and also guess the contents of the box."

Balkis handed the letter to her ambassadors and gave them the following instructions: " When ye arrive near the palace of Solomon, request him to separate the males from the females, because if he be a Prophet, this will not be difficult for him to do. Ask him further to guess the contents of the box, to pierce the pearl, to thread the diamond, and fill the goblet with water which has come neither from heaven nor from earth. If he speaks and acts righteously, then leave these gifts with him, otherwise bring them back to me. If Solomon looks at ye with haughtiness and pride, then know that he is a King and not a Prophet, and ye need not fear his power and bravery. But if he receives ye graciously, meeting ye with affability and kindness, then be on your guard, for he is indeed a Prophet."

The peewit had remained all the time by the side of the Queen, watching the proceedings and listening to her injunctions. Thereupon he flew back to Solomon and acquainted the King with all that had occurred. When the messengers from Queen Balkis arrived and beheld the magnificence of Solomon, they were greatly astonished. Terror seized them when they set foot on a carpet the end of which they could not see, and had to pass between ranks of demons and Jinns, princes, nobles, and soldiers. They were confused and ashamed of the poverty of their own gifts when they beheld the floor of gold and silver and the great magnificence of the King. Solomon received them with a gracious smile, and when they presented to him the letter of their Queen, he told them its contents without opening it.

When the ambassadors offered the box, Solomon guessed its contents. He drilled a hole in the pearl by means of the worm Shamir and threaded the diamond. A Jinn brought him a worm, and Solomon put the end of a silken thread in its mouth and inserted it in the diamond. The worm crept through the winding passage and appeared at the other end. The diamond was threaded. Solomon was anxious to express his gratitude to the worm, and asked it what reward it desired. The worm asked for a tree from which it could draw for ever its nourishment, and Solomon gave to the little creature the mulberry tree, and therefore the silkworm always dwells on the mulberry tree. The King then proceeded to fill the goblet with water that came neither from heaven nor from earth. He summoned a huge and heavy negro slave and commanded him to mount a fiery young horse and gallop it about the plain until it streamed with sweat. When the horse returned, Solomon easily filled the goblet with the sweat pouring down its flanks.

He next bade his servants bring a thousand silver basins filled with water, and commanded the disguised youths and maidens to wash their hands after their journey. He watched intently and saw that the girls washed their faces with both hands, whilst the boys dipped their hands in the water and rubbed their faces only with one hand. He thus distinguished the males from the females.

Having accomplished these tasks, Solomon now turned to the ambassadors and thus addressed them: " Ye have seen that I have answered the riddles set to me by your Queen. Take now back your presents, for ye cannot augment my possessions. What God the magnificent and glorious has bestowed upon me is better than anything ye are able to offer. Return and tell your Queen to submit to my power and profess the Faith, or else I shall come with an army to which she will be unable to offer resistance. I will take possession of her country and lead her into captivity."

The messengers returned to Sheba and informed their Queen of all they had seen and heard. The Queen swore that Solomon was not only a sovereign but a Prophet, and made up her mind to go to him and do him homage. She prepared for her journey and set out at the head of twelve thousand generals and all her army.

When Balkis was a league away from Jerusalem, Solomon summoned a demon of hideous appearance and commanded him to bring the throne of Queen Balkis which the latter had locked up in a hall in her own palace. The Jinn promised to fetch the throne before noon, but Solomon would not wait, for the Queen was already approaching Jerusalem. Thereupon Asaph, the son of Berachiah, stepped forward and thus addressed the King: " Lift up thine eyes to heaven, O King, and before thou canst lower them to earth again the throne of Balkis will be here." Asaph knew the Ineffable Name of God, and by its power he was able to accomplish what he had promised. When the King lowered his gaze, the throne of Balkis stood before him. Although portions of the throne had been quickly changed by Solomon's servants, Balkis recognized it on her arrival. When Solomon asked her if she knew the throne, she replied prudently: " It looks as though it were mine." [1]

Now Solomon fell in love with Balkis and wanted to marry her. The Jinns, however, were envious of the Queen, and spread a rumour that her beauty was far from peerless because she had the feet of an ass, or ass's legs. [2] According to Mirkhond, the rumour had been spread not by Jinns but, what is more likely, by the ladies of Solomon's harem. When Solomon became aware of the intelligence of Balkis, he sent her to live with his sister who apprised him, after the expiration of forty days, of the noble virtues, exquisite qualities, and exalted disposition of her guest. Solomon then determined to " string this royal pearl of the diadem of sovereignty upon the thread of matrimony ". At this news the ladies of Solomon's harem became distressed and, for the purpose of causing the noble prophetic mind to get disgusted with Balkis, enviously spread the rumour that her legs were extremely hairy. [3] The King, anxious to convince himself with his own eyes of the truth of this report, bade the Jinns build a palace with a crystal floor on the surface of the water, so that it should appear to the beholder as if it were also of water. He then called Balkis to himself, and when she reached the edge of the palace and imagined it to be all of water, she raised her garments and bared her legs. Solomon then saw that the lady had been maligned, and that there were only three goat's hairs on her legs. These Solomon was able to remove, thanks to a cure invented by the demons, which consisted in the use of mortar or some other depilatory preparation.

When the Queen approached Solomon she offered him two wreaths of flowers, one natural and the other artificial,

[1] Weil, *loc. cit.*, pp. 258–266; Tabari, *loc. cit.*, pp. 439–441; Mirkhond, *loc. cit.*, pp. 83–91; Grünbaum, *loc. cit.*, pp. 217–219.
[2] Tabari, *loc. cit.*, p. 441; Weil, *loc. cit.*, p. 267.   [3] Mirkhond, *loc. cit.*, p. 91.

and Solomon was rather embarrassed, for he could not distinguish one from the other. He then opened the window and let a swarm of bees fluttering outside enter the room. The insects immediately settled on the wreath of natural flowers, and Solomon chose the latter.[1] Thereupon Solomon married Balkis, and she bore him a son.[2]

According to Mirkhond, Solomon had a throne of gold constructed for Balkis which was surrounded by four lions, invented by the acuteness of those who excelled in talismanic art. The lions were near the supports of the throne, but inside, and vomited fire from their throats. Two vultures were perched on the back of each lion, and their eyes were of rubies and their teeth of pearls. Whenever Solomon ascended this throne and sat on it with Balkis, two eagles came and poured rosewater upon them. On the two upper extremities of this couch a pair of birds were stationed, which so spread their wings around the throne that whenever Solomon desired with Balkis to be seen by no one, they were completely screened. At the sides of the throne four peacocks were erected, whose beaks constantly exhaled a perfume of ambergris.[3]

Queen Balkis went back to her own land, where she bore a son from her union with Solomon.

When Balkis died, Solomon had her body conveyed to the city of Tadmor in the desert, where she was buried. Until the days of the Calif Walid her grave remained unknown. One day, however, in consequence of prolonged rains, the walls of Tadmor fell, and there was found an iron sarcophagus sixty ells long and forty ells wide, on which was engraved the following inscription: " Here lies buried the devout Balkis, Queen of Sheba, wife of the Prophet Solomon, son of David. Converted to the true faith in the thirteenth year of the reign

[1] Weil, *loc. cit.*, p. 267; Tabari, *loc. cit.*, pp. 441–442.   [2] Weil, *ibid.*; Tabari, *ibid.*
[3] Mirkhond, *loc. cit.*, p. 92; cf. Salzberger, *Tempelbau*, pp. 99–109.

of Solomon, she married him in the fourteenth year, and died in the twenty-third year of his reign."

The son of the Calif had the lid of the coffin raised, and he beheld the body of a woman which was as fresh as if she had just been buried. The Prince announced his discovery to his father, and Walid ordered him to leave the tomb undisturbed, and to pile great blocks of marble over it so as to conceal it from the gaze of man.[1]

SOLOMON AND PRINCESS DJARADA

Balkis had a rival for Solomon's affections in the person of Djarada, daughter of the Indian King Nubara. Solomon had heard that on one of the islands in the Indian Sea there lived a mighty King. Mounting his carpet, he at once marched against this King, whom he defeated and slew. In the royal palace he found the Princess Djarada, who was distinguished by elegance and beauty, surpassing not only all the wives of Solomon but even Balkis. Solomon made a prisoner of the Princess and forced her to mount the carpet. Love for the fair Princess was kindled in the heart of the King, and he forced her to adopt his faith and marry him. The Princess, however, " passed her days in grief and her nights in burning pain ", and led a sad life ever since she had been separated from her father. In Solomon she saw the murderer of the latter, and she recoiled from his embrace.

One day the King asked Djarada what he could do for her which might console her, give her comfort, and reconcile her to her fate. The lady immediately asked him to have a statue of her father made by the Jinns and placed in her chamber, so that by looking at it in the morning and evening her sorrowful mind might be comforted. Moved by compassion, Solomon ordered the Jinns to make the statue and set it up in Djarada's apartment. When this was done Djarada, who had been a

[1] Weil, *loc. cit.*, p. 274; Migne, *loc. cit.*, col. 869.

worshipper of idols before she associated with Solomon,
began to worship the statue like an idol in the company of her
maid-servants.   Daily she prostrated herself before it and
offered incense.   This continued for forty days without Solomon being aware of it.   Then the rumour spread among the
people that the Princess was worshipping an idol, and the
case was reported to Asaph.   Thereupon Asaph preached a
sermon before the King and all the people, and narrated in an
eloquent manner the history of the virtues and noble acts of
every Prophet of past times.   Turning to Solomon, he praised
his wisdom and piety during the first years of his reign, and
only mentioned the acts the King had performed in his youth
before the decease of his father David.   Solomon was amazed
and displeased at this brevity and open rebuke, and summoning
Asaph into his presence, asked him to explain why he had
thus rebuked him before all the people.   Asaph replied: " I
cannot laud or praise a man who has suffered his passions to
blind him so that idolatry is practised in his house since forty
days."

" In my house?" queried Solomon.

" Yes, in thy house," replied Asaph, and narrated what was
taking place.

" We all belong to Allah and to him we shall return," said
Solomon, and immediately hastened to Djarada's apartment.
Finding her in prayer before the image of her father, he
smashed the idol and punished Djarada.   Thereupon he put
on his garment of purity, which had been woven and sewn by
virgins, strewed ashes on his head, and went out into the
desert to bewail and repent of his sin.   Thus he wept and
fasted for forty days, and God forgave him.[1]

[1] Weil, *loc. cit.*, pp. 269–271; Grünbaum, *loc. cit.*, pp. 221–222; Tabari, *loc. cit.*, pp.
450–451; Mirkhond, *loc. cit.*, pp. 95–97.

The Lost Ring

Solomon had a female slave Amina, and every time when he went to perform his devotions or ritual ablutions he gave his signet-ring into her charge. One day, when he had entrusted the ring to this female slave (according to Mirkhond the girl's name was Jarada, and Solomon was going to answer a call of nature), one of the Jinns, Haritsu by name (according to Mirkhond it was the mighty Sakhr), took advantage of the King's act. Assuming the dress and guise of Solomon, he went to the girl, obtained the ring from her, and flung it into the sea. He then took Solomon's seat on the throne, whereon genii and men girded their loins in obedience to him. When Solomon returned and claimed his signet-ring from the girl, she exclaimed:

" I have already given it to thee! Thou art not the King," she cried, " but an impostor who has assumed the shape of Solomon for evil purposes. The King is at this moment in his judgment hall."

Whilst he was expostulating with the girl about the ring, Solomon threw a glance into the judgment hall and beheld an individual sitting on his throne. He became convinced that the Lord was angry with him and had therefore wrested the reins of power from him. He no longer asked for the ring, but put on poor clothing, took a staff in his hand, and went forth.

He wandered about as a mendicant, and when people asked him who he was, he replied: " I am Solomon." The people accused him of folly, threw dust at his blessed head and face, and said: " Thou madman art Solomon? Behold the King sitting on his throne in pomp and glory!—Look at this fool," they cried, " who pretends to be Solomon, the son of David." [1]

During his wanderings the exiled monarch came to the

[1] Grünbaum. *loc. cit.*, p. 223; Mirkhond, *loc. cit.*, pp. 97–98.

land of King Hiram of Tyre, who was just building a great palace. According to one source it was to the land of the King of Yram that Solomon came. He asked for employment and obtained it from the overseer, who set him to draw water from a cistern. One day, when he was reposing in the shadow of a tower belonging to the palace, the Princess, standing at the window, saw him asleep. For several days she watched the handsome youth, and with amazement saw that one day two lions came down from the mountains and, placing themselves by the side of the sleeper, kept away the flies from him with their tails. On the next day two eagles came who fanned him with their wings. Whenever Solomon awoke, he exclaimed: " Extolled be God the only one." The Princess asked him who the God whom he extolled was, and Solomon replied:

" To Him belong all things in heaven and earth, in the air and under the earth."

Then the maiden said: " I have heard it said that all things obey Solomon; art thou perchance Solomon?" And when he answered in the affirmative the Princess exclaimed: " Then, O Prophet of God, I have a request to make thee; take me as thy wife, I will renounce my former belief and learn of thy God. My father," she continued, " has long ago promised me to allow me to marry whomever I will."

The King of Yram kept his promise, but bade his daughter leave the palace and go forth without her beautiful robes and her jewels. He left her only two copper dineros. Thus the pair set out on their wanderings. Solomon bought bread and oil for one coin, and some fishermen made him a present of two fish. These he brought to his wife to clean, and she found within one of them the ring which the demon Haritsu had thrown into the sea. Solomon took the ring and exclaimed: " There is no power or might except with God, the great, the exalted." Thereupon he placed the ring upon his finger, and immediately Jinns laden with costly robes and rich food came through the air. They reared a palace, and Solomon and his wife arrayed themselves in costly garments. The King summoned the fishermen who had given him the fish and bade them eat of the rich food to their heart's content. Then he sent for the King of Yram, and when the latter arrived and saw the great wealth and power, he begged his daughter's pardon and confessed the true faith. Thereupon Solomon commanded a cloud to approach, and he and his wife and the King of Yram were immediately conveyed to Jerusalem.[1]

When Solomon returned to his capital, he ordered the Jinns to find Sakhr and to bring him to his presence. They obeyed, and Solomon fettered and shackled the demon with his adherents and cast them all into the sea. According to another version the demon was riding in the sea. Then a troop of female Jinns or Peris came and began to lament in a loud voice: "Solomon is dead." Suspecting nothing, the Jinn came out, and the Peris seized him and brought him to Solomon. At the command of the King, the Jinn was bound between a piece of iron and a stone and cast into the sea.[2]

The Death of Solomon

Solomon knew that the end of his life was approaching, and he was anxious to see the building of the Temple completed. He was sure that if he died and the Jinns knew of it they would at once leave off building, for the demons were only kept at labour by the power of the King's signet-ring. The King was now in the habit of visiting the unfinished Temple very frequently, and he often remained there for one or two months, plunged in prayer. He even took his food in the Temple. When people saw him in a humble attitude before God, with his head bowed, neither man nor Jinn dared

---

[1] Grünbaum, *loc. cit.*, pp. 223–224 and 273–276; Mirkhond, *loc. cit.*, p. 100.
[2] Tabari, *loc. cit.*, p. 453.

approach him; if a Jinn ventured to draw near, then fire fell from heaven and destroyed him.

Now in the garden of Solomon each day a tree grew which was unknown to him. Solomon used to ask each tree what its name was and for what purpose it had been created, and the tree would reply. One day he saw a new tree and he asked:

" What is thy name, and what purpose dost thou serve?"

Then the tree gave the following answer: " I serve for the destruction of the Temple, make me into a staff and lean upon me!" This answer puzzled Solomon.

" No one can destroy the Temple as long as I am alive," he said, and he understood that the tree had warned him of his approaching death. He accordingly cut the tree and made a staff out of it, and henceforth, when he prayed, he used to lean upon the staff.

Solomon now prayed to God and said:

" O Lord, let my death be unknown to the Jinns, that they may finish the work of the Temple."

God granted Solomon's request, for when the angel took away his soul his body remained leaning on his staff with his head bowed in adoration. Those who saw him thus thought that he was alive, and never dared to come near him. He thus remained for a whole year. The Jinns, therefore, continued to work day and night until the Temple was completed.

God, however, had sent a white ant on the day on which Solomon's soul was taken, and commanded it to gnaw the inside of the staff. The white ant gnawed a little every day, and at the end of a year the staff was eaten up and crumbled under the weight of the King, and then all knew that he was dead.[1]

The sages then took the ant and enclosed it in a box with a piece of wood, and thus kept it for twenty-four hours. Comparing the amount that was eaten up in that time with the

[1] Tabari, *loc. cit.*, p. 455; Weil, *loc. cit.*, p. 279.

length of the staff, they could ascertain how long it had taken the ant to gnaw through the entire staff.[1] According to Mirkhond, the Ifrits themselves found out that Solomon was dead. When the stay of the King had become protracted beyond all reasonable expectations, one of the Jinns entered the Temple by one window and left it by another, but, contrary to his previous experience, failed to hear the voice of Solomon reading. He therefore said to the other Jinns: " It is my opinion that Solomon has departed from this world." Thereupon the Jinns, who were anxious to obtain certainty on the subject, procured a beetle whose nourishment is water and earth and made it gnaw the staff on which Solomon was leaning. When the staff broke down, the Jinns were convinced of the King's death and spread the information in the world.[2]

[1] Weil. *loc. cit.*, p. 279.   [2] Mirkhond, *loc. cit.*, p. 103.

CHAPTER XVII

The Prophet Elijah

Among the later Kings of Israel one of the most well-known
rulers was Ahab, the husband of Jezebel. Legends cluster
round this royal pair not only on account of their wickedness,
but because during their reign the famous prophet Elijah
the Tishbite arose. The latter waged a continual war against
Ahab and idol-worship, which had spread in Israel. In the

following two chapters we shall relate some of the many legends told of the Tishbite.

Many prophets arose in Israel after Moses, but the most popular prophet, round whom cluster numerous legends, was Elijah the Tishbite.   The prophet Elijah is represented in Jewish legend as the protector of the innocent, as the guardian angel bringing help to people in distress.   He is ubiquitous, and neither time nor space are obstacles when he is engaged upon his mission of bringing succour to the pious, and especially to the students of the Law and to the scholars.   The prophet is supposed to employ various means and to adopt many disguises.   In the Talmudic legends we see him disguised as an Arab,[1] as a rider upon horseback,[2] or arrayed in the Roman toga.   He appears as a Roman dignitary, especially when he is called upon to revoke an unfavourable law passed against Israel.[3]   One day, legend relates, Rabbi Shila was denounced to the government and accused of administering the law in accordance with Jewish legislature.   The Rabbi was in great distress, but Elijah, disguised as one of the court officials, suddenly came and bore witness in favour of Rabbi Shila and against the informer, so that the Rabbi was saved.[4]

Another Rabbi whom Elijah saved from death was Kahana. He was very poor and earned his living by peddling about with household goods.   A great lady, at whose house he used to sell his wares, cast an eye on him, and one day decided to force him to commit an immoral act.   Rabbi Kahana, preferring death to sin, threw himself out of the window, but the Prophet Elijah appeared just in the nick of time and caught up the Rabbi before he had reached the ground.

" Thou hast compelled me," said Elijah, " to hasten to thee over a distance of four hundred parasangs so as to be in time to save thee from death."

---

[1] *Berachoth*, 6b.   [2] *Sabbath*, 109b.   [3] *Abodah Zarah*, 17b.
[4] *Berachoth*, 58b; see also *Abodah Zarah*, 17b.

" I prefer death," said the Rabbi, " to a life of misery and a trade beset with perils wherein I am always running the danger of committing a sin."

The prophet gave Rabbi Kahana means which enabled him to change his occupation.[1]

Rabbi Bar Abbuha was another student of the law who suffered great poverty. One day he met the Prophet Elijah and complained to him that his poverty was so great and his worries so constant that he had no time to study the law as he should like to.

" Come with me," said Elijah, and he led the Rabbi straight to Paradise where he told him to spread out his mantle and gather the leaves growing in the abode of the blessed, which he could sell on earth at a high price.

The Rabbi did as he was bidden, and was about to depart with his precious load, when he heard a heavenly voice calling out:

" Rabbi Bar Abbuha is already anticipating his reward in the world to come by taking his share during his earthly life!"

When the Rabbi heard these words, he hastily emptied his garment of the celestial leaves he had gathered. He nevertheless sold his mantle afterwards at a high price on account of the wonderful fragrance it had acquired from the leaves of Paradise. The sum he thus realized enabled him to live free of care and to devote his leisure to the study of the law.[2]

As a guardian angel hurrying to save him from certain death and thus bring him help in his hour of need, the Prophet Elijah appeared to the famous Rabbi Nahum of Gimso. This pious Rabbi was one day sent by his co-religionists to Rome on a political mission. As a gift to the Emperor, the Rabbi was carrying a casket full of diamonds and precious stones. He had to pass the night in an inn, where thieves found out

---

[1] *Kiddushin*, 40a.   [2] *Baba Mezia*, 114b.

how precious were the contents of the casket. They robbed
the Rabbi of the jewels, replacing the abstracted gems with
common earth. Unaware of the substitution, Nahum continued his journey. When he arrived in Rome he offered his
gift to the Emperor. The casket was opened, and the anger of
the Emperor knew no bounds when it was discovered that it
contained nothing but common earth.

" Do the Jews perchance wish to mock me?" he exclaimed.
" Let their delegate be put to death at once."

The pious Rabbi never lost faith in God, but, as was his
usual custom, said:

" This, too, is for the best."

But behold, suddenly the Prophet Elijah appeared, wearing
the Roman toga and disguised as a court official.

" Your Majesty would do well," said the supposed court
official, " to test the qualities and the virtues of this earth.
It may be the same earth which their ancestor, the Patriarch
Abraham, once hurled against his enemies and which turned
to bows and swords. Your Majesty can test the virtues of this
earth against the enemy with whom the Romans are now at
war." Thus spoke the Prophet Elijah, and the Emperor
decided to follow his advice.

In vain had the Romans been besieging one city which was
still resisting their onslaughts. The Emperor ordered some of
the soldiers to throw a handful of earth from the casket against
the besieged city, and lo, the earth turned to swords and bows
which worked havoc among the enemy.

Convinced of the great value of the casket and its contents
which worked such wonders and were more efficacious than
Roman valour and Roman weapons, the Emperor loaded the
pious Rabbi Nahum with gifts and treasures and dismissed
him in honour.

When the thieves heard what had occurred, they filled
another casket with the same earth and brought it to the

Emperor as a gift. " Here is more of the earth which the Jew has offered to Your Majesty," they said.

The Emperor gave instructions to test the virtue of the earth the thieves had brought him, but it naturally proved to be ordinary dust, and they were put to death.[1]

When the Prophet Elijah does not immediately bring help to pious scholars in need, he at least inspires them with hope and confidence, making them look at life from a brighter point of view. Thus it happened in the case of Rabbi Akiba, whose romantic marriage to the daughter of a very rich man will be told elsewhere. Before he became a great Rabbi, Akiba had married the daughter of Kalba Shebua. As his daughter had married Akiba against his will, Kalba Shebua refused to have anything to do with the pair, and they consequently lived in great poverty. Once, on a very cold night, Akiba had managed to gather a little straw which he could offer to his wife as a bed to sleep upon.

" My dear," he said, " you have been brought up in luxury and comfort, and now I have neither food nor clothing to offer you, and only a little straw to lie down upon. I wish I were rich and I would place a golden crown upon your head. Be assured, however, that my love for you is great and that you are very dear to me. The privations you are undergoing for my sake are immense, but it will be my constant endeavour to prove myself worthy of your noble love."

Thus spoke Akiba, when suddenly there was a knock at the door. He opened the door of their miserable hut and beheld a poor beggar who was none other than Elijah in disguise.

" My friends," he cried pitifully, " my wife has been delivered of a child, and I have not even a bundle of straw in my hut to make a bed for her. For God's sake give me some straw if you can spare it."

---

[1] *Sanhedrin*, 108b–109a; see also *Hibbur Yafeh*, by Rabbi Nissim, p. 8b.

Turning to his wife, Akiba, who had been full of despair a moment ago, said:

" You see, my dear, there is even greater misery than ours in the world, and we must not lose heart."

He thus consoled himself and his wife, and their courage revived, which was exactly the end Elijah had wished to attain.[1]

The deserving and worthy poor to whom Elijah is supposed to offer his help are not always scholars or rabbis. The Prophet appears even to ordinary folk in the hour of dire distress, as long as they are pious and deserving.

THE SEVEN YEARS OF HAPPINESS

It happened once that a rich man had lost all his wealth and become so poor that he was compelled to hire himself out as a labourer so as to earn his bread for his wife and child. One day, when he was working in the field, the Prophet Elijah appeared to him, disguised as an Arab, and thus he spoke:

" My friend! It has been decreed that thou shalt enjoy seven years of happiness, wealth, and comfort, and thou hast only to tell me whether thou dost want these good years now or at the end of thy existence, as the seven closing years of thy life."

Thus spoke Elijah, but the poor man, taking him for an Arab sorcerer, replied:

" Go thy way, I have nothing to offer thee for thy witch-craft."

Elijah went away but came again three times and repeated the same question.

" I require nothing from thee," he said, " tell me only when thou dost wish these seven good years to come to thee."

At last the man replied:

---

[1] *Nedarim, 50a; Ketubot, 62b.*

" I will talk the matter over with my wife and ask her advice."

Elijah consented to wait for his reply till to-morrow. The poor man now went and told his wife of what had happened.

" Tell the man," said the woman, " to send us the good years at once, for the near is preferable to the far off."

The poor man followed his wife's advice, and when Elijah again appeared and repeated his question, the man replied:

" Let the seven good years come to us at once."

" So it shall be," declared the Prophet. " Go thou home and before thou reachest the gate of thy house the Lord will have blessed thee and sent thee good fortune."

The man went home and, to his great surprise, found that the Prophet's prediction had come true. His children had just informed their mother that whilst digging the ground they had found a treasure, and his wife was coming to meet him and tell him the happy news. The man thanked the Lord for the treasure he had sent them, and he also praised his wife for her excellent advice.

His wife now said unto him:

" We are sure of the grace of God for seven years, let us therefore practise charity all these years, feed the hungry and befriend the poor, perchance the Lord will continue His grace towards us when the seven years are over and send us further wealth or allow us to keep in our possession to the end of our days what he Has given us now."

Thus spoke the pious and good woman, and the husband approved her words. They practised much charity, and whenever they heard of a case where they could do some good they hurried at once to offer their help. Whatever they gave to the poor the woman made her little son write down in a book. Seven years passed, and once more Elijah appeared and thus he spoke:

" The time has now come for thee to return the gift I gave thee."

" My Lord," said the pious man, " when I accepted thy blessing I did so with the consent of my wife. Suffer me now, before I return the gift thou didst bestow upon us, to consult with my wife and to acquaint her with thy request."

Elijah gave his permission, and the man who was about to lose again his fortune went to tell his wife that the old man had come to take away what he had given them.

" Tell our benefactor," replied the woman, " that if he has really found people who are more faithful than we, who will guard better the treasure entrusted to them and make a better use of it, then we are quite ready to return the pledge entrusted to us."

The Lord hearkened to the words of the pious woman, and saw that she and her husband had performed good deeds and made a proper use of the wealth entrusted to them. He therefore continued to bestow His grace upon the worthy people, and allowed them to keep in their possession till the end of their days the wealth He had sent them through Elijah.[1]

THE PROPHET ELIJAH AS AN ARCHITECT

There was once a pious man, the father of five children, who was very poor. One day, when his distress was very great, for he had no food to give to his family, his wife said to him: " Go into the market, perhaps the Lord will send thee some help so that we may live and not die."

" How can I go?" said the poor man; " I have no friend to whom I can address myself in my need."

But the children, being hungry, wept and cried for bread.

" Go into the street," said the wife, " canst thou sit here and see how thy children are dying of hunger?"

---

[1] *Midrash Sutta, Ruth*, 4, 11; *Seder Elijahu Rabba*, p. 28; see also Kuttner, *Jüdische Legenden*, 2, pp. 31–33; Bin Gorion, *Der Born Judas*, Vol. II, pp. 225–226.

" I am almost naked," replied the man, " how can I go out into the street?"

Thereupon the poor woman took her own torn garment, threw it over her husband, and sent him out into the street. The poor man, not used to begging, stood in a corner and, lifting up his eyes to heaven, thus he prayed:

" Lord of the Universe! Thou knowest that I have no friend and have no one to whom I could tell my tale of distress and ask him to have pity upon me and my children. I have neither brother nor friend, and my starving children are crying with hunger. Have Thou therefore pity upon us and send us Thy mercy, and if not, be compassionate and take us away, so that we need no longer suffer."

Thus prayed the poor man, and God hearkened unto his prayers, and suddenly the Prophet Elijah appeared before him.

" Why art thou crying?" he asked of the poor man. The latter told him of his misery and distress and acquainted the Prophet with his tale of woe.

" Cry no more," said Elijah, " but come with me and do as I will tell thee. Take me into the market and sell me as a slave, and the money thou wilt thus receive will suffice for thy needs."

The poor man refused to accept such a sacrifice.

" Master," said he, " how can I do such a thing? Besides, the people here know that I am very poor and they will never believe that I am thy master, but will say that I am the slave and thou the master."

" Be not afraid," replied Elijah, " but do as I am telling thee."

The poor man, thinking of his starving wife and children, gave in and went with the Prophet to the market-place. The people at first thought that Elijah was the master and the poor man his slave, but the Prophet informed them that such was not the case. Thereupon one of the servants of the King passed, saw the slave offered for sale, liked his appearance, and decided to purchase him for his master. He paid eighty *dinars* for the Prophet and took him away.

" Take the money thou hast received for me," said Elijah to his supposed master, " go to thy starving wife and children and feed them; mayest thou never know either want or suffering; and may distress and misery never visit thee."

Full of joy the poor man hurried back to his wife and children to whom he brought food and drink. God blessed him, and he amassed a great fortune which he enjoyed to the end of his days. And neither he nor his children ever knew poverty or want.

In the meantime the Prophet followed the King's servant who brought the slave he had purchased before his master. The King had made up his mind to build a palace, and he was buying many slaves whom he employed to hew and carry stones and cut down trees and prepare everything for the structure.

" What canst thou do?" he asked Elijah.

" I am an architect," replied the Prophet, " and I can build thy palace."

The King rejoiced when he heard these words.

" If thou canst build me this palace, as I wish it to be built, within six months, thou shalt be free then, and I will reward thee royally," said the King. Elijah promised to give his new master satisfaction.

During the night the Prophet offered a prayer to God that He might let the palace be built instantaneously. Before dawn broke, a wonderful palace stood quite ready and complete. Great was the King's amazement when he saw the palace finished. but in vain did he seek for his slave to reward him. Elijah had disappeared. The King realized that it must have been an angel from Heaven who had constructed such a wonderful palace overnight.

Elijah now met the poor man whom he had helped in his need and told him what had occurred.

" I have accomplished," said the Prophet, " what the King had asked me to do. I built him a palace which is worth a thousand times more than the sum which he paid thee for me. I have thus enriched him, as I did not wish to cheat him when I let him purchase me."

The pious man, who was now no longer poor, praised the Prophet and thanked him for his timely help.

" Thou hast given back life to me, to my wife, and to my children," said he.

" Praise the Lord who showed thee grace," replied the Prophet.[1]

This legend has entered the Jewish liturgy, and under the title of *Ish-Hasid* (a pious man) is sung on Sabbath evening.[2]

Another characteristic trait of the Tishbite is his rigour practised towards all those he has relations with. He not only punishes the arrogant, the misers, and evil-doers, but he often rebukes his friends, the scholars, if they fail to come up to his standard of morality. Thus Elijah was in the habit of visiting a pious man. One day the man built a vestibule, constructing it in such a way that the supplications of the needy could be heard only faintly in the house, and immediately the Prophet ceased to be a visitor at the house.

Another story runs as follows: There were two brothers, one of whom was in the habit of attending first to the needs of his guests and servants and then to his own, whilst the other brother first looked after himself and only when his own needs were satisfied did he think of his guests and servants. Elijah frequently visited the first brother, but never honoured the second with his presence.[3]

In another instance he preferred one of two brothers who

[1] *Hibbur Yafeh*, pp. 24a–25a; Jellinek, *Beth-Hamidrash*, Vol. V, pp. 140–141; *Seder Elijahu Rabba*, p. 30; see also Bin Gorion, *loc. cit.*, Vol. II, p. 355.
[2] See Bin Gorion, *loc. cit.*, p. 363.   [3] *Ketubot*, 61a.

was in the habit of providing for his servants as for his own family, permitting them to eat of all the courses served at his own table. He did not, however, consider worthy of his visit the other brother who allowed his servants to eat abundantly only of the first course and only the remnants of the others.[1]

Just as he is in the habit of helping the pious and needy in their hour of distress, Elijah never hesitates to give a lesson, to rebuke, and even to punish severely the arrogant and the greedy, as the following story will show.

ELIJAH AND THE FARMER

There was once a rich farmer who possessed vast tracts of land and many fields, but required cattle to work his fields. Putting a considerable sum of money in his pocket, about 100 *dinars*, he set out to a cattle sale in the neighbouring town with the intention of buying oxen and cows. On the road he was accosted by Elijah.

" Whither art thou going?" the prophet inquired of the farmer.

" I am going to the town to buy cattle," said the farmer, who was not aware that the stranger was none other than the Prophet Elijah.

" If it please God, you should add," said Elijah.

But the farmer arrogantly replied:

" If it please God or not, it makes no difference. I have money in my pocket and I can do what I like with it."

" Quite true," replied Elijah, " but without luck." Saying this he went his way.

Arrived at the market town, the farmer selected the cattle he intended to buy, but when he put his hand into his pocket he discovered to his annoyance that he had lost his purse. He was compelled to return home and provide himself with other money. Remembering the stranger he had met and who

[1] *Ketubot*, 61a,

seemed to have brought him ill-luck, he went to another town and by another road so as not to meet the man. On the road, however, he again met Elijah disguised as an old man, and once more the stranger inquired of him whither he was going.

" I am going to buy cattle," replied the rich farmer.

" Say, if it please God," again said Elijah.

" What has it to do with God?" angrily replied the farmer. " I have money in my pocket and I will buy the cattle I require."

He had walked some distance when he suddenly felt rather tired. He sat down to rest awhile, fell asleep, and when he awoke his purse had disappeared. Amazed at his repeated ill-luck, he returned home to provide himself once more with money. For the third time he set forth on his journey, and for the third time he met a stranger who was none other than Elijah.

" Whither art thou going?" asked the Prophet.

" To buy cattle, if it please God," replied the farmer, who had now learned his lesson.

" Go in peace, and may thy journey prove successful." Thus spoke Elijah, slipping into his pocket the two purses the man had lost on his previous trips. When the farmer arrived at the market town he found two fine red cows which he decided to buy. When he inquired after the price, he was told that it was two hundred *dinars*.

" I have not so much money about my person," said the farmer. Thereupon he put his hand into his pocket to take his purse, and, to his amazement, he discovered the other two hundred *dinars* he had lost. He bought the two cows and also an ox, and later on sold the cattle to the King for a thousand *dinars*.[1]

The Prophet Elijah is supposed to be even more severe in

---

[1] See *Alphabetum Siracidis*, ed. Steinschneider, p. 17; Bin Gorion, *loc. cit.*, Vol II, p. 248, and notes, p. 356.

the case of the scholars and sages whom he censures or dis-
solves intimacy with them, as soon as they fail to come up to
his own moral standard. In the Prophet's opinion it is not
enough for the scholars and students of the law to obey liter-
ally the commandments of the law. They must also listen to
the categorical imperative of their conscience and do more than
merely follow the letter of the law. None of the Rabbis could
boast of such intimacy with the Prophet as Rabbi Joshua ben
Levi, and none did the Tishbite esteem so highly. During his
life-time he led the Rabbi into Paradise and showed him the
place he would once occupy among the blessed.[1] When Rabbi
Joshua, after the close of his earthly life, came to the abode of
the blessed in Paradise, it was Elijah himself who announced
to the inmates the advent of the new-comer. He went before
him calling out:

" Make room for the son of Levi." [2]

And yet, when the Rabbi failed to come up to the moral
standard Elijah had set up, he at once ceased to visit him. It
happened thus:

THE PUNISHMENT OF THE INFORMER

A man named Ulla ben Kishar, being sought by the officers
of the law, escaped to Lydda and took refuge in the house of
Rabbi Joshua. His whereabouts became known to the officers
of the law; they came to Lydda but failed to discover Ulla's
place of concealment. They demanded his surrender and
threatened to wreak vengeance upon the whole city of Lydda
if Ulla was not delivered to them. Rabbi Joshua now urged
the fugitive to give himself up to justice.

" It is better," he said, " that one man should die than all
the inhabitants of the city run the danger of being put to the
sword."

Ulla listened to these arguments and allowed the Rabbi

---

[1] *Sanhedrin*, 98a.   [2] *Ketubot*, 77b.

to hand him over to the officers of the law. After that event Elijah ceased to visit the Rabbi.

Greatly affected by the absence of the Tishbite, Rabbi Joshua fasted many days, and when at last Elijah once more appeared to him, he inquired after the reason of his absence.

" Why has my lord not honoured me with a visit for such a long time?" asked Rabbi Joshua.

" Because," replied the Prophet, " I will have nothing to do with informers."

The Rabbi quoted a passage from the *Mishnah* in justification of his conduct, but Elijah was not satisfied.

" This is the letter of the Law," he said, " enough for the ordinary man, but the really pious must do more, and thou shouldst have acted otherwise.[1]

A similar rebuke the Prophet made to Rabbi Baroka, to whom he proved that it is wrong for men to go by appearances. One day Rabbi Baroka was walking in the crowded market-place when he met Elijah. The Prophet revealed to the Rabbi his identity and they conversed together.

" Is there one among this crowd," asked Rabbi Baroka, " who is destined to occupy a place in Paradise?"

" Not one in this throng," replied the Prophet, " will occupy a place in Paradise." He had hardly spoken these words when a man, whose dress did not at all indicate a pious man, hurried by.

" This one," said the Prophet, pointing to the passer-by, " is destined to occupy a place in Paradise."

Greatly astonished, Rabbi Baroka accosted the man and entered into a conversation with him. He questioned him about his occupation and life, and the man replied:

" I am a prison guard, and I take great care to keep apart the men and women detained in jail, so that no opportunity is offered to them to violate the laws of chastity. I sleep myself

[1] *Talmud Jerushalmi, Terumot,* 8; *Genesis Rabba,* 94.

between the two rooms wherein the prisoners are kept, and I am particularly careful when a Jewess is brought to prison."

" How is it," asked Rabbi Baroka, " that thy dress is not that of a pious man and that thou dost not wear the *zizith* prescribed by the Law?"

" On account of my occupation," said the man, " I often have business with the authorities and I am a frequent visitor at court. It is better that they should remain ignorant of my origin and unaware that I am a Jew. I am thus able to find out whenever new and hostile laws against the Jews are planned. I immediately convey the information to the wise men and leaders of Israel, and they are enabled to take steps to make the authorities in power favourably disposed towards the Jews and to avert misfortune. At the present moment, I am hurrying to court, because I have heard that a council of the princes has been convened and that new and hard laws against the Jews are being planned." Thus spoke the man and hurried away.

Rabbi Baroka then understood that in spite of his appearance this man was doing a great deal of good quietly and unostentatiously and that he was worthy to occupy a place in the abode of the blessed and the pious.[1]

The Rabbi soon again met Elijah and once more conversed with him. Two men were just passing, and the Prophet, pointing to the passers-by, said: " These men, too, will occupy an honourable place in Paradise."

Curious to know the merits of the future occupants of Eden, the Rabbi took leave of the Prophet and hurried after the strangers. He questioned them and found out that their purpose in life was to cheer up and console all those who were a prey to despair and sorrow.

" We visit all those who are sighing and weeping," said the men, " those who are a prey to hopelessness or are suffering

[1] *Hibbur Yafeh.*

from illness. We cheer them up, console and encourage them, and make them look upon the brighter side of life. We make them forget what has occurred, the sorrow that is gnawing at their hearts, the despair that is gripping their souls, and the fear that is paralysing their thoughts and actions. With our comforting words and even jokes we drive away the shadows and call forth brighter visions." Thus spoke the men, and Rabbi Baroka once more understood that it is also possible to do good in a humble station, and even more perhaps than in an exalted one.[1]

THE LAWSUIT AND THE GIFT OF FISH

The Prophet Elijah was very severe in the case of Rabbi Anan. One day someone brought the Rabbi little fishes as a present. The Rabbi accepted the gift and asked the donor: " What can I do for thee?"

" I should like to bring a case before thee and would ask thee to act as judge in my lawsuit," replied the man.

" This I can no longer do," replied the Rabbi. " I cannot act as judge in a lawsuit thou art interested in since I have accepted a gift from thee."

" Well then," replied the litigant, " I no longer ask thee to serve as judge in my case. Take the fish, for a gift offered to a scholar is as meritorious as the firstlings given to the priest, and assign one of thy colleagues to act as judge."

Rabbi Anan sent the applicant to his colleague Rabbi Nachmann, requesting his friend to act for him, as he himself was not allowed, according to Talmudic law, to serve as judge. Rabbi Nachmann now imagined that the reason why his colleague was incapacitated from serving as judge was that of the litigant being a relation of his.

Although strictly just, he nevertheless treated the litigant with some consideration and felt favourably disposed towards

[1] *Hibbur Yafeh*; see also *Taanith*, 22a; cf. Bin Gorion, *loc. cit.*, Vol. II, p. 384.

him. The other party, noticing Rabbi Nachmann's friendly treatment of the opponent, felt somewhat intimidated and failed to plead as convincingly as he might have done under different circumstances. He lost the case as a result of Rabbi Anan's carelessness, although unintentional, both in sending a message to his legal friend and in not explaining fully the reasons why he could not serve as judge.

From that moment the Prophet Elijah, who had been both a friend and a teacher of Rabbi Anan, shunned him and refused to come near him for a long time.[1]

ELIJAH AND THE ANGEL OF DEATH

In several cases the Prophet, by his interference and advice, saved a pious man from the angel of death.

Once upon a time, there lived a pious scholar whose name was Rabbi Reuben. He had a son who was as pious and saintly as himself. One day the angel of death appeared to Rabbi Reuben and informed him that his son would soon have to die.

" Such is the fate of man," said the pious father, " and no mortal can do anything against it. If, however, I have found favour in thy eyes, and thou canst grant my request, allow my son thirty days respite so that I might have the happiness of seeing him under the canopy and married."

The angel of death consented to wait thirty days.

When the appointed time had drawn near, Rabbi Reuben arranged the wedding feast of his son for the thirtieth day.

On that very day, the son, who was on his way to invite the guests to the wedding feast, met the Prophet Elijah:

" Whither art thou going?" the Prophet asked the bridegroom.

" I am going to invite the guests to my wedding feast," replied the bridegroom.

[1] *Ketubot*, 105b; *Sanhedrin*, 113a; *Makkot*, 11a.

" Dost thou know," queried the Prophet, " that the time of thy death is approaching?"

" If such is the decree of the Lord," replied the pious son of a pious father, " I cannot oppose it. Am I greater than Moses, Abraham, Isaac, and Jacob, who, too, had to die?"

" My son," said Elijah, " I will give thee an advice. When the guests will arrive and you will all be seated at the wedding dinner, do thou not taste anything but watch the door. As soon as thou wilt perceive one disguised as a beggar, ragged, dirty, and dishevelled, know thou that it is the angel of death. Hasten to run and meet him, greet him in a very friendly manner, and, seating him beside thee, set at once food and drink before him. If he refuses, insist upon his partaking of refreshment." Thus spoke the Prophet Elijah and went his way, whilst the would-be bridegroom returned home.

He never said a word of what had happened, or of his encounter with the Prophet Elijah, but when he sat at the wedding dinner among the guests, a dirty and ragged beggar suddenly stood in the door. Immediately the bridegroom rose up, greeted him in the kindliest manner and insisted upon his sitting down and partaking of food and drink.

The angel of death, for it was none other, at first refused, but soon was prevailed upon to take a seat. He seemed to be eating and drinking like the other guests, and when he had finished he said to the bridegroom:

" I am the angel of death, and the messenger of God who has sent me to fetch thy soul. It had been lent to thee for a time, and now the Master claims it." Thus spoke the angel of death, revealing his identity.

" Grant me permission," said the son, " to inform my parents, and bid them farewell."

Rabbi Reuben thereupon came and began to supplicate the angel of death and to implore him to spare his son's life, whilst the son was weeping and kissing his father and mother.

THE YOUNG BRIDE AND THE ANGEL OF DEATH

But the angel of death remained adamant, although his heart had been somewhat softened.

" Let me go and bid farewell to my newly-wedded wife," begged the son.

The angel of death gave his permission, and the young husband hurried to his young wife, kissed her and informed her of what had happened.

" The angel of death has come to fetch my soul," he said. Fear and terror seized the young bride, but she was determined to plead and argue and fight for her spouse.

" Wait thou here," she said, " and let me go out and speak to the angel of death."

" Is it true," she asked the latter, " that thou hast come to take the soul of my husband?"

" So it is," replied the angel of death.

" Dost thou not know," asked the young wife, " what is written in the Law with regard to the newly-wed? It is written that he who marries a young wife is exempt from military and other duties, and is to remain at home a whole year so as to enjoy himself and be happy in the company of his young wife. Wilt thou now take the life of my husband, and give the lie to the Torah?"

Thus argued the young bride, for love and despair gave her courage and cunning. Somewhat taken by surprise, the angel of death, who had already been moved by the tears and supplications of the parents and had been touched by the kind treatment of the son, replied:

" I will go before the throne of God and present the matter to Him. He may have pity upon thy husband and grant him a new lease of life."

Spreading out his wings, the angel of death ascended to Heaven, where he found the angels Gabriel and Michael, and other ministering angels, praying the Lord to have mercy upon Rabbi Reuben, and to leave this son. The angel of death now

presented the petition of the young bride, and the Lord had
compassion upon her and upon the unhappy parents, and bade
the angel of death annul the decree of death against the son
of Rabbi Reuben. God then added seventy years to his life,
as against the seven days of the wedding festivities.[1]

The Maiden and her three Husbands

A similar story is told in the *Midrash Tanchuma*. Here it is
related of a pious and rich man who had a beautiful daughter.
She had already been married to three husbands, but every
time, on the day of her wedding, she lost them. She had made
up her mind never to marry again, when one day a cousin of
hers came to their house from a distant land. He fell in love
with his beautiful cousin and wished to marry her. The arguments of his uncle, who acquainted him with the terrible fate of
his predecessors, had no effect upon him, and the wedding
accordingly took place. Whilst he was standing under the
wedding canopy, the Prophet Elijah appeared to him and gave
him the advice to receive in a friendly manner the ragged and
dirty beggar who would soon appear and who would be none
other than the angel of death. The bridegroom did as the
prophet had advised him, and the result was that the pleading,
arguments, and tears of the young bride, who had already
suffered so much, touched even the angel of death. He himself
went up to Heaven and presented the petition, pleading for
mercy for the newly wedded pair. The Lord had compassion
and granted the request of the pious wife.[2]

This legend, to some extent, resembles the story of Sarah in
the book of *Tobit*, where, however, it is the power of Ashmedai
that is broken by some magic means and not by the efficacy
of prayer. The two tales again remind us not only of *Thousand*

[1] *Hibbur Hamassiot Ve-Hamidrashot Ve-Haagadot*, Venice, p. 1; see Bin Gorion, *loc. cit.*;
see also *Mélusine*, Vol. II, col. 573–574, French translation by Israel Lévi.
[2] *Midrash Tanchuma*, section *Haazinu*; *Kav Hajashar;* see also Tendlau, *Die Sagen der
Juden*, p. 108 ff., No. 28; cf. Bin Gorion, *loc. cit.*

and One Nights,[1] but also of the famous story of Savitri and Satyavan; one of the most beautiful episodes in the *Mahabharata*.

SAVITRI AND SATYAVAN

And hearing these words, Yama said: " The words that thou utterest, O fair lady, I have not heard from anyone save thee; I am highly pleased with this speech of thine. Except the life of Satyavan, solicit thou, therefore, a fourth boon, and then go thy way!"

Savitri then said: " Both of me and Satyavan's loins, begotten by both of us, let there be a century of sons possessed of strength and prowess and capable of perpetuating our race! Even this is the fourth boon that I would beg of thee!"

Hearing these words of hers, Yama replied: " Thou shalt, O lady, obtain a century of sons, possessed of strength and prowess and causing thee great delight. O daughter of a king, let no more weariness be thine! Do thou desist! Thou hast already come too far!"

Thus addressed, Savitri said: " They that are righteous always practise eternal morality! And the communion of the pious with the pious is never fruitless! Nor is there any danger to the pious from those that are pious. And verily it is the righteous who by their truth make the sun move in the heaven. And it is the righteous that support the earth by their austerities! And, O King, it is the righteous upon whom both the past and the future depend! Therefore, they that are righteous are never cheerless in the company of the righteous. Knowing this to be the eternal practice of the good and righteous, they that are righteous continue to do good to others without expecting any benefit in return. A good office is never thrown away on the good and virtuous. Neither interest nor dignity suffereth any injury by such an act. And since such conduct ever adheres to the righteous, the righteous often become the protectors of all."

Hearing these words of hers, Yama replied: " The more thou utterest such speeches that are pregnant with great import, full of honeyed phrases, instinct with morality, and agreeable to mind, the more is the respect that I feel for thee! O thou that art so devoted to thy Lord, ask for some incomparable boon!"

---

[1] Cf. Perles, *Monatsschrift*, Vol. XXIII, p. 123; Chauvin, V., *La Recension égyptienne des Mille et une Nuits*, Bruxelles, 1899, pp. 59–60; 116–118.

Thus addressed, Savitri said: " O bestower of honours, the boon thou hast already given me is incapable of accomplishment without union with my husband. Therefore, among other boons, I ask for this, may this Satyavan be restored to life! Deprived of my husband, I am as one dead! Without my husband, I do not wish for happiness. Without my husband, I do not wish for Heaven itself. Without my husband, I do not wish for prosperity. Without my husband, I cannot make up my mind to live. Thou thyself hast bestowed on me the boon, namely of a century of sons. Yet, thou takest away my husband! I ask for this boon: may Satyavan be restored to life, for by that thy words will be made true!"

" So be it," said Yama, the dispenser of justice, untied his noose, and with cheerful heart said these words to Savitri: " Thus, O auspicious and chaste lady, is thy husband freed by me! Thou wilt be able to take him back free from disease, and he will attain to success. And along with thee, he will attain a life of four hundred years. And celebrating sacrifices with due rites, he will achieve great fame in this world. And upon thee Satyavan will also beget a century of sons."

The Mahabharata (*Vanaparvan*, 49, 297: Roy's translation).

CHAPTER XVIII

The Prophet Elijah in the Kabbalah and in Moslem Tradition

The Prophet Elijah in Jewish mysticism—An angel descended from Heaven—Sandalphon-Elijah—The mission of Elijah—Elijah and John the Baptist—Elijah identical with Phinehas, the son of Aaron—The angel of the covenant—The chair of Elijah at the ceremony of the rite of circumcision—The forerunner of the Messiah—Armilaos and the Anti-Christ—Elijah in Christian legend—*The Book of the Bee*—Elijah in Mohammedan tradition—Elijah and El Khidr, the ever-young—The source of eternal life—Rabbi Joshua ben Levi and Elijah—The Prophet Elijah and the wandering Jew—The origin of this legend.

Whilst, however, the Haggadists consider Elijah as a man who had attained immortality, the teachers of the Kabbalah and of Jewish mysticism look upon him as a supernatural being who had never been born by woman. He is an angel descended from Heaven for the purpose of being useful to mankind.

When the Creator of the Universe made up his mind to create man, Elijah, one of the ministering angels, approached the Throne of Glory and thus he spoke: " Lord of the Universe! If it be pleasing in Thine eyes, let me descend to earth where I can be of service to the sons of men." Thus spake Elijah, whose name was really Sandalphon, or, according to other teachers of mysticism, Metatron.

The Lord thereupon changed the angel's name to Elijah, but some time elapsed before this benefactor of humanity was permitted to descend from the regions celestial, assume the shape of mortal man, and abide on earth. This happened in the days of King Ahab.

When Elijah had converted the world to the true faith and belief in the Eternal, God took him again to Heaven and thus He spoke to him: " Be thou now the protector and guardian spirit of My children and spread the knowledge of Me and the belief in Me in the whole world." [1]

This belief is derived from the fact that neither the father nor the mother of Elijah are mentioned in Holy Writ and that he ascended to Heaven, which had never happened to mortal man before.[2]

In the Talmud already Elijah is identified with Phinehas, just as in the New Testament John the Baptist was held to be Elijah.[3] In Mohammedan legend, too, Elijah is identical with Phinehas, the grandson of Aaron, the High-Priest.

In Kabbalistic and mystic lore Elijah is represented as the angel of the covenant, and hence the custom prevalent among Jews to set aside a chair for the Prophet Elijah at the ceremony of the rite of circumcision.[4] He is also supposed to be the fore-runner of the Messiah. Before the advent of the Messiah, he will subdue Armilaos or Hermilaos, the Anti-Messiah who may be compared to the Anti-Christ of Christian legend, and then introduce the true Messiah, the son of David, to Israel. He will then perform the miracle of resurrection.[5] He will slay Sammael or Satan, and then the era of peace, the messianic time, will begin, the principle of evil having been eradicated.

From the Jews the myths and legends about Elijah were taken over by the Christians and the Mohammedans. In *The Book of the Bee* it is related that when Elijah was born, his father saw in a dream that one was born, and that they wrapped him in fire instead of swaddling bands, and gave him some of that fire to eat. He came to Jerusalem and told the priests the

[1] *Yalkut Rubeni, Genesis,* ed. Amst., p. 9b.   [2] *Ibid.*   [3] *Matthew,* 11, 14.
[4] *Pirke de Rabbi Eliezer,* ch. 29; see Friedlaender's translation, p. 214, notes.
[5] *Monatsschrift,* Vol. XII, p. 289; see also Jellinek, *Beth-Hamidrash*; Buttenwieser, *Die hebräische Eliasapokalypse,* 1897.

vision that he had seen. The learned among the people said to him: " Fear not, thy son is about to be a fire, and his word shall be like fire, and shall not fall to the ground; he will burn like fire with jealousy of sinners, and his zeal will be accepted before God." [1]

Mohammed, as we have already pointed out, borrowed largely from the Jews and very frequently applied the legends told of one Biblical personage to another. In Mohammedan tradition, the Prophet Elijah is that mysterious never dying being known as El Khidr, the ever-young. D'Herbelot[2] relates that in the distant and nebulous East there exists a source of eternal life and youth. Whoever drinks of this source is sure of immortality. Mighty kings and rulers travelled to those distant and mysterious regions, but never were they able to reach the spot where the source of eternal life and youth is bubbling. They all failed, and only El Khidr succeeded in reaching the spot. He drank from the source of life and enjoys eternal life and youth.[3] When the Arabs came into contact with the Jews and their legendary lore, and heard of the legends clustering round the person of the Tishbite who never dies, they identified him with El Khidr. All that the Jews told of Elijah, Islam relates of El Khidr, and all the myths and legends current in Mohammedanism and related of El Khidr are transferred to Elijah. El Khidr and Elijah are thus identical. Thus the story of Rabbi Joshua ben Levi and Elijah is told in the Koran of Moses and El Khidr.

RABBI JOSHUA BEN LEVI AND THE PROPHET ELIJAH

For many days did the pious Rabbi Joshua, the son of Levi, fast and pray to his Creator that He would grant him the sight of the prophet Elijah. And lo, one day, Elijah indeed

[1] E. W. Budge, *The Book of the Bee* (Aneed. Oxon. Sem. Series, Vol. I, Part 2), p. 70.
[2] *Bibliothèque Orientale, s.v. Ab Zendeghian.*
[3] See Wünsche, *Ex Oriente Lux*; J. Friedlaender, *Die Chadhirlegende und der Alexander-roman*, Leipzig, 1913.

appeared to him and thus he said: " Is there aught thou dost desire of me? Speak, and I will fulfill it."

And Rabbi Joshua, the son of Levi, replied: " I am anxious to accompany thee in thy wanderings, so that I may see thy works in the world and thus learn great wisdom from thee and profit."

But Elijah replied: " Thou wouldst not be able to endure all that thou wouldst see, and it would be a great worry and trouble to me to explain unto thee constantly the reasons of my conduct and actions."

Thus spoke the Prophet, whereto the pious Rabbi replied: " My Lord, I promise thee that I will never ask or inquire, nor will I weary thee with questions concerning thy deeds. All that I long for is to accompany thee and witness thy deeds."

And the prophet Elijah consented and permitted Rabbi Joshua to accompany him in his wanderings, on condition that he should never ask any questions concerning the reasons of his deeds, or the signs and wonders he might perform. Should he disobey, then they would at once part company.

The two sallied forth and wandered about until they came to the house of a poor and needy man, who had nothing but one cow which stood in the court of his house. When the man and his wife saw the travellers, they at once rushed out to meet them, saluted them and invited them to their house. They offered them the best room in their house, placed before them what meat and drink they happened to possess and made them eat and drink and remain the night under their roof. When it was morning, the Prophet and the Rabbi arose to go on their journey, but before leaving the hospitable roof, Elijah prayed concerning the cow, and she died, and then they went their way.

Greatly did Rabbi Joshua wonder at this deed and he was faint at heart. He said within himself: " All the reward this poor man has received for the honour he has shown us was to lose his cow, that has been killed, and he has no other." Unable to restrain himself, he said to the Prophet: " My Lord, why didst thou kill this poor man's cow, he being a worthy man who has shown us much honour?"

Thus spoke Rabbi Joshua, and Elijah made answer: " Remember the condition I made, that thou shouldst take heed but be silent, hold thy peace, and ask no questions. I am quite ready to give thee the reason of my action if thou art prepared to separate from me." Rabbi Joshua, afraid of being dismissed by the Prophet, was silent and spoke no further.

They continued their journey, and after travelling the whole day came towards evening to the house of a certain rich man. The host, however, never turned to them to do them honour, and the two travellers sat in his house without either meat or drink. Now in the house of this rich but ungenerous man there was a wall that had fallen down, and he had to build it up again. In the morning Elijah prayed concerning the wall, and it was at once built up. Great was Rabbi Joshua's astonishment and trouble when he saw what Elijah had done. Remembering, however, the Prophet's rebuke, he restrained himself from asking any questions and kept his peace.

Thus they travelled all day, and towards evening came to a great synagogue. The seats therein were of pure gold and silver, and each man was sitting on his chair according to his rank and dignity. When they beheld the two wanderers, one of them said: " Who will give food and lodging to these two poor travellers?" Then another man answered: " There is no need; they will have enough with the bread and salt and water which they have brought with them hither."

The two waited for someone to invite them, but none of the men in the synagogue paid any attention to the weary wanderers. Thus they passed the night in the synagogue until the morning. When morning came the two travellers arose, and Elijah said to the men: " May it be the will of the Lord to make you all leaders and chief men of the community."

Thereupon the two continued their way, and Rabbi Joshua greatly wondered and his trouble increased, but once more he held his peace and said nothing. With sunset they reached another town, where they were received with kindness, joy, and cheerfulness. The two travellers were honoured, treated with great courteousness, and lodged in the finest house in the city. They ate and drank and passed the night in great honour. When morning came Elijah prayed, and thus he said: " May it be the will of the Almighty to make only one man among you a leader of the community."

No longer could Rabbi Joshua restrain himself when he heard these words uttered by Elijah.

" My Lord," he said, addressing the Prophet, " tell me now, I pray thee, the reason of thy strange actions, and acquaint me with the secret of all the works thou hast performed."

" As it appears to be in thy heart to separate from me," said the Prophet, " I will explain it all to thee and tell thee the secret of my actions. Know then that with regard to the cow of the poor man which I slew, I did it because it had been decreed that on that very day his wife should die, and I prayed to the Lord to accept the cow, his only possession, as a ransom. Through the woman, I foresaw, great good and profit will arise to the house and the man. As for the rich man whose wall I built up, know that under the foundation of the tumbled-down wall a great treasure lies hidden. Had I left the rich miser to build up the wall himself, he would have laid bare the foundation and discovered the treasure. The wall I have built will soon tumble down and will never be rebuilt again.

" As for the hard-hearted men whom I wished and concerning whom I prayed that there should be many princes, communal leaders, and chiefs among them, I did this because this will turn out to be an evil thing for them. Whenever there are many leaders there is a division in their counsels, and the place is destroyed and goes to ruin.

" It is for the same reason that I prayed concerning the just men who did us much honour that only one of them should be a chief man. It will be a benefit to them and their counsels and works will have unity, and they will be a happy people, for the spirit of division will not come among them; their counsels will not vary, and their plans will not be frustrated. Thus it is said in the proverbs: ' Through too many sailors the ships founder ', and ' Under the protection of one master a city stands firm '."

And Elijah continued: " I am now about to leave thee, but before parting I will tell thee something the knowledge of which will benefit thee. If ever thou seest a wicked man who prospers and upon whom the hour smiles, let not thine imagination entice thee, nor do thou wonder, but know that his fortune is for his hurt. If, on the other hand, thou seest a righteous and just man in trouble and in grief, pained and wearied, going about hungry, thirsty, naked, and lacking everything in this world, suffering greatly and visited by numerous afflictions, then again be neither angry nor provoked in spirit. Beware of letting thy imagination and thy heart delude thee to entertain the slightest doubt of thy Creator. Consider in thy heart and understanding that He is just and right, and that His judgment is right. His eyes are on the ways of men, and who shall say to Him: ' What doest Thou? '"

Thereupon Elijah bade farewell to Rabbi Joshua ben Levi and went on his way.[1]

Tabari relates the following story of Elijah:

Idolatry was general in the land of Israel when the Prophet Elijah appeared. The Lord had sent him to the city of Balbeck or Heliopolis for the purpose of persuading the inhabi-

[1] *Hibbur Jaffe*, pp. 4b–6a; Jellinek, *Beth-Hamidrash*, Vol. V, pp. 133–135; Vol. VI, pp. 131–133; *Seder Eliahu Rabba*, p. 36, § 4; *Serapeum*, XVII, 5; Wünsche, *Aus Israel's Lehrhallen*, Vol. I, pp. 127–130; see Zunz, *Gottesdienstliche Vorträge*, p. 138, note a.

tants to give up the worship of Baal, after whom the city was called. The Prophet preached against idolatry, which had spread among the Jews. The King of the Israelites, Ahab, who had at first believed the Prophet and been induced to reject Baal, soon returned to idol worship. Thereupon the Prophet prayed to the Lord, and He sent a famine upon the land which lasted three years. In those days none but Elijah had bread and many men died. Whenever people smelt the odour of bread, they said to each other: " The Prophet Elijah hath passed this way."

One day Elijah came to the house of an old woman who had a paralytic son named Elisha. Elijah gave bread to the old woman and healed her son. Henceforth the boy accompanied the Prophet. When the famine had lasted three years, Elijah and his companion appeared before Ahab, King of Israel, and thus he spoke: " For three years the famine has now lasted in the land, and thou hast been without bread. If thy god Baal can satisfy thy hunger it is well, but if not, worship the God of Israel, and I will pray to Him that He send thee help in thy distress." Ahab consented. Thereupon the idol of Baal was taken out of the city, and the worshippers invoked the heathen god. Their prayers, however, remained unanswered. Thereupon Elijah prayed to the Lord, rain fell, and the earth brought forth herb and corn. The people, however, soon returned to idol worship, and Elijah prayed to the Lord to take him away from the wicked generation. The Lord granted the Prophet's prayer, but Elijah is not dead, for he will live until the day when Israel shall sound the trumpet of judgment.[1]

[1] Tabari. I, 84.

The Prophet Elijah and the Wandering Jew

The legend of the Prophet Elijah, of his eternal wandering among men, may also have given rise to the legend of the wandering Jew. In Jewish legendary lore Elijah, the eternal wanderer, is active and benevolent. The messenger of peace, he encourages the irresolute, instructs those who are eager for knowledge, and brings succour to the needy. One day he will be the harbinger of salvation to the whole race of Israel. He has never tasted death, is omniscient and ubiquitous.

Mohammed, who drew very largely from Jewish sources, had heard of this legend of the eternal, immortal wanderer and represented him as a sage travelling since thousands of years, watching the eternal geological and social changes of the world and humanity, smiling at human ignorance and watching the march of events from the Pisgah heights of his age and travels. He is Khidr, the eternal-young. During the Middle Ages, the legend came to the Christians when it underwent a certain change. On the one hand, there was a constant desire of the Church to find as many witnesses as possible for the infallibility of the Church, whilst, on the other, hate of the Jews would not admit that the eternal wanderer is Elijah, particularly favourable to the Jewish race. He therefore became the wandering Jew, an eternal witness of Christianity. Called Cartaphilus, at first, he is soon changed to Ahasverus and condemned to bear witness to the Divinity of Christ.[1]

---

[1] See *Jüdische Zeitschrift*, Vol. V, p. 45–46.

CHAPTER XIX

The Romance of Esther, or the Jew-baiter and the Royal Favourite

The throne of Solomon—The King of Persia—Ahasuerus builds a new throne—The royal banquet—Great magnificence—The wealth of Ahasuerus—The copper vessels constructed by Nebuchadnezzar—The treasure at the bottom of the Euphrates—The holy utensils from the Temple—The royal gardens—The Jews as the guests of the King of Persia—The divine banquet in the future world—Customs at Persian drinking bouts—The huge beaker — New regulations introduced by Ahasuerus — The Lord waxes wroth—Beauty unadorned, or the disobedient queen—Jewish and Pagan feasts—The reasons of Vashti's refusal—The marks of leprosy—Punishment for her sin—The Queen's proud message—The advice of Daniel—Memuchan—The beautiful Jewess—Esther-Hadassa, origin of her name—The aged beauty—The portrait of Vashti—The conspiracy of the two Tarsians—The wealthy barber of Karzum—Haman becomes a soldier—The starving Haman and the generous Mordecai—Haman sells himself as a slave to the Jew—The sudden wealth of Haman—The ex-barber becomes vizier—Haman meets Mordecai—The image of an idol on Haman's breast—The bird who tried to dry up the ocean—The casting of lots—The days of the week plead in favour of Israel—The months of the year except the month of Adar unfavourable to Haman—The signs of the Zodiac—The Fishes alone are unfavourable to the Jews—Haman's denunciation—The objections of the King—The two cups of wine—The God of Israel has forsaken the nation—The royal decree—The St. Bartholomew Night of antiquity—Haman's arguments in favour of the annihilation of the Jews—The world will have peace only when the nation is destroyed—The indictment of Satan—The verses recited by the schoolchildren—The argument of Satan—The lament of the Torah—The weeping angels—The Prophet Elijah visits the graves of the Patriarchs—He implores Moses to intercede on behalf of Israel—Moses' advice.

THE ROYAL BANQUET

When Ahasuerus became king over Persia he gave instructions that the famous throne of Solomon be brought to him. Thereupon his counsellors and wise men said unto him:

" Why dost thou do such a thing, O King? Thou wilt surely not succeed."

Greatly surprised, Ahasuerus asked his wise men to tell him the reason of their fear.

" Know then, O mighty ruler," replied the wise men, " that one day Shishak, King of Egypt, captured Jerusalem and carried away the throne of Solomon, the son of David. The throne then came into the possession of Sennaherib, of Pharaoh Necho, and of Nebuchadnezzar, King of Babylon. But neither the kings of Ashur and Egypt nor the ruler of Babylon were ever allowed to seat themselves upon the throne of Solomon, for scarcely had they placed a foot upon the first step of the wonderful throne when the lion dealt them a blow. Thereupon Darius, thine own father, waged war against Babylon, and among the rich booty he carried away the famous throne and brought it to the city of Eilam in Media. Never, however, did thy father dare seat himself upon the throne of Solomon, the great King of Israel. Thy father, O King, was a wise ruler and a pious and god-fearing man, and if he was careful not to seat himself upon the throne of Solomon, why shouldst thou expose thyself to any danger?"

Thus spoke the wise men of King Ahasuerus. Thereupon the ruler of Persia sent for artificers from Tyre and Alexandria and bade them construct a throne similar to that of Solomon, King of Israel. This they did, but it took them three years to build the throne.

When the work of the throne was completed, Ahasuerus made a gorgeous feast for the hundred and twenty-seven rulers of the hundred and twenty-seven provinces of his mighty empire. All the grandees and nobles were seated upon couches of gold and silver set in with precious stones, and daily King Ahasuerus showed to his guests his vast treasures. The ruler of Persia boasted of his greatness and power and pretended that he himself had acquired all the vast wealth which was his personal possession. One day, however, one of the princes said unto his friends:

"In vain doth the King boast of his vast wealth, for it is not his personal property nor hath he himself acquired it. I will tell ye whence Ahasuerus hath his treasures. Ye know that Nebuchadnezzar, the mighty King of Babylon, had waged many wars, conquered many lands and carried away great booty and vast treasures. Now when Nebuchadnezzar felt his end draw near he was greatly reluctant to leave his possessions to his son Evil-Merodach. ' I will hide my treasures ', thought the miserly King of Babylon, ' rather than leave them to my son.' Now what did he do? He constructed vessels of copper wherein he placed his gold and silver and precious stones, and during the night sank the vessels into the River Euphrates. They remained at the bottom of the river until Cyrus came and gave permission to the Jews to rebuild their temple at Jerusalem. As a reward for his pious deed God allowed him to inherit and take possession of Nebuchadnezzar's vast wealth. One day, when Cyrus was crossing the River Euphrates, the waters suddenly separated and the King discovered the copper vessels containing Nebuchadnezzar's wealth. Such is the origin of the wealth of which Ahasuerus is now boasting."

The treasures which Ahasuerus was displaying to his guests were indeed immense, for the King of Persia was wealthier than all the kings of Persia and Media. Ahasuerus erected couches of silver and gold in the streets of his capital in order to let the whole world know how rich he was. All the vessels used at the feast of the King of Persia were not vessels of silver but of gold. When, however, Ahasuerus commanded that the utensils from the temple of Jerusalem be brought in, all the vessels in the palace changed in appearance; they became dim and lost their splendour, looking like lead when brought together with the sacred vessels of the temple. But not only to his princes did Ahasuerus offer a great feast. He also invited the inhabitants of his capital Shushan. The festivities took place in the royal gardens where wonderful trees bore delicious fruit and aromatic foliage wafted a fragrant smell. The pavement consisted of precious stones and pearls, and the guests were seated upon couches made of delicate draperies placed under the trees. Curtains of byssus and royal purple stretched from tree to tree, and servants hastened to do the bidding of the guests, for the King had commanded that every guest be allowed to follow his own inclinations. Walking through the royal gardens, Ahasuerus approached his Jewish guests, for whom separate tables had been set, and thus he said:

"Look at this wonderful scenery, at the golden couches, the pleasant trees and the aromatic foliage, and tell me whether your God will be able to offer you such a banquet in the future world?"

The Jews made no answer, for they thought in their hearts: "How stupid are the words of the King who does not realize the fact that all this scenery, the garden, the trees, the food and the wine are the handiwork of the Creator of the Universe." But when the King of Persia once more repeated his question, the Jews replied as follows:

"Know, O King, that the banquet which the Lord will prepare for the pious in the future world no eye hath seen it but God's. If the Lord, however, were to offer us a feast like thine, we should certainly feel ashamed and say: 'Such a banquet we have already partaken of at the table of Ahasuerus, King of Persia.'"

In spite of his vainglory and foolishness Ahasuerus was a tolerant monarch. He gave instructions to his servants to let every guest follow his inclinations in the matter of drink. Thus it was an old custom of Persia at drinking bouts to compel each guest to drain a huge beaker containing 15 eights and called *Pitka*. And when one of the guests said that he could not do it, the servants forced him to comply with the old custom,

though he lost his reason over it or even died. The guests
therefore at Persian wassails were in the habit of bribing the
butler so as to permit them to drink only according to their
respective capacities. The butler and other servants thus
grew rich. Ahasuerus, however, gave instructions that the old
Persian custom be ignored for once, and that each man should
drink only as much as he could or wished to.

The King also commanded his officers never to use a cup
more than once. The cups out of which the guests had drunk
were also to be kept by them as a royal gift. Moreover the
guests were to be served with drinks to which they had been
accustomed from their youth.

When Ahasuerus issued his famous order " to do according
to every man's pleasure " the Lord, however, waxed wroth.
" Villain," said He, " how canst thou do every man's pleasure
at once? This is only in the power of God to do. Tell me,
what wilt thou do if two men came to thee who are in love
with the same woman, both desiring to marry her? Canst thou
do according to both these men's pleasure? Or suppose that
two vessels are sailing from the port, one of them requiring a
north wind and the other a south wind. Canst thou satisfy the
two vessels at once and produce at the same time a wind that
was both northern and southern?" The Lord alone can
satisfy at one and the same moment the wills and pleasures of
many men, as it is said: " He will fulfil the desires of them
that fear him."[1]

Beauty Unadorned, or the Doom of Vashti

There is always a vast difference between the banquets
and feasts of Jews and the carousals of the pagans. Whenever
the former are gathered for the purpose of feasting on some
momentous occasion, they discuss the Law, the Haggadah or
the Halachah, or even a verse from the Scriptures. They sing

[1] *Psalm,* cxlv, 19.

hymns and praise the Lord. Not so the pagans, who indulge in prurient talk whenever they are of good cheer. Thus it happened at the festive board of Ahasuerus. The conversation began to turn on the subject of women, and Persians and Medians began to praise the charms of their respective women. Thereupon the " fool " Ahasuerus maintained that his own wife, who was neither a Median nor a Persian but a Chaldæan, excelled in beauty all the women in the world. In order to prove the truth of his assertions the King, in his drunken boast, consented to the request made by his boon companions. Vashti, his queen, was to appear unadorned and without any apparel before Persia's grandees and princes, so as to give them the opportunity of judging whether in reality her charms were such as described by her spouse, and whether she deserved the palm of beauty.

The Queen of Persia was not such a prude as to feel shocked at the order she received from her lord and master who had forgotten all dignity in his drunken fit. To appear naked in the company of men and to exhibit her charms to their gaze did not at all offend the moral sense of that queen of pagan antiquity. If the semi-nude is considered as *comme il faut* by the daughters of Eve after twenty centuries of Christianity, why should the nude have shocked the Queen of Persia, who, like her husband, really revelled in carnal pleasures? According to Jewish legendary lore, Vashti's refusal to obey His Majesty's command was due to other reasons than that of an outraged moral sense. When Vashti began to divest herself of her garments, ready to walk into the banqueting hall, she suddenly noticed that marks of leprosy and other diseases had become visible upon her forehead and her body. No puff, powder, or perfume could remove the marks of her disease, and Vashti was compelled to make a virtue out of necessity. Unwilling to acquaint the King with the real reason prompting her to disobey his command, she pretended that her action was dictated by pride and a sense of decency.

Vashti's disease was a punishment meted out to her on account of her sins. She had been in the habit of forcing Jewish maidens to spin and weave on the Sabbath, and often would she strip the innocent girls of their clothing. It was for this sin that she was commanded to appear naked before the King and his drunken guests. Persia's queen would have obeyed the command of her royal spouse and gladly offered her beauty to the gaze of men, but the Lord sent His angel Gabriel, who struck Vashti with leprosy and other diseases.

Thereupon the proud beauty sent the following message to her husband: " I am Vashti, the daughter of Belshazzar, son of the great and mighty Nebuchadnezzar, the proud monarch who laughed at kings and princes. Thou hast never been deemed worthy even to run before my father's chariot. Had my father been alive now, I would never have been given to thee as wife. Even the criminals condemned to death by my father were never stripped of their clothes and led naked to the place of execution. Thou art only a fool and a madman who has lost his reason in consequence of too much drinking. I refuse to appear before thy boon companions stripped of my clothing, and I do it for thine own sake. Knowest thou not, thou fool, that if they are charmed with my beauty, they will kill thee and take possession of me, whilst if they remain indifferent they will simply say that thou art a liar and a boaster."

Such was the message which Vashti sent to King Ahasuerus. The great ladies of the Persian aristocracy, jealous of the queen's beauty, encouraged the latter in her refusal and advised her to persevere and disobey the command of the King. At the advice of the Memuchan—who was none other than Daniel —Vashti was thereupon condemned to death. The Queen was an enemy of Daniel and hated him, because he had once predicted her father's death. Daniel again was hostile to the Queen because it was she who prevented Ahasuerus from permitting the Jews to rebuild their temple at Jerusalem.

The Beautiful Jewess

The Persian court thereupon decided to find a new queen for Ahasuerus, and Esther was chosen. Esther was also called Hadassa, or Myrtle, on account of her good and pious deeds which spread her fame abroad even as the myrtle wafts its fragrance in the air. She was also like the myrtle because just as the myrtle has a pleasant scent but a bitter taste, so Esther was pleasant to her own people, but proved bitter to her people's enemy, the Jew-baiter Haman. She was called Esther, which means the mysterious one, because she jealously guarded the secret of her origin and descent from King and Court. Esther, according to Jewish legendary lore, was not really beautiful, but had grace and a bewitching charm, and all those who beheld her deemed her worthy of becoming Queen of Persia. According to some Jewish legends Esther was seventy-five years of age and it was really a miracle that such beauty was hers that even at an advanced age she charmed the mighty monarch, his court, and his people.

Ahasuerus, it seems, had been regretting his former wife Vashti, and for many years had her portrait in his chamber hung over his bed. None of the maidens brought to him equalled Vashti in beauty and he could not forget her, but when Esther came, Ahasuerus at once forgot the daughter of Belshazzar whom he had put to death.

The Conspiracy

It was at that time that Mordecai, Esther's foster-father, discovered the conspiracy of two officials who had determined to poison the King. The two court-officials were Tarsians, and spoke in their native tongue, Tarsian, never suspecting that Mordecai, who was present, could understand them. They did not know that Mordecai was a member of the Sanhedrin, and as such could converse in seventy languages. The two conspirators somehow got wind that their plot had been discovered, and they speedily removed the poison they had put in the King's cup. But a miracle happened, and when the King had the contents of the cup analysed, lo! it was found that it contained poison.

HAMAN THE JEW-BAITER OF ANTIQUITY, OR THE WEALTHY BARBER

Mordecai the Jew had thus saved his life, but Ahasuerus forgot the service the Jew had rendered him and acted most ungratefully. Instead of rewarding the man who had saved his life, he raised Haman, with whose feelings towards the Jews he was well acquainted, to the highest honours.

Haman was a man of very low origin, and owed his rapid advance and his rise to such high honours to his vast wealth. He was a *nouveau-riche* who became a prince for no other merit than that of having acquired a vast fortune. In Jewish legend the story of Haman's early life runs as follows.

In those days there came to Persia a man named Haman, son of Hamdata. He was a direct descendant of Eliphaz, the son of Esau, the brother of Jacob, and a barber by profession. For twenty-two years Haman exercised his craft in the village of Karzum, but when his family increased and he had ten sons, his small earnings no longer sufficed to provide his wife and children with bread. Thereupon Haman left his wife and children at Karzum, and taking up his staff set out from his village in search of some more lucrative occupation. Thus he journeyed from town to town until he heard that the commander of the King's army was asking for volunteers to whom he promised good pay. Haman immediately sold himself as a soldier and joined the army. A battle was waged, the commander was defeated and his army dispersed. Many soldiers, among them Haman, escaped into the desert, where for many days they suffered the pangs of hunger and the torture of thirst. In vain did Haman implore his brothers-in-arms for a crust of bread and a drop of water. None of them would part with the little he possessed.

One day the former barber came across a Jewish officer, Mordecai by name, who took pity on the starving son of Hamdata and gave him a morsel of bread and a drink of water, sharing with him the little he had himself. Great was the gratitude of Haman and thus he spoke to Mordecai: " Thou hast saved my life, for without thy generous help, I would at this hour have died of hunger and thirst. I shall now be thy slave for ever and serve thee faithfully." Thereupon Haman took a piece of old parchment and pricking his finger with a thorn, dipped a small stick in his blood and wrote out a deed wherein he solemnly declared himself to be the slave of Mordecai who had saved his life.

According to some sources Haman wrote the deed of sale upon Mordecai's knee. In the meantime the King sent out another army and the general defeated the enemy. The mercenaries were now disbanded and Haman returned to the village of Karzum.

" It would be best for us," said the son of Hamdata to his wife Zeresh, " to leave this village and betake ourselves to the capital where, perchance, we might be able to earn our living among the inhabitants. Zeresh agreed with her husband and the family journeyed to Shushan, the capital of Persia. On the way fortune smiled upon the barber, for he found a vast treasure and thus entered Shushan as a very wealthy man. He bought houses, fields, and vineyards, and acquired many friends who honoured him and paid him homage on account of his great wealth.

The fame of the ex-barber, the new-rich, increased, for he was reputed to be the wealthiest man in the land, and the King himself honoured him greatly. Ahasuerus raised Haman, in spite of his low origin, above all his princes and counsellors, and made him his vizier and Prime Minister. He also commanded all his subjects to pay homage to Haman, and to bow to him whenever they met him. Thereupon Haman put the image of an idol upon his breast and wherever he passed the people of Persia bowed low and prostrated themselves before the descendant of Agag.

One day Haman passed the gates of the royal palace and beheld old Mordecai, the generous Jewish officer who had once saved his life and to whom—in an outburst of gratitude —he had sold himself as a slave. The vizier immediately recognized his benefactor, but was annoyed at his discovery. " If the old Jew," thought Haman, " recognizes me and refuses to bow to me, looking upon me as his slave, then I will kill him." Mordecai indeed refused to bow to Haman and to prostrate himself before the vizier, not, however, because he claimed the former barber as his slave, for he had never expected any reward for his generosity. He refused to prostrate himself before Haman because the latter bore the image of an idol upon his breast.

" I would pay homage to and honcur the man whom the King has set above all his princes," thought the pious and law-abiding Jew, " but never will I bow to and prostrate myself before the image of an idol and thus transgress the commandment of the Lord of the Universe." Thereupon the vizier determined not only to kill Mordecai, his former benefactor, the man who had shared with him his bread and water in an hour of need and thus saved his life, but also to exterminate the entire Jewish race. Haman's decision reminds us of the story of the stupid bird who had once made up its mind to dry up the ocean.

There was once a bird which had built its nest on the seashore. One day, when it returned after a flight in search of food, the bird found no trace of its nest and the young therein, for the waves of the ocean had destroyed the nest and swept it

away. Great was the wrath of the bereaved bird and it vowed
in its breast to wreak vengeance upon the cruel ocean.

" I will dry it up," cried the bird, and immediately set to
work to carry out its design. Filling its tiny beak with water
from the ocean it spat it out upon the sands and thus proceeded
to empty the ocean. Night and day did the bird work, but,
alas! perceived no progress. Then another bird came to the
seashore and was mightily surprised to see its friend engaged
upon a strange task.

" Tell me, sister," said the newcomer, " what is the task
thou art engaged upon?"

" I have sworn," replied the first bird, " to empty the
waters of the ocean, to turn the wide expanse of water to dry
land and change the sands upon the seashore into an ocean."

" Thou stupid bird," laughed the newcomer, " it is an
impossible task thou hast undertaken. Dost thou not know
that if all the creatures in the world were to forgather and help
thee in thy task, they would all perish in their enterprise, for
never would they succeed to empty the ocean." Haman knew
the story, but he spoke in his heart: " I am not a stupid bird,
nor are the Jews the waters of the ocean. If only the King will
give me permission, I will soon exterminate the entire race of
Israel and wipe out its memory for ever."

THE CASTING OF THE LOTS

Haman laid out his plan how to destroy the people of
Israel, but being an astrologer he determined first to cast
lots so as to find out the most favourable moment for his purpose. He began by casting lots with regard to the days of the
week. Thereupon the seven days appeared before the Lord
of the Universe and raised a protest. The first day said that
it was the day on which heaven and earth had been created
and these were to exist only as long as the nation of Israel

existed. The second day pointed out that it was the day on which Rakia had been created and on which the Lord had separated the celestial from the terrestrial waters, even as Israel had been separated from the heathen nations. The third day protested against the destruction of Israel, because it was the day on which the trees had been created, and did not Israel offer the tenth part of all fruit, giving it to the widow and the orphan? It also praised the Lord with branches of palm trees during the Feast of Tabernacles. The fourth day refused to lend itself to the destruction of Israel, because it was the day on which the celestial luminaries, the sun, the moon, and the constellations had been created. " Hast Thou not sworn unto the Patriarchs," pleaded the fourth day of the week, " that their offspring will be as numerous as the stars in heaven?" Then the fifth day came and protested against the destruction of Israel, because it was the day on which the birds were created. " Israel," cried the day, " is in the habit of bringing offerings unto Thee, and who will do so when the nation will be destroyed?" Thereupon the sixth day raised its voice in protest and reminded the Lord that it was the day on which He had created the sheep, and Israel is called both sheep and man.[1] Finally the Sabbath came and objected to the destruction of Israel because it was the day called " a sign between Israel and God ".[2] " Destroy me first, O Lord," pleaded each of the seven days in turn, " and then Thou mayest destroy the nation of Israel."

The seven days of the week having thus refused to aid Haman in his plans, each, on the contrary, having pleaded in favour of Israel, the Jew-baiter of antiquity decided to find out which of the twelve months of the year would favour his undertaking. Once more, however, he was baffled in his design. The month of Nissan appeared before the Lord and thus it pleaded: " Lord of the Universe! I have found grace

---

[1] *Ezechiel*, xxxiv, 31.   [2] *Exodus*, xxxi, 17.

in Thine eyes, for in me the Children of Israel were redeemed
from bondage, and now may it be Thy will to vouchsafe Thy
favour unto me and not to turn the month of festivity into one
of mourning." Thereupon the month of Jyar came and thus
it spoke: "In me Thou didst send down heavenly food,
Manna, to Israel in the desert and also hast subdued its enemy,
Amalek." The month of Sivan protested against the destruction of Israel because it was the month in which the Law was
given to the nation on Mount Sinai, the Torah in which it is
written: "It is a tree of life for those who observe it." Thereupon the months of Tammuz and Ab came and pleaded in
favour of Israel because the nation had already suffered enough
during these two months. Ellul pointed out that it was the
month in which the ruined wall of Jerusalem was rebuilt.[1]
Thereupon the month of Tishri came and reminded the Lord
that it was the month in which Israel celebrated the Day of
Atonement and the Feast of Tabernacles. It was also the
month in which Solomon once dedicated the Temple of
Jerusalem. The month of Heshvan was favourable to Israel
because it was the month in which the building of the Temple
of Jerusalem was completed. In Heshvan also Sarah, the
wife of Abraham, died, and the month implored the Lord to
remember Israel for the sake of the merits of Sarah. The
months of Kislev and Tebet pleaded that not only were they
the months in which the Kings Sihon and Og were once
defeated, but in which Israel celebrated the Feast of Lights,
and in which Esra arose and performed good deeds. Thereupon the month of Shebat came and reminded the Lord that
it was the month in which the Children of Israel once set out
to punish the tribe of Benjamin for the misdeeds of Gibbah
and the idol erected by Micah.

At last the turn of the month of Adar came, and the poor
month found nothing to say either in its own favour or in the

---

[1] *Nehemiah*, vi, 15.

favour of the Jews. Curiously enough Adar proved to be the only month of the year in which nothing had happened that could be interpreted in favour of Israel. When Haman's lot fell upon the month of Adar, he rejoiced greatly, for it was a month of misfortune for Israel. Haman knew that during the month of Adar Moses died and Israel remained like a flock of sheep without a shepherd. What Haman, however, did not know was that in Adar Moses was born.

Thereupon the Jew-baiter once more cast lots so as to find out which of the twelve signs of the Zodiac would prove favourable to his plan and unfavourable to Israel. The constellation of the Ram said that Israel was a scattered nation and never would the heavenly Father consent to His son being offered to slaughter. The constellation of the Bull said that Joseph had been compared by his father Jacob to the firstling bullock. The constellation of the Twins said that twins did Tamar bear to Judah who both walked in the ways of the Lord. The constellation of the Crab recalled the merit of Jonah. The Lion said that God being called a lion was not likely to allow the fox to bite his children. It was also under the sign of the Lion that Daniel was cast into the den of lions. The sign of the Virgin said that Israel was often compared to a virgin. It recalled also the merits of Chananiah, Mishael, and Azariah. The constellation of the Balance claimed in favour of the Jews that they obeyed the Torah which forbade unjust balances. It also recalled the merits of Job. The Scorpion said that Israel was also called a scorpion, and it also recalled the merits of Ezechiel. The Archer said that the bows of the mighty men will be broken when directed against the sons of Judah who are masters of the bow. The Goat pointed out that it was a goat that once brought blessing to Jacob, whilst the Water-bearer said that Israel's dominion was like a bucket, and it also recalled the merits of Moses. The Fishes alone appeared to be favourable to Haman and unfavourable to the

Jews. Haman interpreted them as meaning that the Jews would be swallowed up like fishes.

Thereupon Haman urged King Ahasuerus to give his royal consent to a general massacre of the Jews. When Haman finished his long speech of accusation, Ahasuerus, who had listened very attentively, said: " Your advice to exterminate the Jews may be very good, and indeed it is good, but I am afraid lest their God destroy me even as He did destroy the Kings of old when they ventured to wage war against Israel."

" Your Majesty," replied Haman, " need not fear any longer the God of Israel, for He is old and weak, and His power is no longer what it used to be. Besides, the Children of Israel have sinned, and their God has abandoned them and no longer vouchsafes His favours unto them."

Many more objections did the ruler of Persia raise against Haman's arguments, but the Jew-baiter of old had a ready answer to everything.

" If Your Majesty," he said, " were to present to a Jew two cups of wine into one of which a fly had fallen, whilst the King himself had taken a sip out of the other, and bid the Jew drink out of one of the cups, then he would unhesitatingly choose the cup into which the fly had fallen rather than touch that out of which Your Majesty has drunk. Can Your Majesty have any pity with such a people?"

Ahasuerus still hesitated, for he feared the wrath of the Lord who had once destroyed the Kings Sihon and Og and all the rulers of Canaan. Thereupon the King summoned his counsellors and wise men and asked their opinion on the matter. The Persian grandees were inclined to dissuade Ahasuerus from following Haman's advice, for they, too, feared the anger of the Lord who would certainly wreak vengeance on the enemies of His chosen race.

" Chosen race!" mocked Haman, " had their God really loved the Jews, He would not have allowed the mighty Nebu-

chadnezzar to destroy the Temple of Jerusalem, and lead the
people into the Babylonian captivity. I tell ye, that ye need
no longer fear the anger of the God of Israel who has forsaken
the nation." Haman furthermore offered vast sums to the
King of Persia to compensate him for the loss of revenue
derived from taxes paid by the Jews. The heathen sages and
wise men ultimately agreed to Haman's plan, and the Persian
monarch yielded. He gave his signature to a sort of St. Bartholomew night of antiquity, allowing the massacre of the
Jews.

The Decree

Haman now called his scribes and dictated unto them a
decree which he issued to all the heads and princes of the
nation concerning the annihilation of the Jews. Among other
things the Jew-baiter informed the rulers of the provinces
that the world would have rest only when the whole of Israel
was destroyed, men, women, and children.

" The great eagle of Israel," ran the decree, " had stretched
out his pinions over the whole world, and neither bird nor
beast could withstand him. Then Nebuchadnezzar, the great
lion, dealt him a blow and plucked out his feathers, and the
world enjoyed rest for a while. We must not, however, permit
the eagle to let his feathers grow and to gather strength, but
lay snares to him and prevent him from returning to his eagle's
eyrie. It would be useless to destroy only the men, to carry
them into exile or to assign to them another land. If the world
wishes to enjoy tranquillity, then the entire nation of Israel
must be wiped out."

Another decree was sent out by Ahasuerus himself wherein
the King accused the Jews of being presumptuous, ungrateful,
and a stumbling-block in all times. In accordance, therefore,
with the consent of the Satraps and Princes, the King had
resolved to extirpate the Jews. The decree, declared the King

of Persia, was an irrevocable resolution according to the laws of the Persians and Medes.

THE INDICTMENT OF SATAN

Haman left the court full of jubilation, whilst Mordecai, who had learned all that had occurred, was in a state of despair. On his way Mordecai met three Jewish boys coming from school, and he asked them to tell him what verse from Scripture they had studied to-day.

The first of the children replied: " Be not afraid of sudden fear, neither of the desolation of the wicked, when it cometh."[1]

The second boy had studied the following verse: " Let them take counsel together, but it shall be brought to naught." [2]

The third boy had learnt the following verse: " And even to old age I am He." [3]

When Mordecai heard these verses recited by the school-children, he looked upon it as a good omen and was comforted.

" Good news has been announced to me by the school-children," he said to Haman when he met him.

" Is that so?" replied Haman; " then they shall be the first to feel my hand."

Mordecai's prayers almost induced the Lord to have mercy upon Israel, but Satan soared up before the Throne of God and indicted the Jews. When the Tempter saw that the Jews were repenting of their sins and praying to the Lord to save them from destruction, he rushed up to heaven, and standing before the Throne of Glory raised his voice of accusation against Israel.

" Lord of the Universe," argued the accuser, " do not be swayed and influenced by the prayers and lamentations of the nation of Israel, for such has always been their way. When they are left in peace they forsake Thee, but when a calamity

---

[1] *Prov.*. iii, 25.   [2] *Isaiah*, viii, 10.   [3] *Isaiah*, xlvi, 4.

threatens them they at once turn to Thee and plead for mercy. It is not out of love for Thee that they are now repenting and mending their ways, but because they are frightened of the doom that awaits them. It is not love of Thee but fear of Haman that has caused them to turn good and pious. Forty-eight prophets and seven prophetesses have in vain preached to that obstinate nation but it never heeded the words of wise counsel. Now that the Jews have suddenly been informed of the decree issued against them, they are turning to Thee and praying for mercy and divine intervention. Verily, such a nation does not deserve Thy divine mercy. Remember, O Lord, that thousands of these Jews never hesitated to feast at the table of Ahasuerus, although Mordecai had implored them to abstain."

"And who," replied the Lord, "will sing my praises, if I destroy the nation of Israel?"

"Heaven and earth, Thy creations, will praise Thee in all eternity," said Satan.

When the Torah saw that Israel was indeed doomed to destruction, she dressed in black, as a sign of mourning, and raised a bitter wail, and her lamentations resounded through the seven heavens. The angels in heaven, too, shed tears of pity and pleaded for Israel.

"Lord of the Universe," cried the angels of mercy, "if Thou dost destroy the nation of Israel, then destroy us too." And when the sun and the moon heard the bitter cries of the angels they grew dark and withheld their light from the world.

The loud wailings of the angels and the bitter cry of the Torah touched the heart of the Prophet Elijah. The Tishbite hastened to Hebron, where the Patriarchs lie buried, and he called aloud: "Awake, ye sleepers! know ye not that the sun and the moon, heaven and earth and the angels in heaven are weeping and lamenting because your children are to be exterminated? They have forfeited their life on account of their

sins. How can ye sleep in peace and tranquillity! Arise, ye
just and pious men, and intercede for Israel."

Elijah also hastened to the graves of the prophets and to
that of Moses and cried in despair: " O faithful shepherd,
an edict of annihilation has just been issued against thy flock!"
Thereupon Moses asked:

" How has the decree been sealed, with wax or with blood?"

" With wax," replied Elijah.

" Then there is still hope," said the son of Amram.

Moses thereupon asked Elijah whether there were any
saints in Israel in the present generation, to which the Tishbite
replied that there was only one saint among them, namely
Mordecai.

" Then go and tell Mordecai," said Moses, " to pray to
the Lord, whilst the saints and just men who have departed
will unite their prayers with his and thus avert the calamity
that is threatening the nation." [1]

---

[1] The entire chapter is based on the following sources: *Babylonian Talmud, Megilla,*
10b ff.; *Pirke di Rabbi Eliezer,* Ch. 49; *Josippon,* ed. Breithaupt, Gotha, 1707, II, pp. 77–84;
Midrash Esther Rabba; Midrash Lekach Tob, ed. Buber; *Midrash Abba Gorion,* Jellinek,
Beth-Hamidrash, Vol. I, pp. 1–18; *Sifra d'Agadatha,* ed. Buber, 1880; *Targum Sheni to
Esther;* cf. also M. Gaster, *The Oldest Version of Midrash Megillah,* in G. A. Kohut, *Semitic
Studies,* p. 174 ff.; see also Lewner, *Kol Aggadot,* Vol. IV, pp. 87–104.

CHAPTER XX

Mordecai's Dream
and the Downfall of Haman

Mordecai's strange dream—The two dragons—the small nation—The fountain separating the fighting dragons—Mordecai's dream as related in the *Apocrypha*—Esther's prayer—Fast day and festival—Esther appears before the King—Why Esther invited the King and Haman to her banquet —The jealousy of the King—Haman and his friends—The advice of Zeresh —The gallows for the Jews—A sleepless night—The despair of the Jews— Esther has turned traitress to her people—Haman's threat to put the Jewish infants to death—The suspicions of Ahasuerus—The book of records— Shamshai, the confidential secretary—The mysterious voice—Mordecai's reward—Haman's pleading—The vizier turns barber—The Jew-baiter's daughter—Her suicide—The end of the vizier—Harbonah's denunciation —The new decree of the King—The story of Haman in Mohammedan legend—The Feast of Purim—Albiruni and Makrizi.

MORDECAI'S DREAM

When Esther heard from her attendants that her foster-father had appeared in the streets of the capital in sackcloth and ashes, she was greatly alarmed. She immediately sent Hathach, who was none other than Daniel, to find out the cause of Mordecai's mourning. Mordecai informed Esther of what had taken place and of the impending calamity threatening the nation of Israel. He further said to Hathach, Esther's messenger:

" Tell Esther to intercede on behalf of our people, for God has already shown me the future in a dream, and I know that the plan of our enemies will be frustrated if my foster-daughter pleads before the King. If Esther asks thee what is that dream, then answer her as follows:

" In the second year of the reign of Ahasuerus, in the capital of Shushan, Mordecai had a dream. And lo! there was a terrible earthquake and a mighty uproar and tumult in heaven and upon earth. And behold! in the uproar and tumult two dragons were fighting and the noise they made was terrible. And great fear and terror seized the nations of the earth, and they fled before the uproar and scattered themselves on all sides. And behold! there was a small people among the nations of the world, and all the other nations arose against that small people and tried to destroy it and to wipe out its memory from the land. And on that day there was darkness and obscurity for all the inhabitants of the earth, and the small nation was in dire distress. And it cried to the Eternal and prayed to God for its life. And the two dragons were fighting one against the other with great cruelty, but there was none to separate them. And behold! A small fountain issued forth from between the two dragons and separated them. And the fountain grew bigger and bigger until it became a mighty stream flooding the world and discharging its roaring waves over the earth even like the mighty ocean. Thereupon the sun rose up and shed its light over the whole world; then the small nation arose and became great, whereupon peace and truth reigned supreme upon earth and the world was at peace.

" Tell Esther," continued Mordecai, " that the interpretation of my dream is quite clear. The two dragons are Haman and myself, and the nations of the world have risen up to destroy Israel. The fountain of water is the fountain of help from which the people of Israel will draw as soon as it will repent and return to the Lord. The sun is Esther herself whom the King has taken to wife and made her queen in the place of Vashti. It is Esther's duty to go to the King and plead on behalf of her people." [1]

[1] *Esther Rabba; Yalkut Shimeoni, Esther*, Ch. 4; Jellinek, *Beth-Hamidrash*, Vol. V, pp. 1–8; Wünsche, *Aus Israels Lehrhallen*, Vol. I, pp. 149–160; see also E. Kautzsch, *Die Apocryphen und Pseudoepigraphen*, Tübingen, 1900, Vol. I, pp. 193–212, and Ryssel's Introduction, pp. 193–200; P. de Lagarde, *Hagiographa Chaldaice*, 1873, pp. 362–365; A. Merx, *Chrestomathia Targumica*, 1888, pp. 154–164.

It will be interesting to compare the Midrash relating Mordecai's dream with the additions found in the LXX, known as the *Apocrypha*.

2. In the second year of the reign of Artaxerxes the great, in the first day of the month Nisan, Mardocheus the son of Jairus, the son of Semei, the son of Cisai, of the tribe of Benjamin, had a dream;

3. who was a Jew, and dwelt in the city of Susa, a great man, being a servitor in the king's court.

4. He was also one of the captives, which Nabuchodonosor the king of Babylon carried from Jerusalem with Jechonias king of Judea; and this was his dream:

5. Behold a noise of a tumult, with thunder, and earthquakes, and uproar in the land:

6. and, behold, two great dragons came forth ready to fight, and their cry was great.

7. And at their cry all nations were prepared to battle, that they might fight against the righteous people.

8. And lo a day of darkness and obscurity, tribulation and anguish, affliction and great uproar, upon earth.

9. And the whole righteous nation was troubled, fearing their own evils, and were ready to perish.

10. Then they cried unto God, and upon their cry, as it were from a little fountain, was made a great flood, even much water.

11. The light and the sun rose up, and the lowly were exalted, and devoured the glorious.

12. Now when Mardocheus, who had seen this dream, and what God had determined to do, was awake, he bare this dream in mind, and until night by all means was desirous to know it.

Then Mardocheus said, God hath done these things

5. For I remember a dream which I saw concerning these matters, and nothing thereof hath failed.

6. A little fountain became a river, and there was light, and the sun, and much water: this river is Esther, whom the king married, and made queen:

7. and the two dragons are I and Aman.

8. And the nations were those that were assembled to destroy the name of the Jews:

9. and my nation is this Israel, which cried to God, and were saved: for the Lord hath saved his people, and the Lord hath delivered us from all those evils, and God hath wrought signs and great wonders, which have not been done among the Gentiles.

10. Therefore hath he made two lots, one for the people of God, and another for all the Gentiles.

11. And these two lots came at the hour, and time, and day of judgment, before God among all nations.

12. So God remembered his people, and justified his inheritance.

13. Therefore those days shall be unto them in the month Adar, the fourteenth and fifteenth day of the same month, with an assembly, and joy, and with gladness before God, according to the generations for ever among his people.[1]

ESTHER'S PRAYER

For a long time Esther resisted Mordecai's request urging her to intercede on behalf of Israel. Hathach had in the meantime been killed by Haman, and the archangels Michael and Gabriel came therefore to act as messengers from Mordecai to Esther and back again. Esther yielded in the end, but made a request to Mordecai to proclaim a fast on her behalf. Although it happened to be Passover, Mordecai consented and decided to transgress the law which forbids fasting on holidays and festivals.

[1] *The Apocrypha, Esther*, Ch. XI and Ch. X.

Arrayed in silken garments and decked out with diamonds and pearls, but with a heavy heart, Esther betook herself to the monarch of Persia to plead for her people. Before proceeding on her way, Esther uttered a long prayer to the God of her fathers.

" God of Abraham," she sobbed, " of Israel and Jacob, and God of my ancestor Benjamin, Thou art a great God. If I now dare to go and appear uninvited before that ' foolish ' monarch it is not because I consider myself to be without fault or blemish. I do this so that Israel may not be cut off from the world. The whole world has been created for the sake of Israel, and if this nation were to cease to exist, who will exclaim before Thee thrice daily ' Holy, Holy, Holy '? Thou who once didst save Chananiah, Mishael, and Azariah out of the burning furnace and Daniel out of the den of lions, save me from the wrath of that foolish King whom I am now going to approach. For the sake of Abraham protect now his beloved children and call Haman to account for the evil he intends to do unto us. I am now going to the King to plead for my people, but I implore Thee, O God, to send Thy angel of compassion with me and let Thy favour and grace be my companions. May it be Thy will to put the charm of Jacob into my mouth and the grace of Joseph upon my tongue. O Lord, Thou who art called merciful and gracious, lead us out of distress. For the sake of the Patriarchs, Abraham, Isaac, and Jacob, may it be Thy will that my request be not left unfulfilled nor my petition be turned aside."[1]

---

[1] Cf. Jellinek, *ibid.*; Kautzsch, *ibid.*; *Midrash Megillat Esther.*

ESTHER APPEARS BEFORE THE KING

Thereupon Esther, accompanied by two of her faithful maids, betook herself to the royal palace. She entered the inner apartments and soon found herself, though uninvited, in the presence of the ruler of Persia. When Ahasuerus suddenly beheld Esther he waxed very wroth, for the Queen had thus acted against the etiquette of the Persian court, and according to the laws of the Persians and Medes she had incurred the penalty of death. Esther was greatly frightened when she noticed the anger of the King reflected upon his countenance, but the Lord had pity with the poor orphan and increased her grace and beauty so that she found favour in the eyes of Ahasuerus. The King hastily descended from his throne and hurried to meet his beloved wife.

" Esther," he called, " why art thou trembling? Art thou not my beloved wife? Woe unto the man who will dare to do thee harm." When the royal servants heard these words uttered by their master, they refrained from laying hands upon Esther, although she had transgressed the laws of Persia by appearing uninvited in the presence of the King.

Thereupon the King inquired after the cause which had prompted Esther to take such an unprecedented step, to which Esther replied that she had come to invite the King and Haman to a banquet she had prepared. Esther did this for several reasons. " When Haman hears," she said unto herself, " that he has been invited to my banquet together with the King, he will no longer think of speaking ill of my people, and of exciting the King's anger against Israel. He will also cease doing harm to my faithful servants even as he has put to death Hathach who served me as messenger, carrying my messages to Mordecai."

Esther also thought that when the Children of Israel will hear that all that the Queen had done for them was merely to

invite the King and Haman to a banquet, they will lose faith
in her and no longer expect anything from her intervention.
" Esther has abandoned us," they will say, " and it will be
best for us no longer to count upon the help of mortals but
pray to the Lord to save us."

Esther had also another purpose in mind when she invited
the King and Haman to her banquet. " When my royal husband sees," thought the Queen, " that I have invited only himself and Haman to my banquet, he will grow jealous of Haman.

" ' Why,' he will ask in his heart, ' did the Queen invite
only Haman to her banquet? No doubt she is in love with
him and wishes to see him near her. I will cast him down
from his exalted position and then Esther will no longer love
him.' " Such were Esther's reasons for asking the King and
Haman to honour her with their presence at the banquet she
had prepared.

During the banquet the King told Esther to ask him for
whatever favour she liked except the permission to rebuild
the Temple of Jerusalem, for he remembered the promise he
had given to Geshem the Arab, Sanballat and Tobiah, never,
to permit the Jews to rebuild their Temple. Esther, however,
replied that she asked for nothing except the honour of seeing
the King and Haman at another banquet which she would
prepare for them on the morrow. Ahasuerus wondered greatly
at the Queen's strange request, but he said nothing and promised to come.

Haman returned home greatly elated and in high spirits.
He summoned his 365 friends and advisers, and his wife
Zeresh, and boasted to them of his greatness and the many
honours heaped upon him.

" Great is my wealth," proudly said the Jew-baiter of
antiquity, " and all the princes of the Empire are paying
homage unto me. All my sons are governors of provinces,
whilst Shamshai, my son, is confidential secretary and private

reader to our royal master. Even the Queen honours me above all the princes and grandees, for, besides the King himself, I am the only guest she has invited to her banquet." His only sorrow was to see Mordecai the Jew still alive. His friends wondered why he the mighty minister and favourite of the King did not simply kill the contemptible Jew.

Thereupon Zeresh said: " It is all very well for ye to say: ' Kill the Jew,' but have ye forgotten Mordecai's race and nationality? He is a son of that race whom neither water or fire, nor hunger or sword ever affect. Have you not heard what miracles the God of that people worked in favour of Chananiah, Mishael, and Azariah whom he saved out of the fiery furnace? Remember Daniel, whom the God of Israel saved out of the den of lions, and Joseph the son of Jacob whom he delivered from gaol and raised to be King over the land of Egypt. Remember their hero Samson who killed many more Philistines in the moment of his death than he had ever killed when he was alive. I advise thee therefore, O my husband, to decree death by hanging over Mordecai, for in all the history of the Jews I know of none of them whom their God had saved from such a death." Thus spoke Zeresh, and her advice pleased her husband well. Haman determined to put an end to Mordecai's life by hanging him on a tall tree. He immediately gave the necessary instructions to his servants, and during the night the gallows upon which Mordecai was to be strung up was speedily made ready.

A Sleepless Night

That night was a sleepless one for many people in Shushan, the capital of Persia. It was a sleepless night for Mordecai and his fellow Jews. They had heard of Esther's conduct and knew that she had merely invited the King and Haman to her banquet. Ignoring the real aim and purpose of the Queen, the Jews concluded that Esther had abandoned their cause and made friends with their enemy.

" Alas," they cried, " our hope has proved futile. We put our trust in our sister who is in an exalted position and hoped that she would plead for us and save us from destruction, but she has turned traitress."

Great was the distress of the Jews of Shushan, and they turned against Mordecai, accusing him of being the cause of their misfortune.

" Hadst thou not been so obstinate," they cried, " and consented to bow to Haman and pay him homage, our lives and the lives of our wives and children would at this moment not have been in danger."

It was a sleepless night for Esther, for with an aching heart she was busy preparing the banquet to which she had invited her royal spouse and Haman.

It was also a sleepless night for Haman. He remembered his threat, first to put to death the infants and little children of Israel, and decided to carry out this threat at once. Accompanied by a regiment of soldiers, he visited the Synagogue where the children were assembled, reading the Holy Law, weeping and praying. The Jew-baiter commanded his soldiers to count the children and there were twenty-two thousand of them. Haman gave instructions to put the innocent victims in irons and keep them prisoners until dawn when they would be led to the place of execution.

It was also a sleepless night for the King of Persia. Ahasuerus could not forget the fact that the Queen had invited no other guest to keep him company except Haman. He thought in his heart: " Who knows, Esther and her lover Haman are perhaps plotting to kill me and Haman hopes to become King in my place. I wonder whether there is one among my courtiers faithful enough to me to reveal unto me the conspiracy." Thereupon the King fell asleep and had a terrible dream. He saw his vizier bending over him, holding a sword in his hand and ready to kill him. Ahasuerus awoke with a start and was greatly frightened. He thereupon commanded his confidential secretary and reader to bring him the book of records and read out aloud all the important events which had occurred during his reign. The secretary was none other than Shamshai, Haman's son, and he read aloud until he came to the chapter relating the incident how Mordecai the Jew had discovered a conspiracy and saved the King's life. Shamshai was about to skip the pages, when lo! a miracle happened. The writing was read aloud by some invisible person and a mysterious voice.

MORDECAI'S REWARD

The Persian monarch decided to reward royally the man who had saved his life. He summoned his vizier and asked him to suggest some signal honour for a man who had saved the King's life. Haman at first expressed it as his opinion that the man whom the King wished to honour should not only ride upon the King's horse, but also wear the royal crown upon his head. Noticing, however, the great anger reflected upon the King's countenance he wisely refrained from insisting upon the wearing of the crown. " I am now firmly convinced," thought Ahasuerus in his heart, " that Haman is indeed plotting to kill me and to take my place."

When the King at last revealed unto Haman the identity of the man whom he wished to honour, the vizier grew frightened. In vain did he advise Ahasuerus to heap other honours upon Mordecai, in vain did he offer to the King to give the Jew vast sums of money, to let his wife and children be his servants if only the monarch would spare him the humiliation of leading Mordecai riding upon the royal horse through the streets of the capital. The more Haman pleaded the more angry Ahasuerus grew.

" All that thou hast offered to give to the Jew thou wilt
accomplish," cried the King of Persia, " but in addition to all
this thou wilt instantly carry out my command. Hurry at once
to Mordecai and array him in my royal robes and let him mount
my horse which thou wilt lead through the streets of Shushan."

Haman was forced to do as the King commanded him, and
humbly betook himself to Mordecai, to whom he communi-
cated the royal wish.

" I cannot don the royal robes," replied the humble Jew,
" for I must first bathe and anoint my body and trim my
beard out of respect for His Majesty." Haman was in a great
hurry to do the King's bidding, and delay was dangerous.
Unable to find either a bather or a barber, he was perforce
compelled to perform these functions himself. When the
vizier was cutting Mordecai's hair and trimming his beard, he
sighed heavily.

" Why art thou sighing?" asked the Jew.

" Is it not sad," replied Haman, " that I, the mighty vizier,
should now be reduced to perform the humiliating functions
of a bather and barber?" Mordecai smiled.

" Thou seemest to have a very short memory," he replied,
" Hast thou forgotten that thou wast a barber in the village of
Karzum in days bygone before thy sudden rise to power?"

Mordecai, having fasted for many days, was too weak and
feeble to mount the royal horse, and Haman had to bend his
knee and help his enemy into the saddle. When Haman was
leading the Jew through the streets of Shushan, the vizier's
daughter, looking down from the roof of her house, imagined
that it was her father who was riding upon the royal horse,
whilst Mordecai, the despised Jew, was running before him.
Quickly she snatched up a vase full of dirt and excrements
and emptied the contents upon her father's head. When she
realized her mistake she threw herself down from the roof
and was killed.

THE TRIUMPH OF MORDECAI

Facing page 272, Vol. III

The End of the Jew-baiter

Swiftly now followed Haman's downfall. During the banquet the Queen revealed to her royal spouse his vizier's plans.

"The royal treasury," said Esther, "will suffer greatly in consequence of the annihilation of the Jews, for Haman has omitted to inform thee of the vast amount of revenue derived from the taxes paid by the Jews in the Empire."

Ahasuerus, who was already suspecting Haman of plotting to kill him, was glad of an opportunity to get rid of his vizier. Haman rose up to plead for his life and at that moment an invisible hand pushed him forward so that he fell upon the couch on which the Queen was seated. This increased the King's ire who was already suspecting Haman of being the Queen's lover.

Now Harbonah, one of the Persian courtiers, stepped forward and informed His Majesty that it was the vizier himself who had hired the two Tarsians to poison their royal master. Haman had thus hoped to become King himself, and when he heard that the plot had been frustrated thanks to Mordecai, his hatred of the Jew knew no bounds. The insinuations of Harbonah completely exasperated Ahasuerus and he gave orders to put the vizier and his sons to death.

Thereupon the monarch annulled the decree which he had issued commanding the wholesale massacre of the Jews. "For a long time," wrote Ahasuerus to the governors of his provinces, "I firmly believed that Haman, the son of Hamdata whom I had raised to the dignity of vizier, was my faithful servant and always acted in the interests of my Empire. I therefore listened to his words when he counselled the destruction of the Jews dwelling in my dominions. It has now, however, come to my knowledge that Haman was an enemy both of myself and the Empire, and was only inspired by an unjustifiable hatred of my peaceful subjects, the Jews. He even plotted to kill me and to take my place. A just punishment has been meted out to the traitor, who has been strung up on the gallows. It is now my royal wish and command that my loyal subjects, the Jews, be allowed to live unharmed and in peace in all my dominions." [1]

THE FEAST OF PURIM IN ARABIC LITERATURE

Several Mohammedan authors refer to the feast of Purim and the story of Haman and Mordecai. Thus Albiruni quotes the following passage:

" The Fasting of Alburi (Purim), i.e. casting of lots. The origin is this: once a man called Haman, a man of no importance, travelled to Tastar to undertake some office. But on the way thither he met with an obstacle which prevented him from reaching the end of his journey, and this happened on the identical day on which the offices (in Tastar) were bestowed. So he missed his opportunity and fell into utter distress. Now, he took his seat near the temples and demanded for every dead body (that was to be buried) 3⅓ drachms. This went on until the daughter of King Ahashverosh died. When the people came with her body, he demanded something from the bearers, and on being refused, he did not allow them to pass, until they yielded and were willing to pay him what he asked for. But then he was not content with his first demand; he asked more and more, and they paid him more and more, till at last it reached an enormous sum. The King was informed of the matter, and he ordered them to grant his desire. But after a week he ordered him in his presence, and asked him:

" ' Who invested thee with such an office?'

" But Haman simply answered this: ' And who forbade me to do so?'

[1] See note on p. 261; cf. Lewner, *l. c.*, pp. 111–142.

" When the King repeated his question, Haman said: ' If I am now forbidden to do so, I shall cease and give it up, and I shall give you with the greatest pleasure so and so many ten thousand of denares.'

" The King was astonished at the great sum of money he mentioned, because he with all his supreme power had nothing like it, so he said:

" ' A man who has gathered so much money from the rule over the dead, is worthy to be made wazir and councillor.'

" So he entrusted him with all his affairs and ordered his subjects to obey him.

" This Haman was an enemy of the Jews. He asked the *Haruspices* and *Augures* which was the most unlucky time for the Jews. They said: ' In Adhâr their master Musa died, and the most unlucky time of this month is the 14th and 15th.'

" Now Haman wrote to all parts of the Empire, ordering people on that day to seize upon the Jews and to kill them. The Jews of the Empire prostrated themselves before him, and appeared before him, crossing their hands upon their breasts, except one man, Mordecai, the brother of Ester, the King's wife. Haman hated her and planned her destruction on that day, but the King's wife understood him.

" Now she received (in her palace) the King and his wazir, entertaining them during three days. On the fourth day she asked the King's permission to lay before him her wishes. And then she asked him to spare her life and that of her brother. The King said:

" ' And who dares to attempt anything against ye both?' She pointed to Haman.

" Now the King rose from his seat in great wrath: Haman dashed towards the Queen, prostrating himself before her, and then kissing her head, but she pushed him back. Now the King got the impression that he wanted to seduce her: so he turned towards him and said:

" ' Hast thou in thy impudence come so far as to raise thy desire to her?'

" So the King ordered him to be killed, and Ester asked him to have him crucified on the same tree which he had prepared for her brother. So the King did, and wrote to all parts of the Empire to kill the partisans of Haman. So they were killed on the same day on which he had intended to kill the Jews, i.e. on the 14th. Therefore there is great joy over the death of Haman on this day. This feast is also called the *Feast of Megilla*, and further Hâmân-Sur. For on this day they make figures which they beat and then burn, imitating the burning of Haman. The same they practise on the 15th." [1]

Another Arabic author, Makrizi, writes as follows with regard to the story of Haman and Mordecai: " The feast of Purim is of modern date and owes its origin to the following incident:

" When Nebuchadnezzar led away the Jews of Jerusalem into captivity and ruined the city, he led the captives to Irak where he settled them in the city of Djai, known to-day as Ispahan. When Ardeshir, the son of Babec, whom the Jews called Ahasveros, became master of the kingdom of Persia he had a vizier named Haimoun. The Jews had as their chief in those days Mordecai. Ardeshir having learned that the Jewish chief had a beautiful cousin, he took her to wife. She gained the favour of the King who raised his wife's cousin Mordecai to high honours.

" Now the vizier Haimoun grew very jealous of Mordecai and conceived the plan to destroy not only the Queen's cousin but all the Jews who lived in Ardeshir's dominions. He therefore arranged with his lieutenants and the governors of the provinces to massacre all the Jews living in their respective districts on a certain day which was the 13th of Adar. Mor-

---

[1] Albiruni, trnsl. by E. Sachau, quoted by Paul de Lagarde in *Purim, Abhandlungen der Königlichen Gesellschaft der Wissenschaften zu Göttingen*, 1887, Philologisch-historische Klasse Vol. 34, No. 3.

decai discovered the plot and speedily informed his cousin, the favourite wife of Ardeshir. He urged her to use her influence with Ardeshir and thus save her people from destruction. The princess hastened to inform Ardeshir of the doings of his minister and of the instructions he had sent out to all the governors of the provinces to kill the Jews. She excited the King against his vizier so that Ardeshir ordered Haimoun and his family to be put to death.

" Thereupon Ardeshir granted the Jews many privileges, and in consequence the Jews have established a feast which they observe annually in memory of the event. They consecrate this day to fasting and thanksgiving to God and the next two days to merry-making, rejoicing, and giving presents one to the other. They also make the figure of the vizier Haimoun whom they call Haman, and after mocking this figure they burn it."

[1] Silvestre de Sacy, *Chrestomathie Arabe*, I, 95; see also P. de Lagarde, *l. c.*, pp. 12–13.

BIBLIOGRAPHY

I. WORKS IN HEBREW

Alphabetum Siracidis, ed. Steinschneider, Berlin, 1858.
Babylonian Talmud (cf. Bibliography to Vol. I).
Ben Hamelech-ve-Hanazir, Hebrew edition of *Prince and Dervish*.
Bialik and Ravnitzky, *Sepher Haaggadah*, Berlin.
Emek-Hamelech, Amsterdam, 1653.
Exodus Rabba, Vilna, 1902.
Genesis Rabba, Vilna, 1907.
Hibbur Yafeh.
Hibbur Maassiot, ed. Verona.
Jellinek, *Beth-Hamidrash*, 6 vols., Leipzig and Vienna, 1853–1877.
Josippon (Josephus Gorionides), ed. Breithaupt, Halle, 1707, ed. Amsterdam, 1771.
Leviticus Rabba.
Lewner, *Kol Agadoth*, Warsaw.
Likkute Maassiot, by Israel bar Sason, Jerusalem.
Maasse Nissim.
Midrash Esther Rabba.
Midrash Lekach Tob, ed. Buber, Vilna, 1884.
Midrash Mishle, ed. Buber, Vilna, 1893.
Midrash Ruth Rabba.
Midrash Samuel, ed. Buber, Cracow, 1893.
Midrash Shir Hashirim Rabba, Vilna, 1907.
Midrash Tanchuma, ed. Buber, 1865.
—— Stettin, 1865.
Midrash Tehillim, ed. Buber, Vilna, 1891.
Nishmat Hayim, by Manasseh ben Israel, Amsterdam, 1651.
Numeri Rabba, Vilna, 1907.
Ozar Midrashim, ed. Wertheimer, Jerusalem.
Pesikta de Rabbi Kahana, ed. Buber, Lyck, 1868.
Pesikta Rabbati, ed. Friedmann, Vienna, 1880.
Pirke de Rabbi Eliezer, ed. Venice, 1544; ed. Lemberg, 1867.
Sepher Hassidim, ed. Bologna, 1538.
Sifre d'Agadatha, ed. Buber, 1886.
Tanna debe Eliahu (also called *Seder Eliahu Rabba*), ed. Friedmann, 1902.
Targum Pseudo-Jonathan, ed. Ginsburger, Berlin, 1899.
Targum Sheni to Esther, ed. Cassel, 1885.
—— ed. David, 1898.
Yalkut, Vilna, 1898.

II. OTHER WORKS

Academy, The, 1891.
Archiv für Literaturgeschichte, Vol. XI.
Archiv für Slavonische Philologie, Vols. I, VI.
Barbazan, *Fabliaux,* Paris, 1808.
Behrnauer, *Die vierzig Viziere,* Leipzig, 1851.
Benfey, Th., *Orient u. Occident.*
—— *Panschatantra.*
Bergmann, J., *Die Legenden der Juden,* Berlin, 1919.
Bin Gorion, *Der Born Judas,* 6 vols.
Brooke, Stopford A., *English Literature from the Beginning to the Norman Conquest,* London, 1898.
Budge, Sir E. A. W., *The Book of the Bee (Anecdota Oxoniensa, Sem. Series,* Vol. I, Part 2).
Buttenwieser, *Die Hebr. Eliasapokalypse,* 1897.
Campbell, J. F., *Popular Tales of the West Highlands,* London, 1890.
Cassel, P., *Die Symbolik des Blutes,* Berlin, 1882.
—— *Kaiser u. Königsthrone,* Berlin, 1874.
—— *Schamir,* in *Denkschrift der Kgl. Akademie,* Erfurt, 1854.
Chauvin, V., *La Recension égyptienne des Mille et une Nuits,* Bruxelles, 1899.
Child, F. J., The *English and Scottish Ballads,* Vol. IX.
Clouston, *Popular Tales.*
Collier, *The History of English Dramatic Poetry.*
Cosquin, *Contes populaires de Lorraine.*
D'Ancona, *Novelle di Giovanni Sercambi,* Bologna, 1871.
Dragomanow, *Popular Tales and Traditions,* 1876.
Dunlop, *History of Prose Fiction.*
Faerber, *König Salomon in der Tradition,* 1902.
Folklore, Vol. XVI.
Frere, Mary, *Old Deccan Days.*
Friedlaender, J., *Die Chadhirlegende und der Alexanderroman,* Leipzig, 1913.
Gaster, M., *Jewish Sources of and Parallels to the Early English Metrical Romances of King Arthur and Merlin,* 1888.
—— *Literatura Pop. Romana,* 1883.
—— *The Oldest Version of Midrash Megillah,* in G. A. Kohut, *Semitic Studies.*
Geiger, A., *Jüdische Zeitschrift,* Vol. V.
Germania, Vols. XVIII, XXV, XXVI.
Gesta Romanorum, ed. J. G. T. Graesse, Leipzig, 1905.
—— ed. Oesterley, Berlin, 1882.
Hartland, *The Legend of Perseus.*
Hebräische Bibliographie, No. XIII, XVIII.
Hershon, P. J., *A Talmudical Miscellany,* London, 1880.
—— *Treasures of the Talmud,* London, 1882.
Horstmann, *Sammlung Altenglischer Legenden,* 1878.
Kautzsch, E., *Die Apokryphen und Pseudoepigraphen d. A. T.,* 2 vols., 1900.
Kemble, *Anglo-Saxon Dialogues of Solomon and Saturn,* 1848.

Koehler, R., *Kleinere Schriften*, Berlin, 1900.
Kuttner, *Jüdische Legenden*.
Lagarde, P. de, *Hagiographa Chaldaice*, 1873.
Landau, M., *Die Quellen des Dekameron*, 1884.
—— *Hebrew-German Romances and Tales* (*Teutonia*, Heft 27), Leipzig, 1912.
Lemke's *Jahrbuch*, No. XII.
Lightfoot, J., *Horæ Hebraicæ*, Rotterdam, 1686.
Loewy, A., *Miscellany of Hebrew Literature*, London, 1877.
L'Oiseleur Deslongchamps, *Essai sur les Fables Indiennes*.
Longfellow, *Poetical Works*.
Mahabharata, The (Roy's transl.).
Merx, A., *Chrestomathia Targumica*, 1888.
Midrash Hachefetz, Schechter's transl.: *Folklore*, Vol. I.
Migne, *Dictionnaire des Apocryphes*, Vol. II.
Mirkhond, *Rouzat-us-Safa*, ed. Rehatsek, Part I, Vol. II.
Monatsschrift für Literatur und Wissenschaft des Judentums, Vols. 22, 39.
Perles, *Zur Rabbinischen Sprach- und Sagenkunde*, 1873.
Piper, Dr. P., *Die Spielmannsdichtung* (in J. Kurschner's *Deutsche National-litteratur*, II, 1.)
Rambaud, A., *La Russie épique*, Paris, 1876.
Revue des Études Juives, Vols. 2, 8, 11, 17, 25, 33, 45.
Revue des Traditions Populaires, No. 2.
Robert, C. A., *Fables Inédites*.
Rosner, *David's Leben und Charakter*, 1908.
Sacy, S. de, *Chrestomathie Arabe*.
Salzberger, G., *Die Salomon Sage in der semitischen Literatur*.
—— *Salomons Tempelbau und Thron*, Berlin, 1912.
Seymour, St. John D., *Tales of King Solomon*, 1924.
Spectator, The, No. 578.
Strack, H., *Der Blutaberglaube*, Berlin, 1891.
Tabari, *Chronique*, ed. by H. Zotenberg, Paris, 1867-1874.
Tendlau, A., *Das Buch der Sagen und Legenden*, Stuttgart, 1842.
Thousand and One Nights.
Trumbull, H. C., *The Blood Covenant*, Philadelphia, 1893.
Tutti Nameh, G. Rosen's transl., 1858.
Varnhagen, *Ein Indisches Märchen*, Berlin, 1882.
Vesselovsky, *Iz istorii*, *&c.*, St. Petersburg, 1872.
Vincenti, A. V., *Die altenglischen Dialoge von Salomon und Saturn*.
Vogt, Fr., *Die deutschen Dichtungen von Salomon und Markolf*, Halle, 1880.
Von der Hagen, *Deutsche Gedichte des Mittelalters*, Berlin, 1808, Vol. I.
—— *Gesammtabenteuer*, III.
Weil, G., *Biblische Legenden der Muselmänner*, Frankfurt a/M., 1845.
Wünsche, A., *Aus Israel's Lehrhallen*.
Zeitschrift der Deutsch-Morgenländischen Gesellschaft = ZDMG, Vol. 31.
Zunz, *Gottesdienstliche Vorträge*.

ICONOGRAPHY

A list of a few famous paintings, engravings and statues illustrating Biblical stories or Biblical characters, who form the subjects of the post-biblical legends related in this work.

(A) *Adam and Eve*:

1. Statue of Adam, in the Cathedral at Milan.
2. The Temptation, by Lucas Cranach, in the Uffizi at Florence.
3. The Fall, by Raphael, Loggie.
4. Adam and Eve hiding, by N. Pisano, at Orvieto.
5. Expulsion of Adam and Eve, by Raphael, Loggie.

(B) *Abraham*:

1. Abraham driving away Hagar, by Paolo Farinato (1524–1606) at the Historical Society, New York.
2. The Sacrifice of Abraham, by Andrea del Sarto (1486–1531) in the Gallery at Dresden.
3. The Sacrifice of Abraham, by Ghiberti, bas-relief in bronze, Nat. Mus., Florence.
4. Abraham journeying with Lot, by M. Corneille (1642–1708).
5. Abraham and the Angels, by A. van Diepenbeck (1599–1675), at Munich.
6. Arithmetic accompanied by Abraham, in the large group by Taddeo Gaddi in the Dominican Convent of Santa Maria Novella in Florence, painted in 1322.

(C) *Isaac*.

1. Isaac blessing Jacob, by Raphael, Loggie.
2. Eliezer and Rebecca, by Nicolas Poussin.

(D) *Jacob*:

1. Jacob and Esau, by A. M. Seitz (1811–1888).
2. Jacob and Rachel, by J. Führich (1800–1876).
3. Jacob wrestling with Angel, by M. Corneille.

(E) Joseph:

1. Joseph's Coat, by Velasquez (1599–1660) in the Escorial.
2. Joseph sold by his Brethren, by A. M. Seitz (1811–1888).
3. Joseph recognized by his Brethren, by Peter v. Cornelius, at the National Gallery, Berlin.

(F) Israel:

1. The Delivery of Israel, by Michelangelo on the walls of the Sistine Chapel (c. 1480).
2. Hebrews gathering Manna, by Nicolas Poussin (1594–1666).

(G) Moses:

1. The Life of Moses, on the walls of the Sistine Chapel.
2. Moses journeying to Egypt, fresco in the Sistine Chapel, by Pinturicchio (Bernardino di Betto) (1454–1513).
3. Moses rescued from the Waves (1647), by Nicolas Poussin.
4. Moses breaking the Tables of the Law, by Parmigiano (Francesco Mazzuola) (1504–1540).
5. The Finding of Moses, by A. M. Seitz (1811–1888).
6. Moses, scenes from his life, by Johann Schrandolph (1808–1879), frescoes in Church of All Saints at Munich.
7. Moses bringing down the Tables of the Law, by J. Rogers Herbert (1810–1890), in the House of Lords.
8. Moses striking the Rock, by Francisco Herrera the Elder (1576–1656), in the Archiepiscopal Palace at Madrid.
9. Moses, by Pinturicchio, in the Sistine Chapel, Rome.
10. Moses, by Philippe de Champagne, at Leningrad.
11. Moses, by Carlo Dolci, in the Pitti Palace at Florence.
12. Moses, statue by Michelangelo, Pietro in Vincoli, Rome.
13. Moses, life of, frescoes by Michelangelo.
14. Moses saved from the Waters, by Raphael, Loggie.
15. The Lord writes the Commandments upon the Tables of Stone, by Jos. Führich (1800–1876).
16. Moses striking the Rock, by J. A. von Gegenbauer (1800–1876), at Stuttgart.

(H) Joshua:

1. Joshua and the Destruction of Jericho, by Jos. Führich.

(J) David:

1. David, painting by Antonio Pollajuolo (1432–1498), in the Berlin Museum.
2. David (called the Zuccone, Baldheaded), by Donatello (1386–1466).
3. David in bronze, by Verocchio (1435–1488), National Museum, Florence.

(K) *Solomon*:

1. The Judgment of Solomon, by Nicolas Poussin (1649).
2. The Judgment of Solomon, by J. R. Herbert, in the House of Lords.
3. The Building of the Temple, by the same.
4. The Visit of the Queen of Sheba, by the same.

(L) *Mordecai and Esther*:

1. The Coronation of Esther.
2. Esther being presented to King Ahasuerus.
3. The Triumph of Mordecai, by Paul Veronese, in the Church San Sebastiano, at Venice.
4. Esther before Ahasuerus, by Hans Burckmair (1473–1531), at Munich.

INDEX

Aaron, dances at father's wedding, ii, 215; meets Moses, ii, 275; not envious of Moses, ii, 276; in presence of Pharaoh, ii, 277; resembles angel, ii, 278; and Balaam, ii, 280; celebrates Passover, ii, 283; and clouds of glory, ii, 325, 326; death of, ii, 333; as peacemaker, ii, 336, 337; soul lured away by Divine kiss, ii, 340; vizier of Pharaoh, ii, 378; death of, in Moslem legend, ii, 390.

Ab, mouth of, iii, 255.

Abel, story of, i, 193 *et seq.*; burial of, i, 194, 197; twin sister of, i, 195; " the prayer of ", a poem, i, 203; blood of, ii, 295.

Abiel, iii, 1.

Abihu, ii, 302; iii, 129.

Abimelech, ii, 207; iii, 26.

Abiram, ii, 241.

Abishai. iii, 29.

Abner, mother of, iii, 3; flask of, iii, 21.

Abraham, and Sammael, i, 68; death of, i, 69; birth of, i, 226 *et seq.*; leaves his cave, i, 230; before Nimrod, i, 232; sells idols, i, 239; in jail, i, 247; in fiery furnace, i, 250; in the King's dale, i, 259; hospitality of, i, 262; judges men, i, 278; visits Ishmael, i, 283 *et seq.*; tested by God, i, 287; covenant with Jebusites, i, 309; a reader of stars, i, 311; death of, i, 323 *et seq.*; installs artificial light, i, 324; refuses to give up his soul, i, 327; visits heaven, i, 329 *et seq.*; visits Paradise, i, 333; funeral of, i, 335; the ass of, ii, 275; and Og, ii, 329; covenant with the Jebusites, iii, 23.

Absalom, in hell, i, 131; rebellion of, iii, 28.

Academy, the heavenly, i, 8.

Achitophel, jealous of David. iii, 116.

Achseriel, i, 6.

Adam, creation of, i, 6; in nethermost earth, i, 24; and Lilith, i, 77; creation of, in Moslem legend, i, 141 *et seq.*; composes psalm, i, 144; and David, i, 148; marriage of, i, 151; penance of, i, 175 *et seq.*; death of, i, 178 *et seq.*; burial of, i, 185; life in Moslem legend, i, 186; and Iblis, i, 189; watches procession of souls, i, 330.

Adamah, i, 24.

Adar, month of, iii, 255; Moses born in, iii, 256.

Adares and Solomon, i, 105.

Adiel, iii, 12.

Adina, wife of Levi, ii, 213.

Adonai, ii, 273.

Adoniah, ii, 246, 248.

Advel, stone, i, 17.

Af, angel, ii, 317.

Agnias, ii, 173, 176, 179, 181, 192, 194, 195.

Agrath, i, 79.

Ahab, ii, 22; iii, 210, 240.

Ahasuerus, throne of Solomon, iii, 116, 243; and vessels from temple, iii, 244; banquet of, iii, 245; regrets Vashti, iii, 249; decree of, iii, 258; sleepless night of, iii, 270; jealous of Haman, iii, 273.

Ahasuerus, the wandering Jew, iii, 241.

Aheyya, i, 61.

Ahish, iii, 20.

Aishia, wife of Pharaoh, ii, 373.

Akatriel, i, 35.

Akher, i, 44.

Akiba, Rabbi, ii, 311; iii, 214.

Akko, the poor lad from, iii, 109.

Akshid, Sultan, tale of, iii, 60.

Alanad, iii, 101.

Alburi, Fasting of, iii, 274.

Alexander the Great, meets descendants of Cain, i, 203; carries off throne of Solomon, iii, 115.

Altamar, iii, 102.

Amalek, and Israel, ii, 300, 301, 326.